A New System For Public Housing

A New System For Public Housing

Salvaging a National Resource

RAYMOND J. STRUYK

 THE URBAN INSTITUTE
Washington, D.C.

THE URBAN INSTITUTE is a nonprofit research organization established in 1968 to study problems of the nation's urban communities. Independent and nonpartisan, the Institute responds to current needs for disinterested analyses and basic information and attempts to facilitate the application of this knowledge. As part of this effort, it cooperates with federal agencies, states, cities, associations of public officials, and other organizations committed to the public interest.

The Institute's research findings and a broad range of interpretive viewpoints are published as an educational service. The interpretations or conclusions are those of the authors and should not be attributed to The Urban Institute, its trustees, or to other organizations that support its research.

Contents

Tables

Figures

Foreword

Public housing is clearly in trouble, and in the past five years, the U.S. Department of Housing and Urban Development, in an effort to upgrade public projects, has awarded almost half of the available funds under a Target Projects Program and almost 70 percent of the funds under a Public Housing Urban Initiatives Program to projects rated "badly distressed" in the 29 PHAs that are the focus of this report. Staff members of HUD's field offices rated 18 percent of large (operating more than 3,000 units) Authorities as "troubled." Eighty-six percent of the Authorities manage more than 3,000 units. Five PHAs in the largest cities are effectively bankrupt.

Many critics contend that public housing projects, constructed to ensure decent housing for the nation's low- and moderate-income families, are little improvement over the slums they were designed to replace. The original public housing projects were built in Atlanta and New York more than 40 years ago, and by 1970, 29 of the 31 American cities with populations of over 400,000 had developed public housing projects. These 29 Public Housing Authorities (PHAs) administer 373,500 housing units, or 31 percent of the national program; and in the 1976-77 fiscal year they absorbed 58 percent of all operating subsidies provided by the federal government.

Problems in public housing in smaller cities should not be ignored either, since housing projects with a similar profile to that of the projects in the major cities, have a high incidence of depreciation, vandalism, and other significant problems.

Naturally, such problems have been the object of much analysis and various, mostly unsuccessful, patch-up programs created by HUD to turn the tide. Past efforts to analyze public housing and eliminate faults have focused only on individual parts of the system—trends in operating costs, tenant profiles, tenant admission standards, or management organization and practice.

This volume, however, presents a unified picture of the conditions, politics, policies, and management that characterize public housing and describes how they operate to help or hinder good project management, empower or discourage tenants, and strengthen or cripple the public housing program. Neither HUD nor particular Authorities are condemned. Instead, the need to view public housing as a comprehensive system is stressed.

First, the report describes the projects, tenantry, and financial conditions found in the largest cities. Who lives in public housing? Are many tenants "problem" characters? What is a basic flaw in the projects' cost accounting systems?

Second, the report details the relationship between HUD central and its Authorities. What happens when projects comply with HUD's requirements? Are guidelines contained in the HUD handbook realistic?

Third, the report explores "good management." What has HUD done to foster its development? How can PHA officials use their own often unperceived power to control tenant profile, improve tenant/management cooperation, or obtain needed modernization funding?

The last chapter suggests changes needed to improve the whole public housing system. These suggestions, embodying changes in funding of Authorities, development of efficiency incentives for the PHAs, and a critical look at HUD's performance funding system, seriously affect the PHA-city-HUD relationship. This report, building on The Urban Institute's decade of research on public housing, makes clear that implementing a comprehensive response is the only effective way to face the breakdowns occurring in public housing and preserve a valuable housing resource for the nation's low- and moderate-income families.

William Gorham
President
The Urban Institute

Acknowledgments

My greatest vote of gratitude is to Elaine Ostrowski and Morton Isler. Mort Isler introduced me to the early research on public housing at The Urban Institute more than six years ago, and during the past three years has continued our dialogue on the problems and prospects for the program. Elaine Ostrowski, a former colleague in the research office at the Department of Housing and Urban Development, had managed public housing and brought this special real-world knowledge to our extensive conversations. Both had firm but different ideas of the path to improving the public housing system. Their diversity of approaches was extremely stimulating for my thinking and in large part accounts for the structure of this book. It was Elaine who convinced me of the necessity of undertaking this project; Mort seized the idea and created the environment for its execution.

I also want to thank those others who broadly contributed to my education as a student of public housing. The executive directors, staff, and tenants of several PHAs were very generous with their time. Dick Baron and Terry McCormack twice acted as knowledgeable guides at tenant-managed projects, described the process of establishing this type of management, and more generally discussed public housing with me. Numerous people in the Office of Housing and the Office of Policy Development and Research of the Department of Housing and Urban Development shared a wealth of experience with me.

Several colleagues carefully and thoughtfully reviewed the two drafts of the manuscripts: Mary Nenno, Joan DeWitt, Carolyn Zeul McFarlane, Sue Loux, William Millkey, Elaine

Ostrowski, and Mort Isler. I also profited from conversations with Ken Ryder, Roger Faxon, and Cynthia Simon.

Paul Dommel provided data from the Brookings Institution's analysis of the Community Development Block Grant Program; and Steve Gale, Tom Fogarty, and Mike James provided data from the University of Pennsylvania's study of the same program.

Frank Wann ably handled the computer programming chores. Sandra Woodcock oversaw the preparation of the manuscript, and Theresa Walker competently edited the manuscript. Finally, Maureen Ring efficiently handled dozens of administrative problems.

This work was partially supported through funds provided by the Ford Foundation to The Urban Institute and this support is gratefully acknowledged.

Part I
INTRODUCTION

Chapter 1

Big Cities and Public Housing

This book is about improving public housing in the largest cities of the United States. Public housing refers to "conventional" or "low-rent" public housing, that is, housing constructed and operated by local Public Housing Authorities (PHAs) under the United States Housing Act of 1937, as amended.[1] It is the oldest national housing program to assist renter households and until very recently, when the Lower Income Housing Assistance Program (Section 8) replaced it, the 1.2 million units built under it made it the largest such program. Although begun with the triple objectives of generating employment, eliminating slums, and providing good housing for needy households, its present mission is almost exclusively to assist poor households to live in adequate housing.

Public housing should not be confused with other rental assistance programs under which private developers who own the dwellings receive various subsidies to provide good housing to moderate- and low-income households. Public housing is owned and operated by local government Authorities, typically distinct

---

1. It also includes a modest number of units built by the Works Progress Administration before the enactment of this act.

3

from municipal governments, with the cost of construction and some operating expenses borne by the federal government.

The largest cities of the country are the 31 places with populations of over 400,000 in 1970. Arguably, these are the areas most difficult to govern, and many of them have been beset by population and capital declines in the past decade. They are also the location of many of the largest Public Housing Authorities, as measured by the number of units under contract for them to operate. Sometimes these Authorities provide as much as 10 percent of all the housing and an even greater percentage of rental units in the city.

As a group, the Authorities in these cities have secured an infamous reputation, and indeed a miasma has settled over policy discussions on how to improve the distressed among them. Martin Mayer, in his book *The Builders,* describes the results of national policy of the 1950s and 1960s of replacing slums with public housing in the following words:

> And so we got the fifty-acre superblock of Pruitt-Igoe, now demolished, Boston's Columbia Point, mostly now boarded up; Philadelphia's vacated Rosen Apartments; Newark's desolate Columbus Houses; Chicago's menacing Cabrini-Green; the Fort Green Houses in New York that so horrified Harrison Salisbury: the "shoddy shiftlessness, the broken windows, the missing light bulbs, the plaster cracking from the walls, the pilfered hardware, the cold, draughty corridors, the doors on sagging hinges, the acrid smell of sweat and cabbage, the ragged children, the plaintive women, the playgrounds that are seas of muddy clay, the bruised and battered trees, the ragged clumps of grass, the planned absence of art, beauty or taste, the gigantic masses of brick, of concrete, of asphalt, the inhuman genius with which our know-how has been perverted to create human cesspools worse than those of yesterday." [2]

Many others—academics, journalists, and public officials alike— have made similar observations. Leonard Downie has said

> Congressional watchdogs effectively prevented public money from being "wasted" on large lawns, trees, fancy playgrounds, balconies, air conditioning, or other amenities, especially facilities

---

2. M. Mayer, *The Builders* (New York: W. W. Norton and Co., 1978), p. 184.

for the large number of children in public housing projects. In design and construction public housing has been consistently and depressingly spartan. . . . The wear and tear (and vandalism) from so many large, poor families jammed together has overwhelmed most public housing projects and their limited grounds. Many recently built projects are already slums and likely will not last half as long as it will take for their construction bonds to be paid off.[3]

Like most of the conventional wisdom, there is some truth present; but a critical examination of the veracity of the glib characterization of big city public housing is one of several motives for this work.

Public housing in the largest cities is an important share of the whole public housing program. In 1970 there were 31 cities in America with populations over 400,000; 29 of them had developed public housing projects. (San Diego and San Jose were exceptions with their exclusive reliance on scattered-site leased housing.) Table 1 lists the 29 cities, their populations in 1975, and the number of public housing units that their Authorities administered in 1978. When combined, these 29 PHAs are responsible for 373,500 housing units or 31 percent of the national program; the 2,900 other Authorities administer the remaining 814,000 units. Further, under the system used to dispense operating subsidies, these few Authorities absorbed 58 percent of all such subsidies provided by the federal government for the 1976-77 fiscal year.[4]

There are other indicators of the concentration of problems of the public housing system in these largest cities.

- In the past five years, the Department of Housing and Urban Development has had two major initiatives to upgrade public projects that were rated "badly distressed" by HUD field staff. The Authorities in the 29 largest cities were awarded 47 percent of the available funds under the first initiative, the Target Projects Program (TPP), and they were awarded 68

---

3. Leonard Downie, Jr., *Mortgage in America* (New York: Praeger Publishers, Inc., 1974), pp. 54-55.

4. Some of the PHAs have fiscal years beginning in each of the four calendar quarters; hence the 1976-77 notation. This corresponds to the 1976 federal fiscal year.

Table 1

POPULATION AND PUBLIC HOUSING IN THE LARGEST CITIES [c]

Central City	1975 Population [d] (000)	Public Housing Units [a]
New York City	7,481	116,600
Chicago	3,099	38,600
Los Angeles	2,727	8,200
Philadelphia	1,816	22,900
Detroit	1,335	10,300
Houston	1,327	2,600
Baltimore	852	16,200
Dallas	813	7,000
San Antonio	773	7,500
Indianapolis	715	2,600
Washington, D.C.	712	11,200
Milwaukee	666	4,400
San Francisco	664	7,100
Memphis	661	6,800
Phoenix	645	1,900
Cleveland [b]	639	11,500
Boston	637	12,800
New Orleans	560	13,600
Columbus, O.	536	4,800
Jacksonville	535	3,100
St. Louis	525	6,700
Seattle	487	5,900
Denver	484	4,900
Kansas City	472	2,600
Pittsburgh	459	9,800
Atlanta	436	14,700
Cincinnati	413	6,800
Buffalo	407	4,800
Minneapolis	378	6,900

a. Conventional, federal public housing available for occupancy in fiscal year 1978; data from Office of Housing, U.S. Department of Housing and Urban Development.

b. Authority serves all of Cuyahoga County.

c. Other large cities without conventional public housing are San Jose and San Diego.

d. U.S. Bureau of the Census, *Population Reports and Estimates*, Series P-25, Nos. 649-698 (Washington, D.C.: U.S. Government Printing Office, 1977).

percent of funds under the second, the Public Housing Urban Initiatives Program (UIP).[5]

• A recent careful analysis of the physical condition of the public housing stock and the cost of bringing all projects up to various standards found that projects with the characteristics of those in the major cities had higher incidence of depreciation and vandalism than others. Hence, they will require a disproportionate share of rehabilitation funds in the future.[6]

• There is a general consensus among public housing cognoscenti that projects with profiles most similar to those operated by the largest PHAs are in trouble. This has been dramatically demonstrated in a study conducted by HUD's Office of Policy Development and Research in 1978 to determine the number and characteristics of distressed public housing projects, as perceived by "the HUD field office staff members who were most familiar with each project."[7] These staff members rated projects in terms of their overall conditions and then in terms of nine separate categories. A project was considered troubled if "reported to be in bad or very bad condition by the field office (3.8 percent of all projects) or was rated in good or average condition but was reported to have five or more significant problems (2.9 percent of all projects)."[8]

Hence, about 6.7 percent of all projects were perceived troubled. The archetypical troubled project was designed for family (as opposed to elderly) occupancy, more than 200 units in size, more than 20 years old, and located in an urban area.

---

5. Amy Kell, *The Target Projects Program: A Basic Resource Book* (Washington, D.C.: National Association of Housing and Redevelopment Officials, 1978), pp. 60-73. "Distressed Public Housing Projects Receive Additional Assistance," U.S. Department of Housing and Urban Development press release, October 3, 1978. These programs are further described in chapter 8.

6. Perkins-Will and The Ehrenkrantz Group, *Preliminary Cost Estimates: An Evaluation of the Physical Condition of Public Housing Stock* (Washington, D.C.: U.S. Department of Housing and Urban Development, 1980).

7. Division of Policy Studies, Office of Policy Development and Research, U.S. Department of Housing and Urban Development, *Problems Affecting Low Rent Public Housing Projects* (Washington, D.C.: U.S. Government Printing Office, 1979), p. 34.

8. *Ibid.*, p. 38.

To be sure, projects with all of these characteristics account for only 27 percent of all troubled projects, but their rate of distress is three times greater than their share of the project population. Further, half of all *units* in troubled projects are in projects with these characteristics. These are also projects with large households, to judge from the number of bedrooms in the units, and they are projects with a higher-than-average incidence of female-headed households. A separate, unpublished tabulation of troubled status by large Authorities, that is, those operating more than 3,000 units, showed that 18 percent of large Authorities' projects were perceived troubled, compared with 4 percent of projects of other PHAs—86 percent of the Authorities in the 29 cities listed in table 1 manage over 3,000 units.

• Five of the PHAs in the largest cities have no reserves; they are the equivalent of being bankrupt. The Boston Housing Authority has been placed into receivership by a state court because of its inability to provide minimum levels of services.

Public housing in the biggest cities is definitely in trouble. Still, the variance among Authorities should not be forgotten; likewise the problems of public housing in other cities should not be dismissed. Nevertheless, focusing attention on this group of cities and PHAs defines a manageable task and a quite consistent set of problems.

With a situation that begs for analysis and action, it is surprising that a need for this study remains. Public housing has certainly been studied, but the focus of past efforts has been various individual components—trends in operating costs, tenant profiles, tenant admission standards, and management organization and practices. The need, addressed in this volume, is exploiting the existing analyses to create a picture complete enough so that both practitioners and policy elite can see the program as a whole. Public housing is not merely the sum of its parts.

For instance, what happens when consultants attempt to turn around a badly distressed project? They begin by carefully diagnosing problems at the site. Perhaps the "children density" of the project is simply too great for the available facilities; and this leads to high rates of depreciation of the physical stock and other management problems. At this Authority, tenant admissions and assignments are handled centrally and uniformly. A schedule relating household size to apartment size (defined by number of bedrooms) must be strictly followed. The individual project manager coping with "children density" has no control over the schedule. When the consultants recommend a different schedule for this particular project, they are told that the Authority's schedule is the one specified in HUD's occupancy handbooks; deviations require approval from the HUD field office. The field office will consider the request, but HUD, like the PHA's own board of commissioners, is always concerned about potential adverse publicity about "overhousing" the poor. Such "overhousing" brings congressional interest and local citizen outrage.

This pattern is endlessly repeated when one pushes for change at the action level, that is, the project level. Hence, an inquiry initially focused on improving certain distressed projects is inexorably channeled into examining the whole public housing system.

The scenario just sketched touched on a critical area: the powerful interactions among conditions, policies, and management. In the scenario, the tenant profile, caused in part by HUD policies, produced difficult conditions under which to manage. Further, as demonstrated below, many of the projects in big cities were poorly designed. The combination of tenant and project design problems creates an extraordinarily difficult management situation, even if management has a free hand. But management does not: rules and regulations imposed by HUD, at the behest of the Congress, stifle initiative and exacerbate bad situations. Proper management under such conditions is a challenge that few in the vaunted "private sector" would risk. This is not to provide a ready, open-ended excuse for the problems of the Authorities in the largest cities; rather it is to condition the reader to the real world and to ask for a realistic judgment of the current situation and the recommendations for change set forth here.

This monograph explores the complexity of public housing. Chapters two-four document the current status of public housing: projects, tenantry, and financial condition in the largest cities. Chapters five and six show the relationship between the incentives or requirements of HUD's regulations and the outcomes observed in the PHAs. Chapters seven-nine discuss PHA

management, what is known about "good management," how
HUD has tried to foster its development, and to what degree
PHAs manage public housing in isolation from their other activities. The final chapter builds on the previous material in suggesting improvements. If the reader is willing to accept as-
sertions made in chapter 10 about present conditions and has a
working knowledge of public housing, the chapter can be read
directly. The balance of this chapter provides notes on the
broad institutional arrangement, the importance of public housing in the local housing markets of the largest cities, and a sense
of the diversity among PHAs.

Because of the concentration of this monograph on today's
existing public housing stock, it ignores some broad areas.[9] The
history of public housing is not recounted, including the past
decade, except where absolutely essential. We begin with public housing in the 1976-79 time period.[10] Also ignored are fundamental questions often asked by economists: Is public housing
the most efficient way to provide a given level of housing services? Do tenants value the housing benefits as much as it costs
the government to provide them? These questions have been
addressed elsewhere;[11] here, we basically accept the proposi-

---

9. The concentration on the existing stock seems amply justified by
low production levels in recent years, i.e., 11,330 starts in FY 78 and
22,200 in FY 79 or about 1.5 percent of the existing stock in FY 79.

10. Some of the historical overviews of the public housing program are
R. K. Brown, *The Development of Public Housing in the United States*
(Atlanta: Georgia State University, College of Business Administration,
1960); E. J. Meehan, *Public Housing Policy Convention Versus Reality*
(New Brunswick: Rutgers University Center for Urban Policy Research,
1975); H. Aaron, *Shelter and Subsidies* (Washington, D.C.: The Brookings
Institution, 1972), chapter 7; E. White, S. Merrill, and T. Lane, *The History
and Overview of the Performance Funding System* (Cambridge Abt Associates, 1979).

11. J. R. Prescott, *Economic Aspects of Public Housing* (Beverly Hills:
Sage Publications, 1974). D. M. Barton and E. O. Olson, "The Benefits and
Costs of Public Housing in New York City" (Madison: The Institute for
Research on Poverty, University of Wisconsin, paper 372-76). *Housing
in the Seventies: National Housing Policy Review* (Washington, D.C.:
U.S. Department of Housing and Urban Development, 1974), chapter 4.
M. Murray, "The Distribution of Tenant Benefits in Public Housing,"
Econometrica, July 1975, pp. 771-88. E. Smolensky, "Public Housing or In-
come Supplements—The Economics of Housing the Poor," *Journal of the
American Institute of Planners*, vol. 34, no. 2, March 1968, pp. 94-101. S. K.
Mayo, S. Mansfield, D. Warner, and R. Zwetchkenbaum, "Draft Report on

tion that the current public housing program will continue to administer the existing inventory, although some radical alternatives are discussed. Improved efficiency is essential, whatever the present level.

This is a positive review of the public housing program. Positive because for every large Authority with specific management deficiencies, there are others with excellent practices. Positive because much of the power needed by the Authorities to improve their situations is already in their hands; this power must simply be used more wisely, more strategically. Positive because the disincentives transmitted by the central office of the Department of Housing and Urban Development, often following congressional intent and directives of Office of Management and Budget, are found so blatantly harmful when systematically reviewed, that the momentum for improvement should be irresistible. Positive because of the solid, well-managed projects that exist in all these major Authorities. Finally, and perhaps most importantly, this review is positive because there are examples of badly distressed projects being turned around through the combined efforts of staff, a core group of tenants (sometimes through formal tenant management), and carefully conceived and sustained technical assistance to the Authority and its tenants.

A PRIMER ON INSTITUTIONS

A fundamental problem in understanding the public housing program is comprehending its complicated institutional arrangement. While the system is detailed throughout the text, an early overview is essential. At the base, of course, is the local Public Housing Authority, which is typically a political entity independent of the municipal government in which it operates. In order for HUD to agree to provide funds for project development, however, the municipality must sign an agreement to provide certain services for the projects and to refrain from levy-

Housing Allowances and Other Rental Housing Assistance Programs—A Comparison Based on the Housing Allowance Demand Experiment, Part 2: Costs and Efficiency" (Cambridge: Abt Associates, 1979). H. J. Sumka and M. Stegman, "An Economic Analysis of Public Housing in Small Cities," *Journal of Regional Science,* December 1978, pp. 395-410.

ing taxes upon the property.[12] In exchange for assistance, the municipality has generally exercised careful control over where public housing projects are located.[13] The local PHA has all of the management responsibility for developing (i.e., building), operating, and maintaining the projects. Thus, a major element in any measurement of public housing is evaluating how efficiently this management responsibility is discharged and to what extent a project is actually receiving municipally-provided services.

The PHA, however, operates under a considerable set of constraints imposed by HUD regulations, which makes judging its efficiency extremely difficult. The PHA abides by the HUD regulations in order to receive capital financing for its projects. Constraints fall into two classes: financial and regulatory. Besides development funds, HUD allocates operating subsidies and funds for project modernization to local PHAs. For the major Authorities, operating subsidies pay for half of current expenses, and most PHAs rely almost exclusively on modernization funds for project renovation. On the regulatory side, to name a few rules, there are rules about accounting procedures, tenant admission and eviction policies, and rent setting. Clearly, funding policies and regulations can produce strong behavioral incentives to the PHAs—incentives producing actions either constructive or deleterious to the efficient provision of housing to the poor. HUD exercises oversight to make sure its regulations are followed, and it can and does impose (mainly financial) penalties to further compliance. While PHAs generally respond to those penalties, a small group is in such dire condition that further penalties are meaningless. The advent of such PHAs is a recent phenomenon, and it is unclear how HUD will ultimately respond.

Additionally, Congress establishes broad policies for public housing through appropriation levels, amendments to the initial statute, and through its intent as announced in reports accompanying the actual legislation. HUD must convert these broad policies into action through regulations and fund disbursements. Beginning in 1979 the Congress explicitly monitors changes in regulations proposed by HUD, and hence has become more ac-

---

12. Note that this gives the municipality a veto on project development.

13. See, for example, R. M. Fisher, 20 Years of Public Housing (Westport, Conn.: Greenwood Press, 1959), pp. 238-41.

tive. (One assumes that local Authorities lobby their representatives to their advantage.) Finally, in the 1970s, the courts have intervened actively primarily to establish and expand tenant rights. Sometimes these judicial acts have caused systemwide regulatory changes to be promulgated by HUD, often to the chagrin of the local Authorities.

The conclusion that follows from this overview is as obvious as it has been unheeded in the past: in making changes to one part of the system to improve service delivery, be certain not to create disincentives to such improved service elsewhere.

PUBLIC HOUSING AND THE HOUSING MARKET

How important is public housing in the largest cities? The first three columns of table 2 present data for those central cities for which the necessary data were available to respond to the question. For 11 of the 17 cities included in table 2, public housing constitutes more than 5 percent of the entire rental housing stock; in Atlanta and Baltimore it is more than 10 percent, a major share of the market.

If one assumes that all public housing is in large structures, that is, structures with five or more units in them, whether high rise or low rise, it is possible to compute public housing's share of the large housing structures in these cities. In 6 of the 17 cities—Philadelphia, Baltimore, Cleveland, St. Louis, Atlanta, and Buffalo—public housing accounts for more than one in five units in large structures. In Baltimore and Buffalo the share is more than 30 percent. In 4 more cities between 10 and 20 percent of all the units in large structures belong to the Public Housing Authority. Further, the share of very large housing projects, consisting of multiple large structures, is much greater but not measurable because of the lack of data on privately operated projects. Hence, in many of these cities, the casual observer can classify large structures and large projects as public housing with a reasonable likelihood of being correct.

How strong are the housing markets in these cities? There is no simple answer. One way of responding is to look at the central city compared to its suburbs, and the figures in columns 4-6 of table 2 give information in this area. The most general information is the hardship index developed by Nathan and

Table 2

HOUSING INDICATORS FOR SELECTED CITIES INCLUDED IN THE ANALYSIS [a]

	PUBLIC HOUSING AS PERCENTAGE OF			HARDSHIP INDEX [h] (1970)	RATIO: CENTRAL CITY TO ENTIRE SMSA		AVERAGE ANNUAL PERCENTAGE CHANGE [d]		VACANCY RATES	
	Rental Housing	All Housing	All Units in Large Structures [b]		Total Households	Renter Family Income [c]	Households	New Construction	Owner Units	Rental Units
New York	5.6	4.1	7.3	211	.70	.88	-1.0	0.5	2.1	5.2
Chicago	5.4	3.4	10.1	245	.47	.84	-1.2	0.6	1.4	6.6
Los Angeles [f]	1.1	0.6	1.9	105	.47	1.02	0.4	1.4	1.7	7.4
Philadelphia	9.0	0.4	22.4	205	.40	.81	-1.1	0.6	1.7	7.0
Detroit	5.0	2.0	12.3	210	.35	.78	-1.7	0.3	2.1	11.3
Houston	0.9	0.5	1.7	93	.60	.97	2.9	4.2	1.8	8.4
Baltimore	10.3	5.6	32.9	256	.39	.80	-0.1	0.2	1.1	7.0
Indianapolis	2.3	1.0	5.7	124	.65	.99	0.9	2.2	2.3	9.3
Washington, D.C.	5.9	4.1	10.3	[g]	.26	.79	-0.4	0.3	1.8	4.5
San Francisco [e]	2.4	1.5	4.1	105	.36	.85	-0.6	0.8	1.6	9.0
Cleveland	8.6	4.6	23.8	331	.34	.78	-1.2	0.4	2.4	7.6
Boston	8.0	5.7	15.8	198	.22	.83	-2.0	0.4	2.2	10.3
St. Louis	5.9	3.2	24.5	231	.24	.75	-2.4	0.2	1.4	10.2
Seattle	5.4	2.5	9.4	93	.42	.92	-0.2	0.5	0.7	5.8
Denver	4.5	2.3	7.5	143	.39	.89	1.1	2.5	1.1	9.3
Atlanta	14.6	8.7	25.1	226	.29	.77	-1.7	1.6	4.2	13.4

Buffalo	5.8	3.0	32.4	189	.34	.80	−1.4	0.2	1.8	4.8
All central cities	g	g	g	g	.46	.90	1.2	1.9	1.6	6.0

Source: Annual Housing Survey, Metropolitan Area Reports, years 1974-76, and Department of Housing and Urban Development, Office of Housing.

a. All data, except public housing, are for the year in which the SMSA (and central city) were surveyed in the Annual Housing Survey: 1974—Boston, Dallas, Detroit, Los Angeles, Washington, D.C.

1975—Atlanta, Chicago, Philadelphia, San Francisco;

1976—Baltimore, Buffalo, Cleveland, Denver, Houston, Indianapolis, New York, St. Louis, Seattle.

Data for all central cities combined are for 1976, taken from the Annual Housing Survey national reports (parts A and C) for that year.

b. Denominator is all rental housing in structures with five or more units.

c. Median income for two or more person households; data for year of the Annual Housing Survey.

d. Percentage change from 1970 to the year of the Annual Housing Survey, divided by the number of years between 1970 and the AHS for the central city.

e. Data, except for public housing, are for the San Francisco and Oakland central cities.

f. Data, except for public housing, are for the Los Angeles and Long Beach central cities.

g. Entries not tabulated for this analysis.

h. See text for description.

Adams, which essentially provides a measure of potential housing demand of the current residents. The index combines data
on factors like unemployment, education, and income level for
central cities and their suburbs, into a single figure. A value of
over 100 for the hardship index in column 4 denotes that the
primary central city in the metropolitan area is disadvantaged
in relation to the rest of the area; the larger the figure, the
greater the disadvantage.[14] Of the 16 cities included in the table
for which the index is available, only Seattle and Houston were
in a stronger position in 1970 than were their suburbs; 3
others had scores between 100 and 150. The remaining 11 cities
were seriously disadvantaged compared to their suburbs, with
Cleveland, Baltimore, and Chicago being in the worst positions.

A similar discouraging picture emerges if changes in recent
years in these central cities are compared with changes in other
central cities (columns 7-8). While the average central city experienced a 1.2 percent per year increase in households in the
first half of the decade of the 1970s, 13 of 17 cities included in
the table actually lost households over the period. Likewise,
while the average central city experienced a 1.9 percent per
year rate of construction of new housing, 12 of the 17 had ratios
of less than 1 percent per year of new construction; 7 were
under 0.5 percent per year of new construction. Only Los Angeles, Houston, Denver, and Indianapolis appear strong in these
terms. The vacancy rates in the final two columns of the table
tell the same story.[15] In brief, the housing markets in many of
these central cities are soft to stagnant, with public housing
constituting a large and—thanks to demolitions of private housing—growing share of central city stock.

The loss of households from many of the central cities—and
the continuance of some residential construction—means that
housing is being withdrawn from the stock through abandonment or conversion to other uses. Decay in American cities has
tended to be spatially concentrated, with good structures fall-
ing into disuse along with the bad. Public housing projects are

14. For a full description, see R. P. Nathan and C. Adams, "Understanding Central City Hardship," *Political Science Quarterly*, vol. 91, no. 1,
spring 1976, pp. 47-62.

15. For more on the definition of distressed cities, see "The Need for a
National Urban Policy," *Occasional Papers in Housing and Community
Affairs*, vol. 4, U.S. Department of Housing and Urban Development, July
1979, pp. 7-190.

often located in declining neighborhoods or areas which have reached their nadir. In part this is due to the oldest projects being located in areas with the oldest housing and infrastructure, areas that were largely passed by as real incomes rose in the post-War period. In part, this was caused more recently by locating public housing on sites cleared by urban renewal, where the bulldozers so rent the neighborhood fabric that it was never mended. Badly managed public housing in some instances also contributed to decline. Whatever the cause of their present locations, the public housing projects now often represent either the key resource or the worst impediment to neighborhood revitalization.

SERVICE DELIVERY AT THE PHAs

How are the Public Housing Authorities carrying out their tasks? Again, unfortunately, a simple response is not feasible. Indeed, a good part of this book attempts to develop a complete answer. Even at this point, though, one can look at the few indicators in table 3 to get a sense of current status. The five data items in the table come from a 1976 national survey of 119 Housing Authorities conducted by The Urban Institute as part of the Institute's research for HUD on the relation between management practices and good performance in public housing. Data are for the PHAs as a whole. Among the PHAs surveyed are 11 of the 29 in the largest cities; and the figures in the table are the responses of the executive directors at the 11 PHAs based on their perceptions of the situation in their Authorities.

The most startling aspect to the responses is the incredible range. Hence, vacancy rates vary from almost 0 to 14 percent, with a mean of 4.2 percent. Because these Authorities all have extensive waiting lists, vacancy rates reveal more about the speed with which vacated units are made ready for new tenants than they reveal about "market" conditions. Still, PHAs do have difficulty marketing ready-to-occupy units in distressed projects or in projects with poor reputations. Turnover rates are one indication of tenant dissatisfaction. Moving out of a unit usually means leaving public housing and its substantial subsidy. Under these conditions, the mean rate of 18 percent seems high, although it is only half of the turnover rate of all central

Table 3

SELECTED OPERATING CHARACTERISTICS OF PHAs
IN ELEVEN VERY LARGE CITIES [a]

	RANGE		Unweighted Average
	Minimum	Maximum	
Vacancy rate as of December 1975 (percentage)	.03	14.2	4.2
Turnover rate during 1975 [b] (percentage)	8.7	27.2	16.9
Tenants delinquent with rental payment in an average month (percentage)	2.7	39.1	18.5
Number of full-time employees per 1,000 units [c]	22	83	56
Response time to tenant request for routine maintenance (e.g., leaking faucet, cracked window), (in days)	same day	45	7.3

Source: Unpublished data from 1976 Urban Institute survey; executive directors
    as respondents. For a description of the survey, see R. Sadacca and
    S. B. Loux, "Improving Public Housing Through Management: A Tech-
    nical Report" (Washington, D.C.: The Urban Institute, Working Paper
    255-2, 1978).
    a. Authorities included National Capital, Baltimore, Atlanta, Memphis, Detroit,
Columbus, Milwaukee, Houston, San Antonio, Los Angeles, San Francisco.
    b. Number of units vacated in 1975 divided by total number of units.
    c. Number of full-time employees plus one half the number of part-time em-
ployees.

city renters with incomes under $10,000 in 1976. Again, the
range is large with the lowest rate being about one third of
the largest. More disturbing is the high average rate of rental
payment delinquencies, 17 percent; the 39 percent rate reported
by one Authority suggests a complete management breakdown.

The two final indicators are measures of labor inputs (staff
years per 1,000 units) and outputs (maintenance response
times). For both of these measures it is once more the range of
responses that makes an impression. Even granting that the
staffing levels cannot be sensibly interpreted without a measure
of services being provided, the one-to-four ratio of the lowest
staff rate per 1,000 units to the highest seems amazing. On the

other hand, a 45-day response time for routine maintenance requests is as appalling as same-day service is admirable.

Similar data are presented in table 4 for *projects,* selected essentially at random, that were sampled within 2 of these 11 PHAs as part of the survey. Recall that housing projects are the basic management units of *Authorities;* each large Authority manages a dozen or more projects. This time the respondent was the project manager. (The PHAs are not identified because of a pledge of confidentiality made to acquire unbiased responses.) The main point of these data is again the sharp variance within Authorities in performance and staffing. The indicators shown in the last two tables provide hints about serious problems as well as revealing occasions of excellence—a vast range of performance between, and indeed within, Authorities. Exploring causes of this variation is the central task of this analysis.

Table 4

SELECTED OPERATING CHARACTERISTICS OF SAMPLE PROJECTS IN TWO VERY LARGE PHAs [c]

PHA/Project	Vacancy Rate	Employees per 1,000 units	Routine Maintenance Response Time (days)	Routine Maintenance Requests per Month per Unit (percentage)
A. 1	12.5	39	7	.8
2	10.4	40	15	.1
3	1.5	22	3	.8
4	1.9	5	3	.4
5	10.0	40	0 [a]	[b]
6	7.6	8	7	.5
B. 1	5.9	20	1	.8
2	3.3	33	1	.5
3	.5	11	2	1.1
4	1.5	9	2	[b]
5	0	16	1	.5

a. Same day.
b. Less than .05.
c. Responses of project managers; source given in table 3.

A NOTE ON THE METHODOLOGICAL APPROACH

The analysis presented is for the layman. Indeed, even if one wished to go further analytically the quality of the available data would not permit it. The analysis is also characterized by a total reliance on data already collected, either through special surveys or through routine HUD reporting requirements. This reliance means that in many places the ideal measures of performance or operations are not available; close substitutes are cautiously employed where possible; in some instances we must admit ignorance. It also means that a variety of data sets are employed, each collected for a different sample of PHAs for a different purpose. This causes a good bit of discontinuity in the flow of the discussion and limits the strength of the concluding statements. The reader is forewarned of these problems of concatenation; nevertheless, even within these limits, a picture of remarkable resolution emerges.

Part II
CURRENT
PHA
CONDITIONS

Chapter 2

The Projects

Beginning the review of the present circumstances of the public housing program in the largest cities with an inventory of the condition of the projects is highly appropriate. Many Americans have formed their opinions of public housing by looking at projects over the years. One measure of an Authority's health is the condition of the housing it manages. Broken windows, kicked-in doors, layers of graffiti in the public areas, stopped-up toilets, and filthy grounds suggest that management is deficient. But there is more to judging project condition than ratings on needed repairs and deferred maintenance. For one thing, the type and quality of the units when built must be considered. Was the project designed as high-rise family housing, a monster garden apartment complex, housing for the elderly, or a small, low density row-house complex? Clearly, the basic configuration is of fundamental importance. How good were the materials used? What is the quality of the finishing work? Are hot water pipes exposed? Do kitchen cabinets have doors? Was there genuine site planning?

Location also influences a project's condition. Even in instances where a project is set apart from the surrounding neighborhood—both spatially and in terms of social contacts between project tenants and area residents—the neighborhood context strongly influences the project. It creates the project's general environment, either positive or depressing. The neighborhood can be the home of vandals, thieves, and muggers who commute to the project for "work." Simply, the greater social distress in the surrounding area, the more difficult good project management becomes.[1] Finally, the tenants are critical to the project's condition: the more responsibility they take for themselves, each other, and the project, the easier the management task.

The discussion in this chapter begins with a description of the types of projects that have been built. The present condition of the national inventory is then documented, using data from a recent HUD study. Finally, we examine the current characteristics of the neighborhoods in which these projects are located.

WHAT WAS BUILT?

In the 40-year history of public housing, some of almost everything has been constructed, but there is a pattern of major swings among several dominant architectural patterns that deserves attention. To distill this history to manageable dimensions, the review begins by discussing the projects built by the Chicago Housing Authority (CHA), the nation's second largest Authority, from the earliest projects of the 1930s to those of the 1970s. Following this description, some notes on the entire stock are presented. Finally, some of the critiques of public housing architecture are briefly reviewed.

Chicago

The 40 years of development of public housing in Chicago fall into four periods on the basis of distinct architectural styles. For each period, the broad characteristics of the projects built are illustrated, and notes are given on a few specific projects. The review relies heavily on Deveraux Bowley's fascinating and comprehensive study of assisted housing in Chicago.[2] In places, judgments about the quality of design appear in the description. The standards applied are those listed in the critique at the

---

1. For more on this point see chapter 7.

2. D. Bowley, Jr., *The Poorhouse: Subsidized Housing in Chicago, 1895-1976* (Carbondale, Ill: Southern Illinois University Press, 1978).

end of the section; their application is, needless to say, extremely subjective.

Two common elements bind together the projects of the various periods. First, until very recently, the scale was always large: From the outset, hundreds of units, whether high-rise or low-rise, were in a single project. Second, throughout most of its history, the CHA located its projects in deteriorating neighborhoods, either on sites it assembled itself or on urban renewal land. While intense arguments for less concentration at these sites were made over the years, in the end, the CHA generally bowed to the wishes of the city council, and continued building projects in deteriorating neighborhoods. A sketch of the trends for each period of CHA's history follows.

The Early Years. This era begins with the construction of the first projects by the Public Works Administration in the early 1930s, which were soon acquired by the CHA, and ends with the completion of several wartime projects. The projects consisted of either low-rise apartments (none higher than four stories) or 2-story row houses; some projects combined both styles. The following projects are representative of the period:

- The Jane Addams Houses completed in 1938, consists of 32 buildings containing 1,027 units. The 2-, 3-, and 4-story buildings cover more than 28 percent of the site.

- Opened about the same time, the Julia C. Lathrop Homes contains 925 units. The project is again low-rise in character and had only a 17 percent site coverage.

- The Ida B. Wells project consists of 1,662 units—868 apartments and 794 row houses and garden apartments—in 124 buildings. Site coverage is 24 percent. Its apartments had more rooms than the other early projects had.

- Frances Cabrini Homes, built in 1941-42, consists of fifty-five 2- and 3-story buildings, housing 586 units on a 16-acre site.

The large number of similar structures on a well-defined site often gave a regimental appearance to these projects. Further, the actual site improvements on the available open space were indeed modest.

The Middle Years. This period, lasting from about 1947 to 1955, saw a much greater variety of projects: some small, low-rise

projects of better than average design, large additions to earlier
projects, and the gradual dominance of first the high-rise apartment building and then the "super blocks" of high-rise buildings. It also saw the continuation of a policy of replacing slums
with public housing, a policy strengthened in the Housing Act
of 1949. Descriptions of some representative projects follow:

• Racine Courts and Le Clair Courts are smaller row-house
  projects completed in 1950. Racine Courts consisted of 121
  units, the greatest floor space of units built to date, with full
  basements, decent landscaping, and location in a middle-class
  residential area. Le Clair Courts was larger, 316 units; a later
  extension added 300 units to the site and created a more institutional environment.

• Dearborn Homes, completed in 1950, was the first elevator
  project in the inventory. Its 800 units are housed in 16 elevator buildings of six and nine stories in height, all with a cruci-
  form design. While billed as an experimental project, there
  was little innovative about it besides its greater height. Land
  coverage was reduced to a mere 10 percent of the site.

• Prairie Avenue Courts is considered the best designed high-
  rise project of this era. The buildings have exposed concrete
  frames with brick in-fill and the exposed gallery construction
  common to this period. The project was completed in stages
  over the early 1950s and when completed contained 343 units
  in 16 buildings—one 14-story apartment building, 3 buildings
  of 7 stories, 3 apartment blocks of 2 stories, and 6 groups of
  row houses.

• Harold L. Ickes Homes opened in 1955, and is reminiscent of
  other high-rise projects of this period, but it is on a larger and
  less human scale. The 797 units are in eight buildings, three
  are nine stories tall and very long; and the other five are seven
  stories tall.

• Grace Abbott Homes, completed in 1955, is the obvious immediate precursor to the super-block era. The project is dom-
  inated by seven 15-story Y-shaped towers. Thirty-three row-
  house structures are at the edge of the site. In Bowley's
  words, "More than any other project built in Chicago to that
  date, the overall feeling is forbidding, and the human scale is
  completely lost."

The High-Rise Years. This might better be called the era of the super blocks: huge projects, constructed on a colossal scale with extremely low rates of site coverage by the structures and sterile landscaping treatment. From 1957 to 1968, the CHA completed an astounding 15,591 family units; all but 696 were in high-rise structures. What was the rationale behind this form of development? Elizabeth Wood, long-time pioneer executive director of the CHA, in 1945 spoke of the need to rebuild the city and argued that the projects—which would be the first step in rejuvenation—had to have sufficient scale to not be overwhelmed by the surrounding neighborhood. To effect this scale required the isolation of the projects and relocation of streets and transit around the projects. This permitted formation of the super blocks. In Wood's mind, super blocks and high-rise construction went hand in hand. Why this was the case is unclear, although Le Corbusier's ideas on this subject certainly influenced a whole generation. Some notable examples follow:

- Stateway Gardens, completed in 1958, contains 1,684 units in two buildings, each 10 stories tall, and six buildings, each 17 stories high. The structures cover only 12 percent of the 33-acre site. Visually, it is massive and forbidding.

- Brooks Homes Extension is representative of the smaller projects of this period. Completed in 1961, the project contains 449 units in three 16-story buildings on an 8-acre site.

- The archetype of the super-block projects is Robert Taylor Homes. This project was designed for an incredible 4,415 units on a one-half mile by two-mile site. The units are contained in 28 identical 16-story buildings, mostly grouped in U-shaped, 3-building clusters. To quote Bowley again, "The buildings are completely undistinguished, with red or yellow brick veneers, central elevator shaft, and fenced galleries." With site coverage of only 7 percent and the clustering of buildings, there are large open spaces in the site which, unfortunately, were unimaginatively treated.

Nineteen Sixty-Seven To The Present. The burst of activity in the prior decade gave way to seeming exhaustion, not to mention genuine disillusionment on the part of some long-time supporters of public housing. Much less building was initiated and much which was completed was of the single-building, elderly-only type. In the 1970s, the CHA has been engaged in prolonged legal disputes about the location of its projects; and a virtual moratorium has been in effect while the court has sought remedies that would locate projects in nonminority, especially suburban areas.[3] A few small, scattered-site projects have been completed.

- Lothrop Apartments was the first project designed for the elderly. It contains 92 efficiency and 1-bedroom apartments in a single high-rise structure. After 1961, the CHA built eight more such buildings with a total of 1,009 apartments.

The National Inventory. While all of the large PHAs went through their own architectural cycles, the landmarks of the Chicago program provide useful reference points for the nation. Important exceptions exist, however. For example, Cleveland, Pittsburgh, and Los Angeles all avoided elevator family housing.

It is indeed difficult to succinctly describe the projects constructed by various PHAs. The approach here has been to use a sample of 66 projects drawn from 12 of the largest PHAs as part of an intense analysis of public housing management in 120 Authorities. These Authorities are representative of all PHAs and the survey was conducted by The Urban Institute during 1973-76.[4] The sample of projects was randomly drawn for each PHA in such a way as to guarantee that they were representative of all of the PHA's projects along six dimensions.[5] Three of the six factors would reflect some aspect of the projects' design: number of units in the project; whether the project included a high-rise building (five or more stories); whether there were 50 percent or more elderly residents.[6] Thus, while

---

3. For an excellent description see A. Polikoff, *Housing the Poor* (Cambridge: Ballinger Publishing Company, 1978); and M. Meyerson and E.C. Banfield, *Politics, Planning, and the Public Interest* (New York: The Free Press, 1955).

4. The sample approach was necessitated by the lack of any comprehensive set of data on the physical attributes of public housing projects kept at HUD in a readily accessible form. Even the information which was supposedly kept in permanent storage was found seriously incomplete.

5. For a description of the sample, see R. Sadacca and S. Loux, "Improving Public Housing Through Management: A Technical Report" (Washington, D.C.: The Urban Institute, Working Paper 255-2, 1978).

6. The other three factors are whether there were 50 percent or more minority-group residents; whether the turnover rate was greater than 7 percent; and whether the vacancy rate was 3 percent or more.

the sample was not drawn to represent project design per se, it is doubtful that the profile so obtained is highly biased for the individual PHAs.

Basic project descriptions are given in table 5 for the projects sampled by The Urban Institute in four PHAs—Atlanta, Baltimore, Detroit, and Houston. These four were chosen for use here because of the relatively complete information available for them from the HUD files. These should be interpreted as giving a general picture—but not necessarily a statistically reliable one—of public housing in the largest cities. These data reinforce several points made previously. The projects are large: The average project size in three PHAs is close to 700 units; 4 of the 21 listed have more than 1,000 units; and only 4 have fewer than 300 units. It is obviously difficult for projects of such scale to blend into the community. All of the projects with apartment buildings more than three stories tall were built since 1955. Low-rise apartments and row houses are the rule up to that point. Finally, there has been a steady increase over time in the apartment size, as measured by number of bedrooms per unit, implying a steady rise in population per project.

How Good Was the Design?

Enough has already been said to suggest that the most positive possible response to this question is "not very." But what have the experts said? There was an outpouring of architectural critique in the early 1960s, but since then little expert commentary has been forthcoming, in part one supposes because of the enactment of numerous other programs which reduced the importance of public housing. Interestingly, much of the contemporary critique of public housing has come from sociologists like Lee Rainwater, who by studying the lives of the tenants in the projects, such as super-block Pruitt-Igoe in Rainwater's case, documented the mismatch between the structure and its occupants.[7] Even more recently, those trying to redesign projects to make them livable—people like Oscar Newman and William Brill—have indirectly provided sharp critiques of the initial design.[8]

---

7. Lee Rainwater, *Behind Ghetto Walls* (Chicago: Aldine Publishing Co., 1970).

8. Oscar Newman, *Defensible Space* (New York: Collier, 1973). A number of Brill's works are cited in chapter 8.

Table 5

SELECTED CHARACTERISTICS OF SAMPLE PROJECTS IN FOUR LARGE PHAs

| PHA and Project | Total Units | Units by Bedroom Size | | | | | Buildings in Project | | | | | | Year Completed |
| | | 1 | 2 | 3 | 4 | 5+ | Row house | | Apartment | | Other [b] | | |
							No.	height (stories)	No.	height (stories)	No.	height (stories)	
ATLANTA													
Capitol Hms	815	210[a]	451	154	—	—	99	2	—	—	—	—	1941
Herdon Hms	520	116[a]	339	65	—	—	54	2	—	—	—	—	1942
Perry Hms	1,000	203	533	41	107	—	179	2	—	—	13	1	1955
(Addition)	140	—	—	78	46	16	24	2	—	—	2	2	1969
Carver Cmmty	990	116	564	194	116	—	238	2	—	—	—	—	1953
University Hms	675	NA	NA	NA	NA	NA	41	2+3	—	—	—	—	1937
Thomasville Hghts	350	40[a]	120	80	80	30	NA	NA	NA	NA	NA	NA	1970
BALTIMORE													
Murphy Hms	706	184	238	230	44	10	20	2+3	4	14	—	—	1963
Latrobe Hms	701	266	332	103	—	—	—	—	25	2+3	45	2+3	1942
Poe Hms	298	164	108	26	—	—	68	2	—	—	—	—	1940
O'Donnell	900	136	452	244	68	—	—	—	—	—	—	—	1944
Somerset Crt	420	106	197	93	24	—	NA	NA	NA	NA	NA	NA	1944
DETROIT													
Brewster Hms	703	432	247	24	—	—	25	2	10	3	—	—	1939
(Addition)	240	72	100	68	—	—	17	2	3	3	—	—	1941
Douglas Hms	1,006	48	770	134	54	—	25	2	8	6+14	—	—	1955
Jefferies I	462	71	299	92	—	—	4	2	15	3+6	—	—	1956
II	896	—	896	—	—	—	—	—	8	14	—	—	1956
III	252	—	—	200	52	—	37	2	8	14	—	—	1956
IV	560	—	560	—	—	—	—	—	5	14	—	—	1956

Lee Plaza	223	195	28	—	—	—	1	15	—	—	—	—	1969
Charles Terr	428	156	171	89	12	—	—	—	23	2+3	38	1	1941
Herman Grdn	2,106	828	828	386	64	—	—	—	1	—	235	2+3	1943
Warren West	212	105	106	1	—	—	—	—	1	9	—	—	1971
HOUSTON												
Kelly Crts	333	88	129	88	28	—	22	2	—	—	—	—	1942
Irvington Crts	318	108	127	46	37	—	—	—	—	—	27	2	1942
Clayton Hms	348	36	116	112	84	—	11	2	—	—	38	2	1952

Source: Completed HUD forms PHA-1885, various editions, kept at HUD central and permanent storage.

a. Includes some efficiencies.

b. Includes singles, twins, and structures with combination of the other categories.

One might begin the critiques with Nathan Glazer's admonition "that one must avoid the danger of building for the poor under regulations or in a style very different from that to which the middle class is accustomed."[9] In fact, Albert Mayer, in a pair of seminal review articles published in the early 1960s, argues that this is exactly what happened in public housing. He sets out five factors—listed in table 6—that must be considered in judging the success of public housing architecture. They include both design internal to the unit, external appearance, site plans, and its performance in use.[10]

Mayer asserts that local and national officials in attempting to design housing that was politically acceptable, that is, not appearing too good, erred in the opposite direction. The housing so built, while structurally sound, was built as cheaply as possible with very deleterious effects. He lists the following three economies which in particular may have had the most damaging effects on public housing design.[11]

1. *Low fees for architects.* Architect's fees were kept sufficiently low so that designers generally settled for standardized plans. This produced repetition of the one or two structure designs many times on a given site, and in some cases, very similar designs in several projects. This experience discouraged more imaginative architects from seeking public housing commissions.

2. *False space economy.* Apartment units generally had absolutely minimum room sizes and minuscule storage areas. Lobby and other public areas along with spaces for laundry facilities and similar tasks were minimal. As Mayer points out, the marginal cost of pure space is quite low. Hence, the modest savings realized were at the expense of a feeling of comfort by the tenants. Such a savings costs more than its value in higher depreciation because

9. Nathan Glazer, "Housing Problems and Housing Policies," *The Public Interest*, no. 7, spring 1967, p. 38.

10. This set of criteria is similar to that employed by other critics. For example, see R. D. Katz, *Intensity of Development and Livability of Multifamily Housing Projects* (Washington, D.C.: U.S. Government Printing Office, FHA Technical Study no. 509, 1963).

11. A. Mayer, "Public Housing Architecture Evaluated from PWA Days up to 1962," *Journal of Housing*, vol. 19, June 1962, pp. 446-58; and "Public Housing Design," Journal of Housing, vol. 20, April 1963, pp. 133-43.

Table 6

FACTORS TO CONSIDER IN JUDGING PUBLIC HOUSING DESIGN

1. Interior floor plans and site plans, viewed as to their functional, family, and social adequacy or inadequacy, in their actual working. A special point of judgment: are the plans quite uniform— or to what extent do they provide for varying tastes, habits, requirements within a development?

2. Three-dimensional elements and site relationships, judged as to psychological and functional effect on occupants of specific developments and on the kinds of relationships, or "unrelationships," they create with surrounding families and community.

3. The grounds—which are generally barren . . . and usually accurately . . . called "open space." Success or failure here can be judged by whether the "space" is filled with life or stands as a fairly dull vacuum; whether it is a source of varied social stimulation and of private repose; whether it is a link between buildings, between people and with neighborhood; whether it has established a sparkling sense of human scale and incident and light.

4. What might be called exterior "straight architecture"—facade, mass, color; what does it say to the indweller, the citizen, the visitor, in the way of inspiration or depression or repulsion? Public housing has become so ubiquitous in so many cities that its civic visual component is a major plus or minus fact in its public appeal—always true of its appeal to its immediate "neighbors"; frequently true for the city at large.

5. What does it all look like, and how does it perform, three or five years later; how has the human drama affected architecture-in-use; are places used as intended by the design . . . or more used . . . or have they degenerated . . . or been abandoned . . . or are they better, more ingeniously, used than was planned; are they serving more purposes than was foreseen; are they "self-maintained," in the best sense—with local public opinion crystallizing and manifesting itself in an effective pride: indeed, a determinant of the success, or failure, of the new kind of architecture that public housing represents.

Source: A. Mayer, "Public Housing Architecture Evaluated from PWA Days up to 1962," *Journal of Housing*, vol. 19, June 1962, p. 447.

of inappropriate and excessive utilization of the minimal space.

3. *False "open space" economy.* As noted in the descriptions of the projects in Chicago, public housing projects were able to dramatically reduce the fraction of sites occupied by structures. But these spaces were not creatively exploited. In Mayer's words, "The space can become a vacuum, can be depressing—even dangerous." Time and again the opportunity afforded by relatively generous sites was squandered.

The low-rise projects that characterized the early years of public housing building suffered from all these problems, but to widely varying degrees. Perhaps the greatest visual problem was the monotonous, barracks-like feeling given by the rank upon rank of row houses in some projects. The row-house projects, however, while generally having poor site planning, did have the advantage of the tenants being able at some projects to claim, maintain, and beautify their front and rear lawns which greatly softened the starkness of the original treatment. Some of the largest projects, like Altgeld Gardens in Chicago, included a public park within its confines, with the design of the spaces that provides definite visual and use variations. It is interesting to note that in some cities, San Antonio as an example, CDBG funds are now being used to put in parks and play facilities near or on an Authority's property to make up for original design deficiencies.

The penurious character of the original finishing work in these projects is easily illustrated: instead of kitchen cupboards, there were open shelves; closets were without doors; and bathrooms had tubs without provision for showers. A good share of "modernization" funds have gone to provide cupboards, closet doors, shower enclosures, and similar remedial items. The units were small: the Carr Square and Clinton Peabody Terrace projects in St. Louis, completed in 1942, had 1- and 2-bedroom units of 420 and 550 square feet, respectively.[12] Overcoming small unit sizes, especially small rooms, requires very costly rehabilitation and has seldom been accomplished.

---

12. E. J. Meehan, *Public Housing Policy* (New Brunswick, N.J.: Rutgers University Center for Urban Policy Research, 1975), table 3.2.

The design imperfections of the high-rise super-block developments overwhelm those of the low-rise projects. As already noted, site coverage shrank with high-rise construction, but site treatment was not improved. Furthermore, in the interest of economy, units become even smaller and cost-saving features more Draconian. Catherine Bauer's 1957 summary critique is especially good:

> The public housing project therefore continues to be laid out as a "community unit," as large as possible and entirely divorced from its neighborhood surroundings, even though this only dramatizes the segregation of charity-case families. Standardization is emphasized rather than alleviated in project design, as a glorification of efficient production methods and an expression of the goal of "decent, safe, and sanitary" housing for all. But the bleak symbols of productive efficiency and "minimum standards" are hardly an adequate or satisfactory expression of the values associated with American home life. And all this, in addition, often embodied in the skyscraper, whose refined technology gladdens the hearts of technocratic architectural sculptors but pushes its occupants into a highly organized, beehive type of community life for which most American families have no desire and little aptitude.[13]

Tenants of Pruitt-Igoe, the subject of Rainwater's study, were very aware of these architectural problems. When asked what the government had intended when it built the project and how well it worked, tenants responded with "They were trying to put a whole bunch of people in a little bitty space. They did a pretty good job—there's a lot of people here," and, "They were trying to get rid of the slum, but they didn't accomplish too much. Inside the apartment they did, but not outside."[14]

Eugene Meehan, in his 1975 evaluation of public housing in St. Louis, notes the shift in quality with the advent of the super block by saying that "conception and execution changed from small and frugal to mean, cheap, and shoddy."[15] A two-bedroom apartment contained only 500 square feet of usable space; hot water pipes were not adequately shielded; and the list goes on.

In recently designing a security plan for the 612-unit Arthur Capper Homes project (first occupied in 1958) in Washington,

---

13. Catherine Bauer, "The Dreary Deadlock of Public Housing," *Architectural Forum*, May 1957.

14. Lee Rainwater, *Behind Ghetto Walls*, pp. 11-12.

15. E.J. Meehan, *Public Housing Policy*, p. 35.

D.C., William Brill noted several design problems, many of them having to do with site treatment, which are typical of elevator projects of this era. There is substantial unassigned open space around the buildings; and the spaces at the "bases of these buildings are poorly differentiated, no zones of transition clearly distinguish between the public street and the semi-public areas of the high rises."[16] The "super-block" project plan does not provide any real or symbolic barriers to define the buildings' relation to the surrounding neighborhood. The result is a no man's land which can be penetrated by anyone, with the tenants unable to exert any natural authority over the site. Brill also notes problems with the design of the entranceways—both their placement (each building has two which cannot be observed at the same time) and their design.[17] The absence of adequate recreational and community space causes adolescents to take over other areas, like entranceways, making other tenants fearful of using them.

These critiques should not be universally applied to all public housing projects of the (roughly) 1955-67 period. Some well-designed projects were built. The merits of the critiques were sufficient, however, to cause HUD under the strong leadership of Public Housing Administrator Marie McGuire to improve designs.[18] Regulations were issued, for example, calling for the use of "low density housing (e.g., nonelevator structures, scattered sites or other types of low density developments appropriate in the locality)" for family housing.[19]

The important point here is that many of the projects operated by Authorities in the largest cities have serious design problems that make managing them an unusually difficult task, especially when coupled with the presence of even a small number of "problem tenants." Furthermore, it means that substan-

---

16. William Brill Associates, *Comprehensive Security Planning: A Program for Arthur Capper Dwellings* (Washingon, D.C.: U.S. Government Printing Office, 1977), p. 31.

17. *Ibid.,* "It is impossible to see inside the building as one enters it, or to see down the hallway to the elevator. Hidden corners, dark narrow hallways, and uninviting, opaque doors and translucent windows make the entranceways appear menacing and fearful," p. 38.

18. See, for example, M. Nenno, "Public Housing Design Seminars," *Journal of Housing,* 1965, no. 2, pp. 86-89.

19. *Code of Federal Regulations,* Title 24, 841.103, U.S. Department of Housing and Urban Development.

tial amounts of modernization funds will have to be expended to redesign elements of the buildings, particularly in the related areas of security and site treatment.

CURRENT MODERNIZATION NEEDS

One way to judge the physical condition of public housing is to know what it would cost to bring all projects up to some common standard. This is exactly the objective of a two-year study funded by HUD's research office. The study's preliminary results, used here, were received in March 1980.[20]

The HUD study actually produced costs estimates for the three distinct investment areas: regular modernization; changes in existing projects necessary to make the projects accessible to the handicapped as required under federal legislation; and, changes to make the projects more energy efficient. Within each of these areas, the cost of achieving several different standards were estimated.

For present purposes, only the estimates for regular modernization are considered. Three standards were defined within the modernization area. The first is to meet minimum health and safety requirements. The second would upgrade projects to meet the HUD minimum property standards (MPS) for new construction, modified as necessary in light of the major structural characteristics of a project. The third standard embodies changes necessary to make public housing competitive with privately owned and operated rental housing, and as such includes amenities beyond those in the first two standards. Our attention is restricted to the first two standards.

Because the specifics of the standards are key to understanding the cost estimates, some further description is in order.[21] Level I includes those items of emergency work to remedy conditions affecting health and safety of occupants; repair major building code violations; and arrest deterioration of major

20. Perkins and Will and the Ehrenkrantz Group, *Preliminary Cost Estimates: An Evaluation of the Physical Condition of Public Housing Stock* (Washington, D.C., U.S. Department of Housing and Urban Development, 1980).

21. This description is taken from vol. I of the Perkins and Will detailed analysis plan submitted to HUD.

building components or systems where there is an existing or potential threat to health or safety. Level II, by contrast includes those items of rehabilitation required to bring a unit up to the MPS or equivalent standards; remedy conditions caused by deferred maintenance that affect a building's use; and postpone major capital expenditures in the future.

The study's objective was to develop nationwide, statistically reliable estimates of the cost of attaining each of the standards; the sample of projects selected to have their condition evaluated and the associated costs of repairs estimated was drawn for this purpose. Consequently, separate estimates are not available for the 29 PHAs which are our particular focus. The study does, however, provide separate estimates for the eight different types of projects listed on the left hand stub of table 7. The projects are distinguished by their intended occupancy (elderly vs. family), height (low-rise vs. high-rise), size (two groups divided at 200 units) and vacancy rates.[22] These categories were chosen after cost estimates had been developed for 200 of the 400 sampled projects; observations were grouped by the extent of variation in costs between and within groups and the second 200 sample projects were chosen to increase the reliability of the estimates for groups with high within-group variance.[23]

It should be possible to place all the projects in our 29 PHAs in these eight project types and attain an estimate of their modernization needs. As shown, however, the necessary data are not in the HUD files. The contractor making the cost estimates for HUD is developing these data, but these were not yet available when this monograph was completed. Hence, we can only describe the cost estimates by the type of project and make some general link to the projects in our 29 PHAs.

The figures in table 7 show the per unit cost and the total cost (per unit cost times the number of units) required to bring the projects in each of the eight project types up to Levels I and II standards. The final three columns of the table give the ratio of (a) the share of total cost summed over all eight project types for a given project type to (b) that project type's share of all

---

22. Elderly projects and those containing 50 percent or more of units designated for the elderly. High-rise projects are those with buildings with 4 or more stories, including projects with high- and low-rise structures.

23. A brief statement and sampling procedure is given in Appendix A.

Table 7

ESTIMATES OF MODERNIZATION NEEDS OF PUBLIC HOUSING [d]

Type of Project	Units Total (000)	Units As Share of Total	Average Age of Project (Yrs)	Level I Cost Average per unit ($)	Level I Cost Total ($000)	Level II Cost Average per unit ($)	Level II Cost Total ($000)	Ratio: Share of Total Cost to Share of Total Units by Level I	Ratio II
Elderly									
Low-Rise	183.3	.15	14	70	5,909	380	67,235	.13	.26
High-Rise	88.0	.07	10	64	16,704	613	51,777	.78	.72
Family									
Low-Rise									
≧ 200 units ≧ 10% vacant	41.5	.03	20 [a]	444	17,725	1,757	70,156	1.97	1.76
≧ 200 units < 10% vacant	352.0	.29	20 [a]	212	71,746	1,321	447,014	.81	1.17
< 200 units	248.0	.20	14	353	84,498	1,249	298,570	1.40	1.14
High-Rise									
≧ 200 units ≧ 10% vacant	41.6	.03	24 [b]	1,589	62,734	2,677	105,648	6.93	2.67
≧ 200 units < 10% vacant	215.1	.18	24 [b]	182	37,849	1,013	210,082	.69	.89
< 200 units	52.5	.04	18	218	11,058	1,278	64,825	.90	1.22
Total	1,222	1.00		258 [c]	302,316	1,076 [c]	1,315,310		

Source: Perkins and Will and The Ehrenkrantz Group, Preliminary Cost Estimate: An Evaluation of the Physical Condition of the Public Housing Stock.

a. Figure for all family projects of over 200 units.
b. Figure for all family projects of under 200 units.
c. Average.
d. Levels I and II are defined in the text; all costs in 1980 dollars.

public housing units. Separate figures are given for Levels I and II.

A brief examination of the figures in the table reveals several consistent patterns. Projects designed for elderly occupancy, whether low-rise or high-rise, have the smallest modernization needs. At the other end of the spectrum are high-rise family projects of more than 200 units and with vacancy rates of 10 percent or more. For Level II, which includes Level I, the projects require about $2,700 of work; and their share of the aggregate cost for all projects is about 2.5 times their share of all projects. These distressed projects with about 42,000 units constitute only 3 percent of all units, but about 12 percent of all investment need. They are particularly in need of the repairs included in the Level I standards.

It is equally important, however, that high-rise projects with low vacancy rates taken as a whole (group 7 in the table) need little improvement compared not only with the distressed high-rise projects but with low-rise projects as well. In fact, large low-rise projects with high vacancies (group 3 in the table) have the second greatest modernization needs and include the same number of units as the distressed high-rise counterpart. These units need $1,760 per unit to be brought up to Level II.

This suggests that unmarketable units, as evidenced by high vacancy rates—whether caused by poor management, neighborhood conditions, or other factors—are those with the greatest modernization needs. Overall, project height or scale alone is a poor guide to need.

The total systemwide cost of achieving the Level II standard is high—about $1.3 billion. Under recent modernization funding levels, and assuming no additional needs develop during the "repair period," it would take three or four years of regular funding to wipe out this deficit. But in light of past experience, it seems likely that without major management improvements, many of the improvements funded with modernization money will depreciate rapidly. Hence, the total bill will be more than the $1.6 billion estimate.

The overall conclusion of the HUD study is important:

> The vast majority of the housing stock, approximately 85 percent is in good condition. While some of it is not attractive, these units appear to be successfully maintaining the physical standard called for in the MPS (minimum property standard).

Unfortunately, based on the location of distressed projects found in earlier HUD studies (cited in the last chapter), it appears that a large share of the residual 15 percent of units are in the Authorities in the nation's largest cities.

PROJECT LOCATION

The location of public housing projects has consistently been influenced by political considerations as well as site availability, land costs, and the relation to other programs, particularly urban renewal. Furthermore, the results of the complicated decision process that produced the sites and the initial neighborhood characteristics would indeed be difficult to observe today in the face of 20-40 years of inner city neighborhood dynamics. Here the focus is on the contemporary characteristics of the neighborhoods.

The types of neighborhoods in which the projects are located are of obvious importance. Neighborhood conditions strongly influence the attractiveness of public housing just as they are a prime determinant of the rental or home purchase decision in the private sector. Likewise, the neighborhood affects living conditions in the project, most dramatically perhaps through criminal activity being imported to some projects but more generally through the social interaction between project tenants and the rest of the community. Little study has been done of this interaction. One can readily imagine differences in this area between residents in the spatially isolated super-block projects and smaller low-rise units. But similar projects can have vastly different experiences depending on the extent of community acceptance and other factors.[24]

There is no systematic information on the types of settings in which public housing is located. Thus, we have been forced to

---

24. Louis Kriesberg, "Neighborhood Setting and the Isolation of Public Housing Tenants," *Journal of the American Institute of Planners*, vol. 34, no. 1, January 1968, pp. 43-9. An indirect measure of acceptance is the trend in property values in the neighborhood in which a project is located compared to similar neighborhoods without projects. See H. O. Nourse, "The Effect of Public Housing on Property Values in St. Louis," *Land Economics*, vol. 39, 1963, pp. 433-41; and J. deSalvo, "Neighborhood Upgrading Effects of Middle Income Housing Projects in New York City," *Journal of Urban Economics*, vol. 1, 1974, pp. 267-77.

construct a crude profile using data on the census tracts in which projects are located from the 1970 Census of Population and Housing. Because census tracts are large compared to what is usually thought of as a neighborhood, only a rough description emerges. Table 8 presents a few indicators for the projects

Table 8

SELECTED CHARACTERISTICS OF NEIGHBORHOODS IN WHICH PUBLIC HOUSING IS LOCATED IN FOUR CITIES

	Mean Household Income (1970) [a]	Home- Ownership Rate (1970) [a]	Fraction of Households Black (1970) [a]	Vacancy Rate (1970) [a]
Atlanta				
City Mean	$7,494	.50	.53	.05
Capitol Homes	5,451	.40	.96	.07
Carver Cmmty.	4,114	.14	.95	.03
University Homes	3,182	.10	.98	.06
Thomasville Hghts.	8,470	.84	.67	.02
Baltimore				
City Mean	8,084	.44	.39	.06
Latrobe Homes	3,348	.06	.99	.13
Poe Homes	2,741	.02	.92	.18
O'Donnell	6,102	.39	.04	.04
Somerset Crt.	4,658	.21	.57	.10
Murphy Homes	3,440	.08	.99	.18
Detroit				
City Mean	8,984	.60	.39	.06
Brewster—				
Douglas Homes	4,015	.33	.93	.18
Jefferies	4,234	.02	.34	.20
Lee Plaza	6,466	.21	.92	.12
Charles Terr.	8,610	.67	.18	.02
Herman Gardens	7,704	.66	.92	.04
Warren West	5,662	.45	.98	.06
Houston				
City Mean	9,840	.52	.23	.09
Kelly Crts.	4,450	.24	.99	.13
Irvington Crts.	5,216	.36	.06	.10
Clayton Homes	5,162	.18	.15	.08

a. "Neighborhood" is defined as the census tract. Data are from the 1970 Census of Population and Housing, printed report, PHC (1)-h series.

whose locations could be reliably located on tract maps from the same four PHAs used in table 5. In most cases the same projects are included in both tables. In addition, in Appendix I, table I-1 gives the mean characteristics for the tracts in which projects are located in each of the 11 PHAs in the largest cities surveyed by The Urban Institute in 1976.

A quick study of these figures reveals a few broad patterns. Public housing projects are located in low-income neighborhoods, often with mean household incomes being around half of that for the metropolitan area; in areas with substantially higher vacancy rates than the rest of the city or metropolitan area; and in areas with comparatively few homeowners. The variance in specific situations, however, is striking. Contrast, for example, the Baltimore neighborhoods as of 1970 in which the pre-war vintage Poe and O'Donnell projects are located. Poe is in an exclusively rental neighborhood, with a very impoverished black population. The O'Donnell area, by contrast, is one with a substantial representation of homeowners and a household income level equal to three fourths of the city average. Similar contrasts exist in city after city.

Another source of information on the neighborhoods is the response of project managers to a question included in The Urban Institute's 1976 management survey, concerning the extent, if any, to which the neighborhood around the project causes problems for the project. The responses range from no problem to a big problem. As noted earlier, many factors will affect the response to this question, including the project's physical isolation and the manager's biases if any. Most managers did not rate the neighborhoods as causing anything greater than a small problem. But in 8 of the 11 PHAs, at least one project manager responded that the neighborhood created real problems for the project.

Chapter 3

Who Lives In
Public Housing?

The answer to the question posed as the chapter title is obviously important for each administering Authority separately as well as for the public housing program in the aggregate. The tenant profile can strongly influence the degree of acceptance in the community. The closer the tenant profile resembles that of the community, the greater the acceptance and support are likely to be. This support can be a critical matter to the Authority because of its dependence on the local jurisdiction for the provision of certain services, for example, police protection or garbage collection, which it would otherwise have to purchase in whole or in part for itself. In fact, it is difficult to get a firm grasp on actual community attitudes because of the contradictory answers generated in various surveys to related but not identical questions.[1]

---

1. For example, on the one hand, surveys show strong disapproval of the welfare program and welfare recipients (J. R. Feagin, "America's Welfare Stereotypes," *Social Science Quarterly,* March 1972, pp. 921-33). On the other hand, public officials and the public support the concept of providing housing assistance to low-income households, although their type of low-income status (e.g., welfare recipient) is not specified; see Carolyn E. Setlow, "A Survey of the Attitudes and Experience of State and Local Government Officials and Federal Housing Programs," and

Even more important, however, is the effect of tenant composition on the manageability of the projects. The greater the project's population density, the larger the number of unsupervised children, and the larger the adolescent daytime population, the greater will be the difficulties of managing the project. Furthermore, the poorer the tenants, the greater will be a PHA's dependence on federal operating subsidies. The greater the dependence on public assistance, the more the PHAs will be subject to shifts in the rental payments from state and federal legislative changes to income support programs.

In fact, as documented in chapter 6, the PHAs have considerable control over the composition of their tenant populations. Data presented in this chapter provide one indication of the extent to which this control has been used. The description given here is limited to demographic and economic characteristics of the tenants. No attempt has been made to review the sociology of the tenants, although a rich literature exists, because it is simply beyond our expertise.[2] The final section, however, considers the profile of the "problem tenant."

Because of data limitations only a broad picture of tenant composition can be given here. The Department of Housing and Urban Development actually gathers a vast amount of data annually on tenant incomes and other characteristics (the so-called SHACO data); but recent analysis has shown these data are unreliable due to variations in reporting between and within PHAs.[3] As a consequence, this chapter relies on special tabulations of data gathered in a survey of 10,000 tenants conducted in 1976 by The Urban Institute for HUD. The survey was designed to provide a reliable national picture of public housing

"A Study of Public Attitudes Toward Federal Government Assistance for Housing for Low and Moderate Income Families," in *Housing in the Seventies: Working Papers* (Washington, D.C.: U.S. Government Printing Office, 1976), vol. 2, pp. 1326-83, and 1433-81.

2. Cf. Wm. Moore, Jr., *The Vertical Ghetto: Everyday Life in an Urban Project* (New York: Random House, 1969); Lee Rainwater, *Behind Ghetto Walls: Black Family Life in a Federal Slum* (Chicago: Aldine Publishing Co., 1970); and Alvin Rabushka and Wm. G. Weissert, *Caseworks or Police: How Tenants See Public Housing* (Stanford: Hoover Institution Press, 1977).

3. Memorandum from Robert Sadacca (The Urban Institute) to Carolyn McFarlane (HUD, Office of Research), "Usability of HUD Data (SHACO) Tapes," (Washington, D.C.: The Urban Institute, May 15, 1979).

tenants.[4] Among the PHAs included in the survey were 22 of
the 29 that are the focus of this study.[5] While the existence of
the special survey is certainly good news; there is bad news as
well: it is not possible to know whether the profiles of the 22
PHAs for which we have data are representative of all 29 PHAs;
and the sample sizes in all but a handful of the 22 included
PHAs are too small to permit PHA-level analysis. Most frustrat-
ing, however, is that no project level analysis within the PHAs
is possible. Thus, it is not possible, for example, to closely link
the physical attributes of the projects with the characteristics
of the occupants. Despite these problems, a broad and quite
consistent profile emerges from the data at hand.

To understand how the public housing tenancy compares
with the population of lower-income households generally, the
data from Annual Housing Survey (AHS) that are available for
20 of the 22 central cities which are the jurisdictions of the
PHAs have been employed.[6] Since the AHS contains substantial information on the characteristics of the individual households included in its sample, it was possible to select those
households who met approximate program eligibility rules, but
who were not living in public housing at the time of the survey,

---

4. For a description of the survey, including the sample design and
sample sizes for individual PHAs, see S. Loux and R. Sadacca, "Estimates
of Rent and Income Levels in Public Housing Under Various Definitions"
(Washington, D.C.: The Urban Institute, Contract Report 247-1, 1977).

5. The 22 cities included are Boston, Buffalo, New York City, Wash-
ington, Baltimore, Philadelphia, Pittsburgh, Atlanta, Memphis, Chicago,
Detroit, Minneapolis, Columbus, Cincinnati, Milwaukee, New Orleans,
Dallas, Houston, San Antonio, St. Louis, Los Angeles, and San Francisco.

6. Although the AHS is fielded in the metropolitan areas of Memphis
and San Antonio, disclosure rules of the Bureau of the Census forbid dis-
closing data for a geographic area less than the full SMSA. So, Memphis
and San Antonio were dropped from this analysis because the PHAs
included in this analysis have jurisdiction (generally) only over the central city, using the SMSA-wide data would yield an inaccurate comparison between participant and eligible households in this jurisdiction. In
the few instances where PHAs have broader jurisdiction, a correspond-
ingly broader geographic area was used in making the tabulations. For a
description of the AHS, see U.S. Bureau of the Census, Current Housing
Reports, Series H-150-76, Annual Housing Survey: 1976, Part A, General
Housing Characteristics of the United States and Regions (Washington,
D.C.: U.S. Government Printing Office, 1978).

as the reference group.[7] Finally, the portion of the AHS that gathers large samples for individual metropolitan areas surveys only one fourth of the 60 included SMSAs each year; this staggered surveying has meant that the data for the 20 cities that are compared with the public survey data are for calendar years 1974-76. This variation in the timing of the surveys, combined with differences in the income definitions used by the PHAs and the Bureau of the Census (who conducts the AHS), makes it infeasible to compare the incomes of tenants and eligible but nonparticipating households.[8]

THE BROAD PICTURE

A profile of households eligible for public housing—divided between those actually living in public housing and "eligibles"—is given in table 9. Using the five categories of race, household type, age of household head, household size, and income source reported with the greatest frequency, the archetypical household is black, headed by a female under age 65 living in a household of four people, and has AFDC payments as the primary income source.

Of course, only a minority of households actually has all five characteristics; but the common image of public housing tenants is accurate to some degree. In the big cities, almost three fourths of the tenants are black, and half of the households are female-headed families, and half of all households have three or more members.

But is the profile just described the profile of the poor of whom public housing tenants are simply a representative subset? No; public housing tenants are a special group of the poor. Columns 2 and 3 of table 9 show, respectively, the profiles of

---

7. There is a question in the survey that asks respondents if they live in public housing, and it was the response to this question that was used to separate recipients from the eligible population. Eligibility was defined as eligibility for the Lower Income Rental Assistance Program (Section 8)—described in chapter 9—although there is variance in income eligibility limits among PHAs. One limitation of the AHS is that nonelderly, handicapped persons cannot be identified. For this reason, all one-person, nonelderly households were classified as ineligible. This may cause some slight bias in the comparisons made.

8. Public housing income definitions are discussed in chapter 6.

Table 9

COMPARISON OF PUBLIC HOUSING TENANTS AND OTHER PROGRAM ELIGIBLE HOUSEHOLDS IN TWENTY LARGE CITIES

(percentage)

	Public Housing Tenants [a]	Eligible Households [b] Total	Renters
Ethnic Distribution			
White	16	53	48
Black	73	37	40
Spanish	10	8	10
Household Types			
Husband-wife, no children	8	19	14
Husband-wife, children	13	18	17
Female-headed family	49	32	36
Single individuals	29	24	24
Age of Household Head			
65 or older	26	38	32
Under 65	74	62	68
Size of Household			
1 person	29	24	24
2 persons	18	34	32
3-4 persons	30	26	28
5 or more persons	23	16	15
Primary Income Source			
Wages, salaries, etc.	30	42	45
Welfare (AFDC, SSI)	43	16	21
Social Security	27	41	34

a. Special tabulations of 1976 tenant income survey data.

b. Income eligibility based on Section 8 income limits; eligibles exclude non-aged single-person households, although handicapped persons are eligible, as in special cases are other single persons. Eligibles exclude households currently in public housing. (Special tabulations of data from the metropolitan Annual Housing Survey).

all eligible households and eligible renter households. In this discussion, renter eligibles are used as the reference group because a good share of eligible homeowners are elderly owner-occupants with reduced incomes but substantial assets; further, it seems less likely that homeowners will move into public housing even though they could technically apply to do so. The contrast between public housing tenants (called "tenants" below) and renter eligibles ("eligibles") is strong in the following four areas:

- Blacks constitute 73 percent of tenants but 40 percent of eligibles;
- Forty-nine percent of tenant households are female-headed families but 36 percent of eligibles are female-headed families;
- Fifty-three percent of tenant families have 3 or more members (23 percent, 5 or more) but 43 percent of eligible families have 3 or more members; and
- Forty-three percent of tenants have AFDC as their primary income source but 21 percent of eligibles have AFDC as the primary income source.

Furthermore, this pattern seems to hold for the individual PHAs as well, to judge from the few for which sample sizes are large enough to give reliable figures.[9]

VARIATIONS AMONG PHAs

The subject here is the tenant mixes in different Authorities, quite aside from how they compare with the pool of those eligible to live in public housing. The sample in the 1976 national survey was drawn such that samples of tenants for most individual PHAs are too small to be reliable, that is, to give mean values with acceptably small variances. Aside from New York, however, samples were large enough for five PHAs—Los Angeles, Atlanta, Chicago, Baltimore, and Philadelphia. Tenant profiles for these five Authorities are given in table 10. In examining these figures, it should be clear that variations among the profiles can result from several causes: the variations in the pool of those eligible for the program, differences in those eligibles who actually apply for the program, differences in the type of units available (especially in terms of bedrooms), and variations in the PHAs' tenant selection policies. In this regard, Mayo and his colleagues have observed that the racial composition of the tenants in the assisted housing programs, including public housing, in Phoenix and Pittsburgh is sensitive to the racial

---

9. See Appendix I, table I-2.

Table 10

SELECTED CHARACTERISTICS OF TENANTS IN LARGE AUTHORITIES: 1976 (percentage)

	Twenty-two cities [a]	Five cities [a]	Los Angeles	Atlanta	Chicago	Baltimore	Philadelphia
Racial Distribution							
White	15	10	6	16	9	14	6
Black	66	85	54	84	89	86	90
Spanish	10	4	33	—	1	—	4
Household Types							
Husband-wife, no children	8	3	3	3	2	6	2
Husband-wife, children	13	10	25	4	11	9	8
Female-headed family	49	61	59	64	58	56	68
Single individuals	28	24	13	29	26	27	20
Age of Head							
65 or older	26	20	11	26	25	20	13
Under 65	74	80	89	74	75	80	87
Size of Household							
1 person	29	24	13	29	26	27	20
2 persons	18	14	18	21	11	15	12
3-4 persons	30	32	32	30	29	35	37
5 or more persons	23	30	37	20	34	22	30
Income Distribution							
Under $1,000	1	2	—	10	—	—	—
$1,000-1,999	10	13	4	33	7	17	10

$2,000-2,999	24	24	10	33	3	37	18
$3,000-3,999	18	19	28	9	25	11	16
$4,000-4,999	13	14	15	6	11	10	25
$5,000-7,999	18	20	32	8	21	14	23
$8,000 and over	16	10	11	1	12	12	8
Primary Income Source							
Wages, salaries, etc.	30	21	36	21	16	24	20
AFDC	34	49	45	35	53	38	59
SSI	9	7	12	9	5	11	6
Social Security	27	23	7	34	26	27	15

Source: Special tabulations of 1976 tenant income survey data.
a. Weighted average; weights are number of units managed by the PHA.

composition of the neighborhoods around the projects. Hence, project location may affect tenant profiles generally.[10]

Note that the composite of these five differs significantly from the characteristics of all 22 Authorities just reviewed; hence, they are not representative of all Authorities in large cities.

The figures in the table show both consistency and differences among the five PHAs. Whites are universally a small minority of the tenants, although in Los Angeles, Chicanos account for a third of the residents. Another consistency is the dominance of the female-headed family. Divergence comes in the related areas of elderly occupants, single individuals, and household size. So, for example, in Los Angeles only 11 percent of the households are headed by someone aged 65 or older, and 13 percent are single-person households; on the other hand, 37 percent of the households are 5 or more members. Atlanta, by contrast, has 26 percent elderly-headed households with a corresponding large number of single-person households; and only 20 percent of its households are very large. There is sharp divergence in dependency, as indicated by the percentage of households whose primary source of income is some form of earnings. The share of those with earnings as the major income source ranges from 36 percent in Los Angeles to a mere 16 percent in Chicago. With the majority of households in all five PHAs dependent upon welfare for income, the differences in the income distributions depend mainly on the relative generosity of federal and state income support payments that are available to households in alternative circumstances. In brief, while there are important differences among the five PHAs for which reliable data are available, the consistencies dominate; the facts reviewed for the 22 large PHAs as a group appear to give a fair picture for at least some of the largest Authorities.

VARIATIONS BY HOUSEHOLD TYPE

In this section, the image of public housing tenants is sharpened by detailing three characteristics of individual household types:

10. Indeed, minority households who move into public housing in Pittsburgh—one place for which we have the necessary data—on average move into neighborhoods with a greater concentration of minorities than their pre-program neighborhood. S. Mayo et al., "Draft Report on Housing Allowances and Other Rental Housing Assistance Programs," chapter 2.

household size, primary source of income, and income level. The first panel in table 11 shows the distribution of family sizes by household type. Husband-wife families, which account for 22 percent of all resident households, have the largest household size: nearly half have five or more persons in the family. Female-headed families are also large, having almost four members on average. The final group, constituting only 2 percent of resident households, has sharply smaller families.

The figures on primary source of income by household type and age of head are especially interesting. Among households headed by someone under the age of 65, 79 percent of the husband-wife families have earnings as the primary income source; for female-headed families the corresponding figure is 24 percent. The vast majority of elderly-headed households have social security payments as the primary income source. This is not the case, however, among female-headed elderly families, a good share of whom work, presumably because they never acquired the necessary calendar quarters employment covered by social security, nor were they ever married long enough to someone contributing to the program to obtain entitlement to survivors' benefits.[11]

The final panel of the table displays the mean 1976 incomes of public housing tenants in the largest cities by household type. A glance at the figures tells one that nonelderly husband-wife households are significantly raising the average income level; in fact, their income exceeds the median for all central city renter households in 1976 ($8,800). Female-headed families lived on an average of $4,600, or a per capita income of about $1,200. Single-person households, on the other hand, received about $3,200. The overall mean income for nonelderly households in 1976 was about $4,900, very moderate by any standard; for the elderly it was even lower.

THE PROBLEM TENANT

A good deal of the troubles of public housing have been attributed to "problem tenants." While no one has been able to iden-

11. For a description of women's rights under social security, see Nancy M. Gordon, "Institutional Responses: The Social Security System," in Ralph Smith, ed., *The Subtle Revolution: Women at Work* (Washington, D.C.: The Urban Institute, 1979), pp. 223-55.

Table 11

CHARACTERISTICS OF TENANTS IN LARGE AUTHORITIES BY HOUSEHOLD TYPE: 1976

A. Household Size by Household Type for Multiperson Families with Nonaged Head

Household Type	Persons			Total
	Two	Three or Four	Five or More	
Husband-wife	.12	.40	.48	1.00
Female-headed family	.22	.47	.31	1.00
Other, multiperson households	.31	.38	.31	1.00

B. Primary Income Source by Household Type by Age of Head

Household Type	Wages salaries	AFDC	SSI	Social Security	Total
Elderly-headed household					
Husband-wife	.13	.01	.08	.78	1.00
Female-headed family	.23	.14	.19	.44	1.00
Single person	.04	0	.14	.82	1.00
Other family	0	0	.13	.87	1.00
Non-elderly-headed household					
Husband-wife	.79	.11	.04	.06	1.00
Female-headed family	.24	.67	.04	.05	1.00
Single person	.33	0	.37	.30	1.00
Other family	.47	.35	.04	.14	1.00

C. Mean Income by Household Type and Age of Head

Household Type	Age	
	65 or older	Under 65
Husband-wife	$5,492	$8,979
Female-headed family	5,182	4,600
Single person	2,797	3,214
Other family	6,334	7,289

Source: Special tabulations of 1976 income certification survey data.

Table 12

DISTRIBUTION OF PROBLEM TENANTS IN FOUR BOSTON PUBLIC HOUSING PROJECTS

	All	McC	Chas	So E	Col
Total families (May 1971)	3,935	1,016	1,118	506	1,295
Total problem tenants	196	31	77	29	59
Percentage of total families	4.9	3.1	7.1	5.7	4.5
Problem types:					
Administrative Rules	64	9	35	14	5
Percentage of total problems	32.7	29.0	45.5	48.3	10.2
Animals	8	4	2	1	1
Failure to clean halls	0	0	0	0	0
Unauthorized tenant	0	0	0	0	0
Rent arrears	53	5	31	13	4
Housekeeping	2	0	2	0	0
Sloppy waste disposal	0	0	0	0	0
Health	28	4	5	6	13
Percentage of total problems	14.3	12.9	6.5	20.7	22.0
Senility	11	4	1	1	5
Mentally ill	8	0	1	3	4
Alcoholic	9	0	3	2	4
Child neglect	0	0	0	0	0

Interpersonal	65	17	30	4	14
Percentage of total problems	33.2	54.8	39.0	13.8	23.7
Child abuse	1	0	1	0	0
Verbal harassment	6	5	1	0	0
Conflict: hallways	0	0	2	0	0
Conflict: child handling	6	4	2	0	1
Person being harassed	0	1	3	0	2
Racial conflict	12	2	8	2	2
Chronic complaining	15	3	5	1	5
Loud noises	6	2	1	1	2
Uncontrolled child	13	0	9	1	2
Severely Disruptive	39	1	7	5	26
Percentage of total problems	19.9	3.2	9.1	.17.2	44.1
Multiproblem family	21	0	3	3	15
Theft	3	0	1	0	2
Assault	1	1	0	0	0
Sexual offenses	2	0	0	0	2
Intimidating gang activity	0	0	0	0	0
Narcotics	8	0	0	2	6
Vandalism (extreme cases)	4	0	3	0	1

Source: Richard Scobie, Problem Tenants in Public Housing (New York: Praeger Publishers, 1975), table A.1.
Note: McC = McCormack; Chas = Charlestown; So E = South End; Col = Columbia Point.

tify the independent role of the problem tenant in causing management problems, there have been analyses of the membership of this special group. Indeed, the sociological literature on multiproblem families is immense. Here Richard Scobie's analysis of the situation in 1971, in four projects, chosen in part for their diverse tenant populations, in the Boston Public Housing Authority is briefly reviewed.[12] Problem tenants were identified in two ways: (a) by the project manager[13] and (b) from a special log of complaints, maintained for a ten-week period, against tenants by other tenants, staff, community organizations, or agencies. About two thirds of all of the problem tenants were identified by the managers by going over tenant lists with Scobie (with the obvious possibilities of misclassification). Table 12 displays the types of problems exhibited by the tenants and their incidence. The overall incidence of problem tenants is low in all four projects—only about 5 percent, consistent with other analyses. There is, however, sharp variance even among these few projects in the type of problems recorded: problems with administrative rules dominate in Charlestown and South End; interpersonal problems in McCormack; and multiproblem, severely disruptive tenants head the list at Columbia Point. Overall, though, the low average incidence of problem tenants is consistent with Scobie's thesis that low-income households in dense public housing need not create adverse social conditions.

Who are these tenants? Scobie's analysis finds differences between race only for certain categories: whites have more health problems and blacks were a disproportionate share of multiproblem households. The elderly (predominantly white) have a higher incidence of health problems, but the younger households dominate in the other problem areas. Female-headed households have a generally higher incidence of problems, but very large families seem to have only a greater incidence of interpersonal problems than other households, for example, uncontrolled children, chronic complaining, and racial conflicts. Finally, problem tenants tend to be relative newcomers to the

12. Richard S. Scobie, *Problem Tenants in Public Housing: Who, Where and Why Are They* (New York: Praeger Publishers, 1975). This book also reviews other germane studies.

13. One criterion for selecting a project was the reputation of the manager at the central office for being aggressive and alert enough to know his tenants.

projects, which suggests that they eventually learn behavioral norms or move out. (As discussed in chapter 6, it is extremely difficult for Authorities to evict tenants for most types of problem behavior; so voluntary leaving rather than eviction is the probable cause of the pattern observed.) Overall, the socially disruptive tenants tend to be found more often in female-headed households and to a lesser degree in very large households than in other household types. This profile, however, is only for a single PHA and may not be a reliable guide to the situation in other Authorities.

*   *   *   *   *

The prototypical image of the public housing tenant in the largest cities being black and living in a female-headed family whose primary income is from welfare payments does have a certain validity. On the other hand, households with all these characteristics are relatively few, and there are sizable representatives of husband-wife households and single individuals in all Authorities. The public housing population is far from universally dependent on welfare, but household sizes are large both for husband-wife and female-headed families. The population is certainly poor on average, and a major segment is desperately impoverished, especially in light of the large family sizes. Finally, the available evidence suggests that "problem tenants" are a small minority—perhaps 1 household in 20.

The large number of children per household and the large number of children per adult imply that unless projects are especially well designed and adults particularly vigilant, children are likely to be a continuing management problem. Further, the low rates of employment among many adults also suggest high "housing utilization rates." In short, combined with the project design problems reviewed in the last chapter, the tenant profile creates serious potential management difficulties.

Chapter 4

Financial Conditions

This chapter concentrates on the actual expenditures and receipts of the very large Public Housing Authorities. More specifically it presents data on the distribution of operating expenditures by functional category and the sources of revenues for recent years; all the finances discussed might be called "current account" items, in the sense that costs and revenues associated with development and major renovations are excluded. Under the funding policies for public housing—described in detail in chapter 5—development, operations, and modernization are treated separately; we have adopted the same convention here for ease of presentation.

Throughout this chapter the extraordinary problems of accepting cost data at face value must be kept in mind. Normally, the cost of some item means the product of the price per unit of the item and the quantity being purchased. Hence, the cost of a barrel of no. 2 diesel oil is the gallon price times 42 gallons. Among PHAs, quantities, especially quantities of output, are extremely difficult to measure. PHAs offer different levels of services; some furnish more protective services, a high level of maintenance, a solid social services program while others do not. Complicating things further is the variance in support from the cities, which means that the Authority itself finances varying shares of a given level of services. Table 13 presents some data

Table 13

RESPONSES TO QUESTIONS ON SERVICES PROVIDED TO
TWELVE PHAs BY THEIR LOCAL GOVERNMENTS;
(Respondent is executive director)

1. City, state, other outside agency or organization provides services specifically for the tenants in the Authorities' projects:	*Yes*		*No*	
a. Recreational programs for youths	10		1	
b. Recreational programs for adults and elderly	11		0	
c. Day care	11		0	
d. Homemaking services	8		3	
e. Health services	7		2	
f. Job referral on training programs	7		4	
g. Family counseling	8		3	
h. Adult and/or youth educational programs	8		3	
2. Do police provided by the local government patrol project property at all your projects, most, some, or none of your project:	*All* 0	*Most* 6	*Some* 5	*None* 0
3. Is street lighting on project property provided by the local government at all, most, some, or none of your projects?	*All* 5	*Most* 2	*Some* 2	*None* 2
4. Is the local government involved in hauling trash and garbage away from the projects?	*Yes* 8		*No* 3	

Source: Tabulations of unpublished data from 1976 survey of public housing
executive directors conducted by The Urban Institute for the U.S. Department of Housing and Urban Development.

on this point for 1976 from The Urban Institute's survey of 119
Authorities cited earlier. The responses for the 11 very large
PHAs included in the sample are recorded here. Of particular
interest is the wide range of response to the questions of the
city provision of police patrols, lighting, and trash hauling.
These figures make clear the problems of judging service provision, and interpreting cost data, for PHAs. Beyond these problems, providing a defined output requires different levels of

inputs depending on operating conditions: vintage of the buildings, tenant profiles, etc. This again causes cost differences even between equally efficient PHAs.

The composite price of providing a unit of some service also varies because of area wage differentials and differences in the price of materials. These variants can be statistically accounted for to a certain degree and have been in some prior analyses; but such analysis is almost inevitably imperfect, and so the data presented must be considered with some caution. As a practical matter, the data at hand can tell us very little about the way in which PHAs are managed because of the lack of any standard against which to judge these figures. Their role for HUD management is realistically limited to very detailed analysis of an individual PHA's expenses for a given year against its recent history. It is a case study approach—the only feasible one under the circumstances.

It would have been preferable to examine operating cost and revenue data for projects within PHAs; unfortunately, project-based budgeting has been discontinued at most PHAs for some years, and the data are unavailable. Because of the data limitations, this chapter provides only a brief overview.

CURRENT ACCOUNTS

The figures presented in this section are also for 11 very large PHAs included in The Urban Institute's data base for 119 PHAs. Tests for difference in the mean values of several key financial variables, such as total operating costs per unit month, between these 11 Authorities and a group of 25 of the 29 PHAs which constitute the population under study showed no significant differences. Hence, the mean values for these 11 PHAs can generally be taken as representative of those of the study population.

Despite the presence of an official "accounting handbook," PHAs have a good deal of discretion in allocating expenditures by category. So, for example, over time a PHA with financial problems can noticeably reduce administrative expenses, since this demonstrates belt tightening, by shifting expenses among accounts. They also have the option of keeping records on a cash or accrual basis. Under a cash system, payments of utility bills may be postponed from one year to another, for instance, and eventually paid off in a lump, which can make figures for a specific year misleading. The patterns presented below for the 11 PHAs appear to be reasonably stable for a 2- or 3-year period. Still, though, other problems are embodied in the data that make comparisons over time or between PHAs difficult. Modernization funds are sometimes used to fund nonroutine maintenance; although this is permitted under the modernization program, it makes the statement of operating costs and revenues difficult to interpret. Similarly, funds furnished under the Comprehensive Employment Training Act and the Community Development Block Grant programs are not recorded. This is consistent with the regulations, which are designed to encourage local assistance, but it is not possible to judge the resources being used by Authorities from the data that are routinely available. Again, caution is warranted in reviewing the data presented.

Expenditures
Figure 1 shows the distribution of expenditures of the major PHAs by a few main categories. The largest component, accounting for 34 percent of outlays, is "administration and general." This component includes administrative salaries, legal expenses, staff training, and the like as well as insurance payments, payments in lieu of taxes, and collection losses.[1] The other very large elements are expenditures for ordinary maintenance and operations (32 percent) and utilities (29 percent). Two small items are broken out in the chart. Outlays for protective services are only 2 percent of the total or about 6 percent of ordinary maintenance and operation expenditures; although as just noted, some cities provide substantial in-kind services in this area, other PHAs like Boston have virtually no such services. Nonroutine and capital expenditures that are financed from funds available for current expenses are the second small item, only 3 percent of total operating expenditures.[2]

---

1. All terms are defined in Appendix B.

2. It would be desirable to contrast the distribution of expenditures by these PHAs with those of privately operated units. A careful examination of the data on private projects showed that even at high levels of aggregation, the differences in the allocation of expenses among expense categories between the PHA system and other accounting systems (or at least the reporting systems) were too great to make the comparison.

Figure 1

AVERAGE DISTRIBUTION OF EXPENDITURES FOR
1976-77 FISCAL YEARS [a]

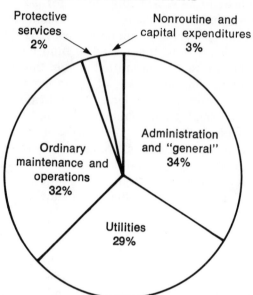

a. All terms defined in Appendix B.

More important than these mean values is the tremendous variance in the relative importance of specific elements among PHAs. Table 14 presents operating data for 10 PHAs.[3] It is divided into two panels. The first panel displays figures for the 1976-77 fiscal year (fiscal years can end in any quarter) and selected ratios of operating costs and revenues. All of the figures in the table are calculated on the basis of outlays divided by the number of (dwelling) unit months, that is, per-unit-month (pum), the PHA had available. The second gives percentage changes in selected outlay and revenue elements for the FY 1973-74 to FY 1978-79 period. The size of the variance among PHAs in the outlay categories is surprising: for ordinary maintenance and operations the range is from $20.59 (Houston) to $50.94 (San Francisco); utilities from $14.01 (Los Angeles) to

---

3. National Capital (Washington, D.C.) is excluded because of the confusion caused by its changing its fiscal year in 1976.

$51.01 (Baltimore); total operating expenses from $76.58 (Houston) to $143.03 (Detroit). Furthermore, there is sharp variance in the distribution of expenditures within PHAs. Ordinary maintenance and operation outlays vary from 25 percent of total expenditures in Atlanta to 41 percent in Los Angeles; utilities from 12 percent in Los Angeles to 43 percent in Baltimore. Finally, salaries as a percentage of total operating expenses net of utilities range from 49 percent (Milwaukee) to 79 percent (Detroit); and there is no obvious relationship between a greater reliance on labor with total operating expenses.

In addition to the variance across PHAs at a point in time, the variance over time is impressive, as shown by data in panel B of the table. In the FY 1973-74 to FY 1978-79 period, the increase in total operating expenditures varied from 4 percent in Baltimore to 102 percent in Houston. For those eight SMSAs for which Consumer Price Index (CPI) data are available and which are the locations of some of the PHAs in the table, total outlays went up less than the CPI housing component in only two cities: Baltimore and San Francisco.[4]

How does one explain such amazing disparities? Some aspects are readily understandable; utility outlays, for example, depend on the climate, the price of fuel inputs, and whether the units are individually metered. Other variations between Authorities are much less easily understood. Analyses done by de Leeuw and by Rydell of operating expense variations across PHAs and over time, summarized in Appendix C, provide some limited insights on the role of project and PHA size, types of tenants, and age of the building.

The divergence in cost over time is in large part attributable to the size and the timing of the introduction of federal operating subsidies. In particular, some significant dislocations were caused by the introduction of the performance funding system

---

4. The CPI housing component includes both owner-occupied and rental units. The full housing shelter index was chosen instead of the rent index because of the general consensus that the rental index is biased downward to some degree. On the other hand, the homeowner index is biased upward in inflationary periods because of the treatment of house prices and mortgage interest charges. Use of the composite index is thought to provide a more general representation of the cost of housing in the market than either of the separate components. Because both the owner and renter indices include capital costs, they are not ideal for the comparison being made.

Table 14

SELECTED FINANCIAL DATA FOR TEN PHAs FOR THE 1973-74–1978-79 FISCAL YEARS [d]

(All figures on a per-unit-month basis)

	Authority										
	Balti-more	At-lanta	Mem-phis	De-troit	Colum-bus	Milwau-kee	Hous-ton	San Antonio	San Fran-cisco	Los Ange-les	Unweighted Mean
A. Data for 1976/1977 fiscal year dollar amounts											
Outlays											
Utilities	$51.01	$43.92	$27.05	$47.40	$26.12	$28.27	$22.74	$30.11	$26.79	$14.01	$30.25
Ordinary M&O	37.63	29.19	31.89	40.68	26.38	28.42	20.59	24.40	50.94	47.05	34.22
Protective services	.18	1.68	—	2.21	3.16	—	6.52	1.03	3.75	4.74	2.12
Routine total expenditures	121.76	110.54	82.81	141.30	81.70	96.98	76.51	81.79	129.15	109.08	101.40
Total Nonroutine expenditures	.14	3.51	1.00	.93	2.66	2.64	—	1.36	4.16	4.00	1.77
Capital expenditures	.39	4.13	1.47	.80	.03	4.33	.07	1.96	.37	2.43	1.62
Total operating expenditures	122.29	118.13	85.28	143.03	84.39	103.95	76.58	85.11	133.68	115.52	105.44
Total salaries	52.38	45.52	38.03	81.56	38.19	37.57	40.45	36.60	71.10	68.77	51.42

Revenues

Op. receipts	$65.58	$40.18	$45.09	$74.64	$46.15	$75.26	$44.11	$46.49	$66.05	$72.30	$57.97
Op. subsidies	86.35	81.41	40.52	70.69	41.71	39.06	40.91	45.45	95.83	53.35	57.17
Selected Ratios											
Op. receipts: Op. subsidies	.76	.49	1.11	1.06	1.11	1.93	1.08	1.02	.69	1.36	1.01
Op. receipts: Total op. expnd.	.54	.34	.53	.52	.55	.72	.58	.55	.49	.63	.55
Utilities: total Op. expnd.	.42	.37	.32	.33	.31	.27	.30	.35	.20	.12	.29
Ord. M&O: total op. expnd.	.31	.25	.37	.28	.31	.27	.27	.29	.38	.41	.32
(Nonroutine and cap. expnd.): Total op. expnd.	.01	.06	.03	.01	.03	.07	a	.04	.03	.06	.03
Salaries: (total op. expnd.- Utilities)[e]	.73	.61	.65	.79	.64	.49	.75	.66	.66	.68	.67

Table 14

SELECTED FINANCIAL DATA FOR TEN PHAs FOR THE 1973-74—1978-79 FISCAL YEARS [d] (cont'd)
(All figures on a per-unit-month basis)

					Authority					Unweighted Mean
	Balti-more	At-lanta	Mem-phis	De-troit	Colum-bus	Milwau-kee	Hous-ton	San Antonio	San Fran-cisco	Los Ange-les
B. Percentage Changes Between FY 73/74 and FY 78/79										
Outlays										
Utilities	29	132	125	108	91	69	276	186	72	50	108
Ordinary M&O	−13	54	60	55	39	84	188	38	35	50	57
Total Op. Expnd.	4	72	86	72	70	76	102	75	44	59	63
Revenues										
Op. receipts	21	33	21	43	40	45	81	46	22	42	40
Op. subsidies	102	85	120	56	98	113	185	211	102	326	129
Consumer Price Indices [b]										
All items	48	47	c	44	c	46	57	c	50	49	
Housing	56	44		43		48	70		55	54	

Source: Tabulations of Data submitted to HUD by the PHAs on HUD Form 52599, as compiled by The Urban Institute.

a. Less than .05.
b. For 1973-78.
c. Not availabe for this area.
d. Definition of accounting terms are in Appendix A to this chapter.
e. Utilities net of associated salary costs.

(PFS) in the 1975-76 fiscal year to allocate operating subsidies. Equally important, though, has been the PHAs' reaction to funding shortfalls—some have simply gone into debt, others have cut services dramatically, and still others have effected needed management improvements and prospered within the budget. The PFS is discussed in the next chapter where its pervasive effect will become more clear.

Revenues

There are two sources of current revenues to the PHA: operating receipts (mostly rent collections) that depend on tenant characteristics, and operating subsidies now provided through the PFS. A fundamental problem with the reported "dwelling rental" figure is that it is not the actual receipts; rather it is the rent roll, based on 100 percent of rent charges being collected for occupied units. The complementary accounts receivable figure, needed to derive net dwelling rents, is often not filled in on the form sent to HUD (Form 52599). Hence, the discussion that follows necessarily assumes full collections, which is a serious problem indicated by the number of rental delinquencies reported by executive directors (see table 3).

Also, the reader may have noted that for all of the Authorities in the table, total revenues exceed total costs for 1976-77 (panel A). The basic reason for this event, which is by no means routine, is that revenues, mostly from rent rolls, went up at a higher rate than forecast when the budgets were prepared in accordance with HUD guidance. Since the planned budget balanced, the additional revenue was at least officially unexpected and some of it was not spent in the year it was received. More is said on this in the next chapter.

For the "average" very large PHA, the tenant contributions and operating subsidies are of roughly equal importance. In other words, the ratio of operating receipts to operating subsidies is about 1.0. This ratio is reported in table 14 for the 10 PHAs for FY 1976-77; and it ranges from .49 for Atlanta, implying a heavy dependence on subsidies, to 1.93 for Milwaukee, implying a comparatively high degree of independence.

On average over the FY 1973-74 to FY 1978-79 period, operating subsidies went up 129 percent, and operating receipts rose by about one third of this amount. Again, however, there is considerable variance. In Detroit, increases in operating re-

ceipts and subsidies were about evenly matched, but in San
Antonio, a 211 percent rise in subsidies dwarfed a 46 percent
increase in operating receipts.

The Balance Sheet

What can one conclude from these data about the financial
health of large Authorities? Not much. In order for HUD to approve the PHA's budget—a requirement for receiving operating
subsidies—planned outlays cannot exceed revenues from all
sources. So actual outlay data must be used to evaluate these
events. Even here the data are murky. Because of the time lags
inherent in the performance funding system for a final settling
of the utilities component of the operating subsidy for a specific
year, total revenues and outlays found in the budget may not be
identical, as illustrated by the figures in table 14.[5]

It is generally agreed that the best single indicator of a PHA's
financial status is the level of its "operating reserves," which
are probably best thought of as savings earmarked for expenditure on nonroutine maintenance items. The HUD field office
establishes the maximum amount of operating reserves that an
Authority can accrue, usually set at 50 percent of annual operating expenses. Excess reserves are placed in other reserve accounts and, if large enough, are ultimately returned to the federal Treasury.

Like the other figures discussed here, operating reserves have
problems of quality and interpretation. Operating reserves are
a balancing item, that is, surpluses are placed in them. Hence,
accounting accuracy problems affecting size of the surplus distort the reserves figure. Furthermore, special project funds, that
is, from the Target Projects Program or Urban Initiatives Program (described in chapter 8) are placed here prior to expenditure. This creates year-to-year variations in reserve levels that
have nothing to do with the ability of the PHA to "save" from
its own operations, which undermines their use as a barometer
of financial conditions. In concept, all of the necessary adjustments can be made to get to a "net reserve" figure; but the pre-
cision of even these accounts is questionable.

The figures used here are for the 1977-78 fiscal year and were
sent to HUD central by the public housing specialists in the

---

5. This is described in chapter 5.

area offices.[6] These figures were explicitly to exclude funds for special projects and modernization. As such they should be reasonably reliable. Table 15 lists the operating reserves as a percentage of the maximum allowed for all of the 29 PHAs that are the focus of this monograph. Five PHAs had no operating reserves whatsoever, and there is wide agreement that these are distressed PHAs. Some of them are deeply in debt. Another eight PHAs had reserves ranging from 2 to 20 percent of the maximum. Seventeen of the 29 had reserves of less than one third of the maximum, a thin defense against an especially harsh winter or emergency repairs. At the other end of the spectrum, only three Authorities had reserves in excess of two thirds of the maximum; these three—Phoenix, Seattle, and Minneapolis—are obviously in very strong positions. While the overall variance is striking, even more impressive are the relatively comfortable reserve levels of Authorities like Baltimore, St.

Table 15

RESERVE LEVELS OF PHAs IN LARGE CITIES
FOR THE 1977-78 FISCAL YEAR

Authority	Reserve Level [a]	Authority	Reserve Level [a]
Nat'l Capital		New York	28
(Washington)	0	Los Angeles	31
Chicago	0	Indianapolis	33
Boston	0	Denver	39
Detroit	0	Baltimore	43
Columbus	0	San Francisco	46
Atlanta	2	San Antonio	47
Memphis	3	Dallas	48
Jacksonville	5	St. Louis	48
Houston	11	Cincinnati	50
Kansas City (MO)	11	Milwaukee	50
Philadelphia	18	Buffalo	61
Pittsburgh	19	Phoenix	68
Cleveland (Cuyahoga)	20	Seattle	81
New Orleans	25	Minneapolis	100

Source: Tabulation of responses to HUD Field Notice H78-122(HUD).
    a. Actual operating reserves as a percentage of the maximum reserves allowed by HUD.

6. HUD Field Notice H78-122(HUD).

Louis, and San Francisco. And these cities certainly have had major problems over the years. For some PHAs, these figures suggest that they may be sacrificing providing current services to avoid being pushed into the public housing equivalent of bankruptcy by unforeseen circumstances. Those with low or zero reserves may be pursuing the opposite strategy: spend now and assume HUD or the city will bail them out later. Again, the lack of any service standard against which to measure financial performance causes fundamental problems in interpretation.

CONCLUSION

No one really knows the financial health of the major Public Housing Authorities in this country. This chapter has established that most PHAs spend the revenues that are available. But it is not possible to use these figures to judge performance. To be sure, there are very difficult conceptual problems having to do with developing service standards that must be overcome before concise meaningful figures can be developed. But the accounting problems at the Authorities and the recordkeeping problems within the Department of Housing and Urban Development cannot claim this reason as a source of the malady. Amazingly, HUD central is "managing" the public housing program without a usable set of books. As a result, special requests for data are often made to field offices for rudimentary data, that is, operating reserves; and special teams of area and central office personnel are dispatched to crisis Authorities to *really* find out about their financial status. To be sure, no financial statement can be a substitute for site visits, but currently available information seems unnecessarily ambiguous.

The available data indicate that about half of the PHAs in the largest cities are presently in serious financial difficulty; a few are in desperate condition. Furthermore, because many PHAs may be maintaining reserve levels by cutting back on routine maintenance and other services, some may be headed toward "bankruptcy" as well.

Given the primitive state of the basic data systems, it is hardly surprising that HUD has devoted very few resources to trying to understand the basis for variations in operating costs and revenues, and, consequently, the amounts in the reserve levels. The work completed to date offers broad explanations for the observed variance, but it is not yet adequate to be used as a basis for detailed policy prescriptions. Of course, given the weakness of the operating data, results of further analysis could be badly misleading. Hence, there is a need to make fundamental accounting improvements throughout the entire system.

Part III
HUD AND THE PHAs

Chapter 5

HUD FUNDING POLICY

The federal funding of public housing is divided into three separately administered components covering development costs, operating subsidies, and expenditures to "modernize" aging projects. Not every PHA receives funding through all three components, although all of the large PHAs do. About 700 of the 2,900 Authorities in the country can meet operating expenses from rental receipts. Those Authorities with projects in good condition and/or the ability to fund their own replacements do not have to compete for modernization funds. In addition to federal funding, Authorities receive income from tenant rental contributions and in some cases from municipal funds for modernization. Also, under the agreement between an Authority and municipality required prior to project development, the city provides certain services to the project and accepts "payment in lieu of taxes," which is a fraction of the full property tax liability.[1]

This chapter concerns federal funding. The description focuses on the funding of modernization and operating expenses;

---

1. For a description of the value of foregone property taxes see S. K. Mayo et al., "Draft Report on Housing Allowances and Other Rental Housing Assistance Programs," Appendix III.

development costs are briefly discussed in the opening section. The incentives and significant disincentives produced by current funding processes for the efficient management of PHAs are considered.

DEVELOPMENT COSTS

The most important point is that the federal government effectively pays for the full cost of developing, that is, planning and constructing, public housing projects. Tax laws, funding mechanics, and economic considerations, however, ensure that the financing is not simply a federal grant for the needed funds. A PHA is advanced short-term construction period loans necessary to bring a project to the point at which it is ready for permanent financing; these advances are then folded into the amount permanently financed. Near the end of construction, HUD enters into an "annual contributions contract" (ACC), with the Authority, which obligates the federal government to pay both the interest and principal amortization on bonds that the PHA sells to obtain permanent financing. Normally, the ACC is for 40 years. In short, HUD guarantees to retire the debt.[2]

Why this particular financing? First, it substantially lowers the direct subsidy outlays. The ACC by itself assures a lower-than-market interest rate on the PHA-issued bonds. In addition, federal tax provisions exempt the interest payments received on instruments issued by local government entities from federal income taxes, and this causes the interest rates to be even lower. A second reason is that it spreads actual government outlays over the 40-year period, a feature that is politically attractive and reduces the discounted present value of the federal costs.

Originally, the only federal subsidies were for development

---

2. If the PHA is able to more than pay for operating expenses out of its rental receipts and other incomes, those extra funds—after accumulation exceeds a specified maximum reserve level—are returned to HUD and applied against capital costs. Today this is not the case for the Authorities included in this study, but it was the case historically and still is for some smaller PHAs.

Also note that the fiscal year 1981 budget for HUD contains proposed changes to 30-year taxable bond financing.

costs. Under this situation it stands to reason that the PHA would have a considerable incentive to build the highest quality, most maintenance-free structure possible. And, within the substantial cost constraints imposed by HUD (or its predecessor agencies) in the form of public housing building standards, this is exactly what happened. Muth has estimated that the average project embodied about 20 percent more capital than would have been the case if the subsidy had been neutral between operating and capital costs.[3] Today, since the operating subsidies in the system and the minimum property standard applied to privately operated, HUD-insured projects are used for public housing, the distortion in favor of capital is probably much smaller.[4]

OPERATING SUBSIDIES

Although public housing was initially structured so that the only subsidy was for development of the project, changes in the 1960s and the early 1970s in tenant composition and restrictions on PHAs as to the amount of rent they could charge (the "Brooke amendments") made it impossible for many PHAs to meet expenses without further subsidies.[5]

HUD responded by agreeing ex post to make up the first year's shortfall. In subsequent years this amount was adjusted for inflation by a judgmentally determined, single, national inflation factor. This procedure resulted in continuing inequitable treatment of Authorities. For example, those who tried hard in the base year to make ends meet were permanently penalized for their effort.

---

3. R.F. Muth, *Public Housing: An Economic Evaluation* (Washington, D.C.: The American Enterprise Institute, 1973).

4. Because there has been considerable unhappiness about how operating subsidies have been allocated, a number of PHA officials interviewed indicated that uncertainty about the level of subsidies was retarding the development of more projects. This would also argue for a "capital intensive" approach to development still being pursued. The interview results are reported in M. J. Schussheim and A. M. Smith, "The Future of Public Housing: Some Views of Local Housing Officials" (Washington, D.C.: Congressional Research Service, 1979).

5. For additional history, see E. White, S. R. Merrill, and T. Lane, *The History and Overview of the Performance Funding System* (Cambridge: Abt Associates, 1979).

By 1972, in the face of ballooning subsidy payments, the Office of Management and Budget was concerned that under this arrangement there was no incentive to the PHAs for efficient management, and that inequities would persist. Consequently, it insisted that the Department of Housing and Urban Development develop a system for disbursing operating subsidies that would be equitable and have strong incentives for good management. During 1972, work had begun on what was to become the system actually adopted—the performance funding system. By 1974, the Congress had also mandated a system be put into place. Under this intense pressure, HUD implemented the PFS. Both The Urban Institute, which had worked with HUD to develop the system, and HUD viewed PFS as an interim system that needed substantial refinement in the years ahead.

Chapter 4 documented the importance of the operating subsidies to meeting expenses. This section gives a description of the structure and rationale of the PFS. It is not a simple system. The description is divided into two parts. The first part describes in general terms how the subsidies for individual PHAs are calculated. The second part discusses several key elements in the PFS in some detail. A final section discusses the incentives for good management embodied in the system. Keep in mind that the PFS is a system composed not only of the funding equation but of certain rules for decisionmaking and administrative practices which have been equally important in determining the actual subsidy received by a particular Housing Authority.

The Basics [6]
The PFS establishes a separate per-unit-month (pum) operating subsidy payment level for each PHA. The subsidy level is determined in part by applying a funding formula derived from the actual operating expenses of a set of PHAs classified as "high performing."[7] (This term is defined in the next section.) Under

6. This description paraphrases and quotes material from the *Request for Proposals* issued for the evaluation of the performance funding system in April 1978 (Solicitation H-2862), pp. 5-10.

7. Actually the equation was initially estimated using data from the high performing Authorities. After the system had been implemented and the funding levels it generated reduced the variance in operating expenditures, the distinction for estimation between high and low performing was blurred and data for the full set of sample PHAs used.

the PFS, the subsidy for any given PHA is set at the difference between the PHA's total approved operating expenses and its expected total income for the year involved.

The complete PFS funding formula for calculating individual agency subsidy entitlements is defined now and explained more fully in the next section.

$$\text{Subsidy}_x = ([\text{AEL}_{x-1} + (\text{FEL}_x (I))] I + U_x - R_x + A_x) \text{ UMA}_x$$

Where: Subsidy_x = The subsidy payment to which the PHA will be entitled in the fiscal year X.

AEL_{x-1} = The PHA pum Allowable Expense Level for fiscal year X-1. This is the sum of the (updated) Formula Expense Level plus utilities allowance plus audit expenses, for the previous year.

FEL_x = The Formula Expense Level for the PHA using PHA characteristics in fiscal year X and the updated (latest) prototype equation. The prototype establishes an FEL using regression coefficients which relate operating expenses (except utilities and audits) to PHA characteristics for a set of "high performing" PHAs. These weights are recalculated each year based on the latest available data.

FEL_{x-1} = The Formula Expense Level for the PHA using a PHA's characteristics in fiscal year X-1 and the same weights used in calculating FEL_x.

I = The inflation rate which the PHA is expected to incur in its operating expenses between fiscal years (X-1) and X.

U_x = The PHA's allowable pum Utility Expense during FY (X).

R_x = The PHA's projected pum Rental Income plus estimated other income during FY (X).

A_x = The expected pum Audit Expenses for FY (X) plus approved add ons.

UMA_x = The expected Unit Months Available during FY (X).

Since PHAs must submit worksheets with their PFS subsidy

request before the beginning of the fiscal year to be funded, FY (X-1) refers to the fiscal year just ending.

Under current PFS regulations, it is intended that each PHA use this formula to calculate its subsidy payment before the beginning of its fiscal year. (PHA fiscal years begin either in January, April, July, or October.) Using a budget worksheet provided by HUD, each PHA first enters its then-current allowable expense level (AEL_{x-1}) and updates it to take into account changing conditions of the PHA and its projects. The PHA then multiplies this amount by the inflation factor (I) supplied by HUD. This figure then becomes the AEL for the requested year. The next step is to enter the allowable utility expense level for the upcoming year (U_x); this factor is determined by taking the annual average consumption during the fixed utilities base consumption period and applying the current or future approved utility rate. Any HUD-approved costs of independent public accountants plus approved add ons (A_x) is then added. The PHA then calculates its expected pum income (R) by taking its then-current rental income, multiplying it by an estimate of next year's occupancy rate, and then multiplying it again by a HUD-provided rate at which rental income will increase from FY (X-1) to FY (X). To this amount the agency adds other anticipated income to arrive at a total expected pum figure. The difference between expenses and income, both of which are on a pum basis, is multiplied by the anticipated number of unit months, UMA_x. After all of these factors are applied, a subsidy level for the upcoming year is determined.

Subject to the availability of funds, the PHA's subsidy is obligated by HUD upon receipt of the PHA's operating budget which includes the PFS worksheet, supporting documentation, and the certification of their accuracy. The agency must live within the constraint that the approved subsidy represents. However, some exceptions that may alter rental income or utility costs are explained later.

For each PHA, it is intended that the subsidy calculation be made before the beginning of its fiscal year. Because PHA fiscal years are staggered, subsidy amounts are calculated and obligated for approximately one fourth of all agencies every three months, and the total actual subsidy requirement of the department is not known until near the end of the federal fiscal year involved. The PFS is also used to estimate the total subsidy needs of the public housing system as described in Appendix D.

More on Specific Elements

The Formula Expense Level. As noted earlier, the formula expense level provides an estimate of the operating costs, except utilities and audits, that a well or "high" performing PHA, with projects of certain characteristics located in a particular part of the country, would incur. This is the amount that all similar PHAs are expected to operate on if they are organized to operate efficiently. The equation itself is an estimated regression model based, like other PFS elements, on the extensive research done at The Urban Institute by Robert Sadacca and his colleagues.[8] The model relates actual operating costs to variables affecting costs; originally it was estimated using data only for the high performing Authorities, but more recently all of the sample Authorities have been included in the data base used in the annual reestimation.

Defining high performance was a central step in the development of the PFS. The initial preference was to measure performance against some absolute standards, that is, maintenance response time, rental payment delinquencies, etc. Such standards, however, were thought difficult to develop and requiring more time and financial resources than were available for the construction of the PFS. Earlier attempts at specifying standards, such as in the "ratio analysis point evaluation" system of the mid-1960s, bear this out.[9] As a substitute, performance was measured primarily by the satisfaction with the project and the PHA of several groups—tenants, project managers, and other personnel, PHA central office employees, and HUD personnel. The particular set of 24 measures (listed in table 16) was selected by a HUD committee of departmental officials and representatives from the National Association of Housing and Redevelopment Officials, the National Tenant Organization, and The Urban Institute. Once these variables were selected, detailed data to measure them and a host of background and control factors were gathered at a sample of 119 Authorities; the sampled Authorities were stratified into three groups (two with 40

---

8. A complete description of this equation is in R. Sadacca, M. Isler, and J. DeWitt, *The Development of a Prototype Equation for Public Housing Operating Expenses* (Washington, D.C.: The Urban Institute, 1975).

9. "The Road to Determining Financial Stability of Local Housing Authorities," *Journal of Housing*, 1960, no. 2, p. 97.

Table 16

VARIABLES USED IN 1973 TO MEASURE PHA
PERFORMANCE IN ANALYSIS BY THE URBAN INSTITUTE [a]

Resident Evaluation
1 Residents' satisfaction with project
2 Residents' satisfaction with neighbors
3 Residents' satisfaction with safety and security
4 Residents' satisfaction with cleanliness of buildings and grounds
5 Residents' satisfaction with maintenance
6 Residents' satisfaction with management
7 Residents' perception of their present and future quality of life
8 Residents' evaluation of the condition of their unit
9 Residents' evaluation of neighborhood acceptance of the project

Manager Evaluation
10 Manager's evaluation of the condition of the dwelling units
11 Manager's evaluation that resident failure to maintain dwelling units is no problem
12 Manager's evaluation of the seriousness of the effects of deferred maintenance
13 Manager's evaluation of the condition of building systems

Authority Personnel Evaluation
14 Executive director's evaluation of Authority staff
15 Job satisfaction of Authority employees
16 Authority employees' evaluation of how well Authority is meeting its objectives
17 Authority employees' evaluation of community acceptance

HUD Area Office Evaluation of
18 How well Authority is meeting its objectives
19 How effectively Authority cooperates with other agencies

Operating Information
20 Occupancy rate
21 Proportion of units that are rent delinquent
22 Ratio of delinquent rents to dwelling rent schedule
23 Average vandalism cost per unit
24 Estimate of burglaries and personal victimization per unit

Source: R. Sadacca et al., *Management Performance in Public Housing*, Appendix II.
a. Data on operating costs are averages for the 1970 and 1971 fiscal years.

observations) based on the number of units under management: large (over 1,250 units); medium (500 to 1,249); and small (100 to 499). As part of the ensuing analysis, for each PHA, the values of the criterion variables, that is, those measuring performance, were adjusted through a statistical process to purge them of the effects of factors beyond the control of the PHA; these factors included such things as the quality of municipal services provided, the size and age and density of the project, and project design problems. These adjusted performance variables were then used to divide the PHAs into "high" and "low" performers. Those PHAs with above average scores on many of the variables were classified as high performers. Importantly, these analyses were conducted for the PHAs divided into the three size groups.[10]

The equation determining the formula expense level, the "prototype equation," regressed the adjusted operating costs variable against factors largely beyond the control of the Authority. Thus, while it was recognized that costs would vary with tenant composition, this type of variable was excluded from the analysis on the grounds that it would give Authorities incentives to shift the tenant mix in potentially undesirable ways. Other factors which had conceptual arguments for being included were excluded when essential data were not readily available at the local level.

The following five variables were included in the initial (1975) equation: age of the project buildings, height of the buildings, average number of bedrooms per unit, relative regional costs of operating a PHA, and size of the population area served by the PHA. With few new public housing units being constructed, it is apparent that the values of those five variables will change very little from year to year. This simple fact has two important implications for the functioning of the PFS: (a) the base year value of the FEL is critical as subsequent year-to-year adjustments to it will be small; and (b) after the first year, it is the inflation factor and utility allowance that really determine the amount of subsidy a PHA receives. (The base year is further considered in the following paragraphs.)

The Inflation Factor. Each year, HUD issues a table of local inflation factors based on an annual survey of local government

10. For a detailed description, see R. Sadacca, S. B. Loux, M. Isler, and M. Drury, *Management Performance in Public Housing* (Washington, D.C.: The Urban Institute, 1975).

employees' wages conducted by the U.S. Bureau of Labor Statistics. PHAs are required to use these in calculating their subsidy entitlements.[11] The inflation factor is applied to each PHA's
AEL as described earlier. Thus, it has to account for inflation
in both personnel and nonpersonnel expenditures. Finally, since
the regulations are published in the fall of each year for use in
the following calendar year, it is necessary to project the expected inflation rates.

Utilities. The utility estimates are calculated by taking the annual average consumption during the fixed utilities base consumption period and applying the approved utility rate. HUD
compensates PHAs dollar-for-dollar for any cost overruns that
result from unexpected rate increases which they experience
during the funding year. HUD also compensates PHAs for 75
percent of any cost increases that result from an increase in
consumption over the average consumption during the base
period. If the PHA consumes less than is expected, it keeps 25
percent of the allocated subsidy related to the savings and re-
turns the remaining 75 percent to HUD. These adjustments take
place after the end of the funding year.

Income and Occupancy. The PFS regulations require the PHAs
to use standard factors for these elements when making this
subsidy estimate. Their approximate per-unit-month rent is
multiplied by 1.03. This is adjusted for the expected occupancy
rate, which cannot be lower than 97 percent without sufficient
justification. To this figure is added PHA income from nonrental
sources. If the estimated rent is too high, the PHA can apply to
the field office for an adjustment; but granting the adjustment
is, within the regulations, at HUD's discretion (unlike the utilities adjustment).[12] If the PHA succeeds in increasing rents by
more than 3 percent, it keeps the difference for that year only.
The actual rent roll this year becomes the base for the next
year's estimate.

---

11. Separate factors are published for counties in 74 major SMSAs
and for counties with populations of 200,000 or more that are outside of
these SMSAs. Those PHAs that are not located in the listed areas use a
statewide average computed by excluding the data from counties lying
within the 74 SMSAs and the populous counties outside of these SMSAs.

12. Examples given in the regulations (*Code of Federal Regulations,*
Title 24, 890-110) of factors beyond the PHA's control that would justify
an adjustment are substantial increase in unemployment in the area
or a HUD-approved revision in the PHA rent schedule.

Decision Rules. Three decision rules adopted by HUD have been key to the subsidies received by individual Authorities: the choice of the base year (1974), as this may have not been a typical year for some Authorities; the "range test" described below; and, the process established for PHAs to appeal their initial subsidy levels. While all three decision rules are important, the range test was critical for some of the largest PHAs.

This test was necessary because although the prototype equation gives an operating cost level for an Authority with a particular set of characteristics, the estimate is not accurate to that particular value. Rather there is an interval around it, and there is a specified statistical degree of confidence of the true value being within that interval. The confidence interval for the estimate was set so that about 90 percent of all PHAs with those characteristics would be statistically expected to be within the interval. For those whose estimated allowable expense levels fall within the interval, this value was taken as their allowable expense level. However, for those whose estimated expense levels were *higher* than the upper end of the confidence interval, the AEL was set at the high end of the range; and a transition funding increment sufficient to raise their allowed nonutility expenses to the previous year's budgeted nonutility expense level was provided. In effect, expenses were held fixed until inflation brought the AEL in line with actual PHA expenditures.

For some Authorities this was a large and painful adjustment. Table 17 shows the budgeted expense levels for the fiscal year prior to PFS implementation, the calculated AEL, and the actual subsidy payments in the first year of PFS for the 11 PHAs we have examined most careful. Nearly half of them exceeded the range and received transition funding in the first year of PFS. For San Francisco and Washington, D.C., the discrepancy between the calculated AEL and the prior year's expense was very large. All of the "overrange" PHAs had to reduce expenses in real terms over the next year. Indeed, in response to questioning in 1976 about the effects of the PFS on operations, executive directors of these same 11 PHAs were quite negative about their early experience; seven directors said operations had been made less efficient while only 2 directors reported improvements, and only one director agreed that the PFS provided sufficient funding to sustain "reasonable levels of services." These responses should, though, be discounted because the system was very new at the time of the 1976 survey.

Table 17

FIRST YEAR OPERATING SUBSIDIES UNDER THE
PERFORMANCE FUNDING SYSTEM FOR
SELECTED AUTHORITIES [a]

Authority	Base Year Expense Level	Calculated Allowable Expense Level (AEL)	Actual Subsidy Payment
National Capital (D.C.)	$ 84.33	$ 71.20	$ 84.33 [b]
Baltimore	72.14	76.37	76.37
Atlanta	66.26	62.43	66.26 [b]
Memphis	46.48	49.99	49.99
Detroit	79.49	76.96	79.49 [b]
Columbus	45.18	48.31	48.31
Milwaukee	76.00	75.38	76.00 [b]
Houston	49.31	53.04	53.04
San Antonio	53.80	57.54	57.54
Los Angeles	95.49	100.18	100.18
San Francisco	112.59	89.29	112.59 [b]

a. All figures on a per-unit-month basis.
b. Received transition funding.

Analysis of the first two years' experience under PFS, by the large PHAs (managing 1,250 or more units) in The Urban Institute's sample, gives a positive overall picture.[13] As shown in the first set of columns in table 18 most had revenues greater than their worksheets for the forthcoming budget year. This was a direct consequence of HUD's directive that the prior year's rent roll be multiplied by 1.03, when a higher rate of income growth was expected. Many PHAs experienced an excess revenue of over $3 pum. In the second year, 7 of these 44 PHAs had overestimated revenues. An examination of the net funds left over at the end of the year, that is the balance between revenues and expenditures shows a more mixed picture. By the second year of PFS almost 40 percent of these PHAs had increased outlays more rapidly than receipts; by contrast a few were piling up over $12 pum in excess receipts. These receipts were, of course, going into reserves to finance nonrou-

13. Memorandum from Robert Sadacca (The Urban Institute) to Carolyn McFarlane (Office of Research, HUD), "Distributions of PHA Income and Expenditures Under PFS," October 20, 1978.

Table 18

DISTRIBUTION OF DIFFERENCES IN DOLLARS PUM
BETWEEN ACTUAL AND WORKSHEET AMOUNTS FOR
LARGE PHAs IN THE UI 1976 SAMPLE

		Total Operating Receipts Exclusive of Hud Contributions		Funds Left Over At End of Year [a]	
		Year 1	Year 2	Year 1	Year 2
BELOW	−9.00	0	1	0	2
−9.00 −	−6.00	0	0	1	5
−6.00 −	−3.00	1	0	1	4
−3.00 −	0.00	1	6	4	6
0.00 −	3.00	16	14	7	9
3.00 −	6.00	16	12	12	9
6.00 −	9.00	7	6	4	3
9.00 −	12.00	1	3	5	3
12.00 &	ABOVE	2	2	3	3

Source: Memorandum from R. Sadacca to Carolyn McFarlane, "Distributions of PHA Income and Expenditures Under PFS," tables 12 and 18.
   a. Operating receipts plus operating subsidy eligibility minus worksheet utilities and nonutility expenditures.

tine expenditures. The point to be made is the range of experience under PFS. Experience may have changed in later years, either for the better or worse depending in good measure on the management changes implemented by the PHAs in a negative net position in the early years.

Incentives
The performance funding system has some notable incentives for improved management, although some are rather clumsy; the system also misses at least one genuine opportunity. The clearest example of a strong positive incentive is the treatment of utilities. It is evident that the sharing of savings with the PHA should have a desirable effect. It might be strengthened by raising the fraction of savings kept by the PHA from its present 25 percent level. If this were done, only the reward for conservation should be increased. The 25 percent cost to PHAs on overconsumption should remain; it provides a serious penalty

and, importantly, a very severe winter could badly deplete reserves for a reason beyond their control.[14]

There is also an incentive for good management by the treatment of overall savings, that is, from operating the Authority at less than the allowable expense level. The PHA is allowed to keep the difference, subject only to increased reserves not exceeding the maximum allowable amount. Before funds would be added to reserves, however, the PHA would probably use savings realized from efficiently performing its straight operating functions to fund some of the backlog of deferred maintenance or to fund an increased level of preventive maintenance. A difficult problem is the distance between improvement in a specific area, for example, tenant screening or maintenance response time, and the reward. Indeed, improvement in some areas can be offset by deterioration elsewhere, possibly for reasons beyond the Authority's control. Unfortunately, a closer tie between specific performance and incentives would almost certainly require that real standards be available against which improvements could be measured; and work on determining these standards is just beginning.

A universally praised feature of PFS is that it provides known subsidy levels that can be used for realistic planning. To many executive directors the consistency of funding under PFS, when averaged over 5-8 years, is better than a somewhat higher, but much more variable subsidy level. (Problems with a more variable system are noted in the discussion of funding for modernization.)

One area of negative incentives concerns the treatment of rent increases beyond the HUD-specified adjustment factor. As it is now, the PHA keeps any "excess" only for the first year it is realized, since the next year's base is this year's actual collections. The Congress has given strong impetus to achieving a more economically balanced tenantry in public housing, and achieving economic integration is one of HUD's self-imposed goals. This being the case, the PHA should be permitted to realize a larger gain from raising incomes. Mechanically, this could be done by not incorporating the full "excess" into the next year's rent base. Guaranteeing the low-income character

---

14. This seems preferable to the proposal made by HUD in the winter of 1979 for a 50-50 sharing arrangement for both savings and consumption increases.

of public housing could be accomplished by establishing that a minimum fraction of tenant households at each project has very low incomes.[15]

Despite its strong features, the PFS has a host of detractors who argue that some of the underlying research was flawed, that lack of performance standards is a critical limitation, that the unique circumstances of the individual PHAs cannot be appropriately treated, and that the inflation factor does not accurately cover PHA expenses. For these reasons HUD has launched a carefully designed comprehensive evaluation of the PFS and its operations to date. This is a first step toward the development of an improved system. Early findings indicate genuine problems with the inflation factor that has been used, apparently especially biased against PHAs in the largest cities. This seems quite understandable given the constraints which fiscal crises have imposed on these cities' ability to grant wage increases in recent years.[16] Discovery of this problem, given the central role of the inflation factor after the base year, merits immediate attention (see chapter 10).

While awaiting the final findings, the integrity of the system should be maintained, and ad hoc changes in the system avoided. It might be feasible to quickly develop and implement a new inflation factor. In the meantime, some discretionary funding should be provided outside of the PFS for those few other PHAs who clearly cannot remain solvent under the existing funding arrangements.

MODERNIZATION

Modernization means improvements such as alterations, additions, replacements, or major repairs that "appreciably" extend the useful life of the property or make the property more suit-

---

15. Very low income for a family of four is defined by HUD as 50 percent of the areawide median family income. Nationally in 1976, this was about $6,100 on an annual basis.

16. S. R. Merrill, J. Cromwell, D. Napior, and D. Weinberg, "A Preliminary Working Paper on the Technical Components of the Performance Funding System" (Cambridge: Abt Associates, U.S. Department of Housing and Urban Development, 1979), chapter 5. See also memorandum from Robert Sadacca (The Urban Institute)) to Carolyn McFarlane, "PFS Inflation Factor for Use in 1980 and Other Issues," October 19, 1979.

able for its intended use. The HUD handbook (7485.9) explicitly
states that "mod" funds are not to be used to make repairs that
are a "result of PHA failure to perform adequate maintenance."
This stricture notwithstanding, the mod program, as it is popu-
larly known, is generally the only source of funds available for
meeting needs caused by deferred maintenance; and the funds
are used for this purpose. Hence, the modernization program
should be thought of as a general capital improvement program
used to meet needs arising from a range of causes: normal wear
and tear; construction defects discovered long after completion;
tenant vandalism and destruction; and natural disaster. Further
modernization will often entail qualitative improvements; when
kitchens are modernized, open shelving is replaced by cupboards; bathroom modernization includes initial installation of
a shower enclosure. Obviously, how this all-purpose program
is administered is of critical importance to the well-being of the
large Authorities.

Funding
The total resources available for the mod program are set by
annual congressional appropriations. These are based on Ad-
ministration-provided estimates of funding needs. The actual
funding process is like that for new construction; to defer outlays and to reduce direct subsidies, HUD enters into an annual
contributions contract (ACC) with the Authority to pay for the
interest and amortization of bonds sold to investors by the
Authority. All ACCs for modernization now have a 20-year
term.

The figures in table 19 show that for the five fiscal years
1976-80, about $2 billion worth of repairs could have been ac-
complished with the appropriated funds. Systemwide this is
equivalent to $302 per year per dwelling unit. This compares
with the $52 per year figure reported by Eisenstadt for replace-
ments for privately owned New York City apartments over
1965-68.[17] On the other hand, if major rehabilitation is required
for part of the stock, the picture changes. For example, if over
5 years, 20,000 units were substantially rehabilitated at a cost of

17. This figure has been adjusted for inflation to be comparable with
the 1976-1980 fiscal years. See K. Eisenstadt, *Factors Affecting Maintenance and Operating Costs in Private Rental Housing* (New York: New
York City Rand Institute, R-1055-NYC, 1972).

Table 19

MODERNIZATION PROGRAM ACTIVITY
($ in 000s)

Fiscal Year	Contract Authority	Capital Costs Financed
76	$ 20,092	$ 215,999
77	37,608	347,660
78	42,632	448,180
79 [a]	50,000	545,500
80 [a]	37,500	409,200
Total 76-80	$187,832	$1,966,539

Source: U.S. Department of Housing and Urban Development, *Justification for 1980 Estimates*, Housing Section, Tab C, 1979.
a. Estimate.

$25,000 each, then the per unit funds available for the remainder of the stock would fall by about 25 percent. Still, the size of the appropriations appears to have been substantial.

The allocation of funds to specific projects and Authorities involves a complex process, including a good deal of judgment and discretion on the part of those at the HUD field office. After set-asides for special projects, the remaining annual appropriation is allocated to the field offices, most recently on the basis of the fraction of all public housing units over 15 years old within each office's jurisdiction. With the funds at the field offices, the decisions on which projects to fund are made based on two sets of priorities, everything else being the same. First, HUD has set out priority "work items," which include those relating to the following: energy conservation; compliance with federal, state, and local laws relating to health and safety; preservation of the basic integrity of the structures and systems; and provision of immediate and demonstrable cost-savings to PHA. The second set of priorities has to do with project age. New projects (under 10 years old) should not expect to need much in the way of modernization, if they are being properly managed; those over 30 years old, and hence nearing the end of their ACCs are to be repaired to ensure that they do not have any "major physical deficiencies"; it is those projects between 10 and 30 years old that receive funding priority. PHAs are, then, to focus their applications on certain types of improvements to middle-aged projects.

Other Administrative Provisions

Four other program provisions are worthy of mention: first, the regulations require an "economical approach" to making improvements. This appears to mean a parsimonious expenditure of federal funds generally and an explicit account of the remaining useful life of the project before making the funding decision. It is important to note the narrowness of the definition employed. Absent, for example, is any notion of demolishing a building in order to reduce project densities to a level conducive to effective management.[18]

Second, management practices must be considered in funding decisions. Specifically, the PHA is required, as a condition for funding, to correct management deficiencies identified by HUD.[19] While the regulations are explicit on this at one point, at another place they give the area office the right to "deemphasize the review of PHA management practices" as part of its detailed view of the application for modernization funds. Thus, considerable discretion—and potential inequity in treatment—is in the hands of the field office to use modernization funding as a carrot to achieve critical management improvements. PHAs are also required to demonstrate an ability to prudently control and manage the expenditure of the mod funds within a two-year period; the timely disposition of funds is a simple performance standard heavily relied upon by area office personnel.

Third, the regulations require tenant participation, although the handbook's language concentrates much more on the participation process than on the rights and responsibilities of the tenants. Finally, in the application review process, the "relationship of the project to the adjacent neighborhood" must be considered. No amplification of this statement is provided; and the role of the project as a possible catalyst for neighborhood preservation or revitalization as a basis for priority funding is never mentioned. This illustrates again the narrow treatment of public housing as an entity separate from the community and other housing assistance programs.

---

18. During Secretary Harris's tenure, it was official HUD policy to destroy no public housing, regardless of circumstances.

19. Specific management areas listed in the handbook are routine maintenance operations; preventive maintenance; rent collection policies and practices; tenant selection policies; and PHA progress in achieving resident employment.

Finally, the reader should note that none of the guidance and regulations just reviewed apply to modernization activities funded out of a locale's Community Development Block Grant funds. The meaning of this exception becomes clear when one realizes that in 1979 the Boston Public Housing Authority received about equal funding for modernization from HUD and the city's CDBG allocation. This is certainly not to argue that CDBG funds should be made subject to current regulations; indeed the supplementary funds may go to fund critical improvements that are too low on the HUD priority list.

Incentives and Possibilities

There are any number of aspects of the present modernization program that cause highly inefficient use of available funds. The most obvious is the uncertainty of funding levels from year to year. Table 20 shows the modernization funding received by 14 of the 29 PHAs in the largest cities during the FY 1975-78 period. Note that these exclude the special funding made under the Target Projects Program (described in chapter 8). These data, taken from internal HUD records, should be considered suggestive not definitive; there were sufficient omissions for the other 15 PHAs that they were thought to be wholly unreliable.[20] The figures in the table illustrate a tremendous year-to-year variance in the funds received by the same Authority; changes by a factor of three or four are common.

This kind of variance is justified only if the area office is following a long-term improvement plan for each PHA. But this is not the case. There is reason to doubt that area offices could implement long-term plans at their discretion, given personnel turnover and political interventions that result in special allocations to some PHAs. Rather, the proximate cause is the enormous discretion available to HUD in making its annual allocations. The question remains as to why the PHA could not have the discretion of retaining its own funds for big projects from steady annual funding levels.

---

20. These missing entries might be accurate, i.e., no mod funding to a PHA which had not obligated substantial amounts of loan authority given to it in prior years; but the frequency and pattern of zero funding make this doubtful. An additional problem was that for several PHAs the TPP mod funding was greater than the total mod allocation for a year. These two sets of data are kept by separate offices and have apparently never been reconciled.

Table 20

LOAN AUTHORITY MADE AVAILABLE TO SELECTED
PHAs FOR MODERNIZATION ACTIVITIES FY 1975-78 [a]

	Annual Loan Authority (000)				Average	
	FY75	FY76	FY77	FY78	Total (000)	Per Unit
National Capital (Washington)	$ 5,309	$ 749	$ 4,555	$5,695	$4,079	$364
Chicago	13,319	4,589	8,983	8,974	6,722	174
New Orleans	5,546	13,048	3,219	3,500	6,328	465
Baltimore	4,258	3,477	3,920	6,255	4,477	276
Kansas City	1,533	287	966	702	872	335
Milwaukee	502	418	1,808	1,474	1,050	239
New York	7,030	1,942	18,269	1,358	7,149	61
Cincinnati	1,080	2,190	4,418	1,134	2,205	324
Cleveland	2,948	330	2,963	5,172	2,853	248
Columbus	521	3,390	2,426	8,463	3,700	771
Pittsburgh	—	1,321	3,147	4,000	2,117	216
San Antonio	1,802	1,548	2,533	6,975	3,214	428
Seattle	—	375	3,976	2,030	1,595	270
St. Louis	6,381	392	1,257	1,542	2,393	357

Source: Program Control Branch, Fiscal Management Division, Office of Public Housing, Office of Housing, U.S. Department of Housing and Urban Development, unpublished data.

a. Excludes special disbursements for the Target Projects Program.

But this merely begs the question of the reasons for the lack of a genuine system. A system would require that reliable estimates of the modernization needs of the public housing inventory be known, both in the aggregate and for specific types of projects, defined by age, structure, size, and tenant characteristics. The aggregate estimate would be the basis for a multiyear congressional appropriation, and the data on project types would determine the allocations to PHAs. Surprisingly, until the summer of 1979 no such estimates existed. Amazingly, after being developed by HUD's research office, they were largely ignored by the program and budget offices in preparing the fiscal year 1981 budget proposal.[21] To be sure, these estimates could not be used in a totally mechanistic way. Some projects would require less than predicted; others more. If possible, though, the funds could be shifted within the same PHA.

The approach just outlined is also consistent with management improvement. Currently, if a PHA's management practices are found wanting and prospects of immediate improvement are small, the PHA could lose this year's allocation of modernization funds. If it improves, it can receive funds next year.

If funds were set aside this year to be released (in whole or in part) when the improvements were made, the positive incentive for change accumulates over time. At present the incentive is a negative one—the further deterioration of projects will occur until management is improved. Beyond this, there is the incentive for PHAs to adopt the posture that under these conditions accelerated deterioration will help ultimately secure funds: HUD will "save" the project when demolition is the only alternative to rehabilitation.

A second feature of the present program that causes inefficiency is the lack of a comprehensive approach to modernizing projects. Nowhere in the HUD handbook is comprehensive planning mentioned. Only as part of the application review is the "general physical condition of the project's systems and structures" taken into account. Thus, some essential items for a project may not be HUD priority items, and they will be omitted from the application. More commonly, work will be done sequentially over several years as distinct work items, even

---

21. Perkins-Will and The Ehrenkrantz Group, *An Evaluation of the Physical Condition of Public Housing Stock* (Washington, D.C.: U.S. Department of Housing and Urban Development, 1979).

though it would be much less costly in terms of both actual work efficiency and management costs to do all the work at one time. There is yet another factor at work: PHAs often receive a lower level of funds than they apply for, even though they work against targets given to them by the HUD field office. When this occurs, it is typical for a less costly and less urgent work item to be done instead of making only a start on the more urgent task. Thus, for example, replacement of wiring might be the most urgent improvement needed; but with a lower level of funding, new linoleum floors are installed rather than rewiring half of the units in the project. A comprehensive, efficient approach is simply impossible under the HUD priority work item—variable funding regulations.

The link between adequate management and modernization funding in the present regulations is good in principle. But in application, as noted earlier, it is too punitive, since funds are often permanently lost. Because of its punitive character, especially with the tenants being the real losers, field office personnel frequently do not use it. Given the primitive state of the modernization program, it is perhaps not surprising that the reverse linkage—from modernization outlays to reduced operating subsidies—has not been seriously considered.

Overall, it is difficult to think of the current modernization program as a program at all. It is a set of disparate elements that have been stapled together with the result being severe impediments to the efficient use of the appropriated funds. Furthermore, the new information on aggregated PHA needs (information costing well over $1 million to develop) has not been seized as a basis for making funding requests, let alone serving as the basis for a comprehensive "catch-up" effort. Executive directors and those responsible for modernization at the major Authorities are acutely aware of these shortcomings. Still, HUD is their major source of funds. But the intensity of the frustration can be appreciated when the St. Louis Authority with over $60 million in modernization needs and the Boston Authority with over $100 million receive less than 10 percent of the necessary funds in a year; the deficit continues to mount. Clearly, the modernization program requires fundamental change.

Chapter 6

PHA Management: Local Initiative versus Central Control

The prior chapters have documented the control of the Department of Housing and Urban Development over the great majority of large PHAs finances, that is, that part coming from various subsidies. This de facto control exists despite language in the 1959 housing legislation that vested "maximum initiative and responsibility" in the Authority. What is the extent of HUD guidance and intervention into other aspects of PHA operations? Because HUD can require certain management changes as a condition for modernization funding, pervasive intervention into local operations is certainly possible.

This chapter begins with a broad overview of the HUD-PHA relationship and then illustrates actual practices by considering two areas critical to proper administration: (a) tenant admission and eviction policies; and (b) establishment of rents paid by tenants. The conclusion is that while PHAs are subject to a great deal of guidance, such guidance is not overly restrictive. Indeed, in some areas, substantial latitude is possible if the PHA chooses to take advantage of it. PHAs have clearly not

used their power in any systematic fashion to screen out the
more difficult-to-serve households or to obtain a more hetero-
geneous tenant population. On the other hand, local initiative
has been thwarted by uncertainty about whether these specific
policies would be acceptable to HUD and to the courts.

THE RELATIONSHIP IN GENERAL

HUD's orientation guide to the low-rent public housing program characterizes the PHA as follows:

> It functions in the capacity of developer and manager of a low-
> rent public housing program. It has the responsibility for planning,
> financing, constructing or purchasing, leasing and managing the
> properties, subject only to applicable laws and contractual rela-
> tionships with HUD and the local governing body.[1]

The guide also contains a list of seven social objectives that
should distinguish a PHA's operations from the operations of
private developers. These include attaining a broad mix of
households in projects, having special respect for tenants' dig-
nity, helping to attain social services for residents, and providing training and employment opportunities for tenants.

The critical document, which spells out the actual relationship between HUD and the local Authority, is the annual contributions contract, signed before the acquisition of property
(by purchase or development) by the PHA.[2] Most importantly,
the ACC makes the PHA's activities subject to both existing and
future HUD regulations. In fact, the "terms and conditions"
section of the ACC is a good precis of the regulations. Because
of the open-ended nature of the commitment, the PHAs are
somewhat at the mercy of HUD. On the other hand, through
the regulation review process, including the public comment
period and explicit congressional review, the PHAs and their
national organizations have an opportunity to change any deleterious features of these issuances.

---

1. U.S. Department of Housing and Urban Development, "Low-Rent
Housing Guide: Orientation to the Program," HMG 7401.3, 1971, chapter
3, p. 1.

2. Also executed at this time is the Cooperation Agreement, a binding
contract between PHA and the governing body of the locality in which the
housing is to be located. It provides for the extent and type of local
cooperation in the development and management of the project.

The regulations, then, are key. Before examining specific cases, some idea of the coverage of the regulations may be helpful. Figure 2 shows in which areas HUD regulations require

Figure 2

OCCUPANCY POLICIES REQUIRED TO BE
ADOPTED BY PHAs

Descriptive Title	Tenant Comment Required [b]	HUD Approval Required [b]	Posting Required	References For HUD Requirements [a]
I. Admissions				
A. Tenant selection and assignment plan	X		X	Appendix 13
B. Noneconomic selection criteria			X	Appendix 2 (24 CFR section 860.204 (d))
C. Verification of non-economic selection criteria			X	Appendix 2 (24 CFR section 860.204 (d))
D. Verification of income for eligibility and rent			X	Appendix 10 (ACC section 206)
E. Income limits	X		X	Appendix 1 (24 CFR section 860.3), Appendix 10 (ACC section 204) and Appendix 10 (ACC section 206) respectively
F. Definition of income for eligibility				Appendix 1 (24 CFR section 860.2(b)) and Appendix 10 (ACC section 206) respectively

Figure 2 (cont'd)

OCCUPANCY POLICIES REQUIRED TO BE ADOPTED BY PHAs

Descriptive Title	Tenant Comment Required [b]	HUD Approval Required [b]	Posting Required	References For HUD Requirements [a]
G. Asset limitations (if any)		X	X	Appendix 1 (24 CFR section 860.2 (d)) and Appendix 10 (ACC section 206)
H. Receipt and initial processing of applications			X	Appendix 10 (ACC section 206)
I. Applicant notification			X	Appendix 10 (ACC CFR section 806.204 (d))
II. Rents				
A. Initial rent schedule or revised rent schedule decreasing rents		X	X	Appendix 10 (ACC section 204), and Appendix 10 (ACC section 206) respectively
B. Revised rent schedule increasing rents	X	X	X	Appendix 4 (24 CFR sections 861.402, 861.401), 861.402 and Appendix 10 (ACC section 206) respectively

Figure 2 (cont'd)

Descriptive Title	Tenant Comment Required [b]	HUD Approval Required [b]	Posting Required	References For HUD Requirements [a]
III. Occupancy				
A. Reexaminations	X		X	Appendix 5 (24 CFR section 866.4(c) and section 866.5)
B. Interim redeterminations	X		X	Appendix 5 (24 CFR section 866.4(c) and section 866.5)
C. Transfers	X		X	Appendix 5 (24 CFR section 866.3) and Appendix 10 (ACC section 206) respectively
D. Lease	X		X	Appendix 6 (24 CFR sections 866.50 and 866.3)
E. Grievance procedure	X		X	Appendix 10 (ACC section 206) respectively
F. Standards and criteria for continued occupancy	X		X	Appendix 1 (24 CFR section 860.2(c)(2)) and Appendix 10 (ACC section 206) respectively

Source: Public Housing Occupancy Handbook (7465.1 Rev.); figure 1, (Washington, D.C.: U.S. Department of Housing and Urban Development, 1978).
  a. References to Public Housing Occupancy Handbook (7465.1 Rev. H, and the *Code of Federal Regulations*).
  b. Prior to implementation by PHA.

PHAs to adopt occupancy policies. Figure 2 shows those areas in which tenant comment and explicit HUD approval before implementation of the policies are required, and the final column gives references to regulatory statements. In addition, the HUD field offices monitor the substance and implementation of the PHA policies. The information in figure 2 makes evident that HUD regulations apply to seemingly every area of occupancy policy. Yet the fundamental question remains: how restrictive are these regulations?

One source of suggestive information on this point is the opinion of executive directors. Table 21 tabulates the responses of the executive directors of 11 of the largest PHAs that were included in The Urban Institute's 1976 survey of 119 Authorities. The survey asked three questions regarding relationships with HUD. When asked about flexibility under the existing reg-

Table 21

EXECUTIVE DIRECTORS' OPINIONS
ON RELATIONS WITH HUD

QUESTION	OPINION				
	A Lot	A Fair Amount	A Little	None	Total
How much flexibility do you feel you are given by HUD regulations in running this Housing Authority?	0	7	4	0	11
	Very Helpful	Fairly Helpful	A Little Helpful	Not at All Helpful	Total
How helpful is the HUD area office in helping to solve Authority problems?	0	6	4	1	11
How helpful is the HUD area office to this Authority in gaining operating subsidies and the like?	2	2	7	0	11

Source: Special tabulations of 1976 Urban Institute survey data.

ulations, none thought they had "a lot," with the majority responding "a fair amount." Half of these respondents viewed the HUD area office as "fairly helpful" in solving the PHAs' problems; but one director found area offices "not at all helpful." On the other hand, all responded that the area office was at least "a little helpful" in securing subsidies, and 2 of 11 rated them "very helpful." Overall, no strong pattern emerges. This fact may reflect various interpretations of the regulations by HUD area offices and variation in creativity by the PHA directors.

ADMISSIONS AND EVICTIONS

Admissions

Policies must first establish who is eligible to live in public housing. Guidelines must be considered for restrictions or preferences that the PHA might exercise, at the discretion of either HUD or the PHA itself.

There is a two-part test for eligibility: an income and asset limitation, and a restriction on single-person households. HUD will accept without documentation the use of income limits set at 80 to 90 percent of those used in the department's Housing Assistance Payments Program (Section 8). These, briefly, are set at 80 percent of the areawide median family income for a family of four and adjusted up (down) for larger (smaller) households. For a lower (higher) income cutoff, the PHA must submit documentation on the presence (absence) of adequate, affordable housing in good condition for the marginal group being excluded (included). With this burden of proof, the incentive is clearly for the PHA to adopt the Section 8 standard. However, data in table 22 show that in 1979 only 9 of 22 of the PHAs in large cities for which we have information have income limits equal to at least 80 percent of the Section 8 program limits. Some PHAs have set very low income limits—notably Chicago and Detroit. These PHAs have, inconsistent with the regulations, adopted a policy of serving only very low-income households. By contrast, some Authorities—including those in New York, Pittsburgh, San Antonio, and St. Louis—allow households with incomes very close to the Section 8 limits to be admitted to their projects.

The PHA has wide discretion on the treatment of assets, either to establish maximums (which could differ for families

Table 22

PUBLIC HOUSING AND SECTION 8 INCOME LIMITS
IN 1979 FOR A FAMILY OF FOUR PERSONS

Public Housing Authority	Income Limits		
	PHA Defined [a]	Section 8 Defined [b]	Difference S.8 minus PHA
Buffalo	$11,100	$14,000	$ 2,900 [c]
New York	15,350	17,050	1,700 [c]
Washington, D.C.	14,600	19,350	4,750
Baltimore	11,250	15,850	4,600
Philadelphia	11,500	15,050	3,550
Pittsburgh	11,750	14,000	2,250 [c]
Atlanta	12,450	15,300	2,850 [c]
Chicago	6,500	17,300	10,800
Detroit	6,225	16,650	10,375
Minneapolis	12,400	16,850	4,450
Columbus	12,100	14,700	2,600 [c]
Cincinnati	10,900	14,700	3,800
Milwaukee	11,125	16,150	5,025
New Orleans	8,750	12,650	3,900
Dallas	10,500	14,800	4,300
Houston	12,350	15,350	3,000 [c]
San Antonio	10,300	12,550	2,250 [c]
St. Louis	12,400	14,900	2,500 [c]
Los Angeles	9,900	15,050	5,150
San Francisco	11,500	16,550	5,050
Boston	12,350	15,500	3,150 [c]
Memphis	9,200	12,700	3,500

a. From 1979 PHA (Re) Certification Policies and Procedures Survey.
Response to the question
    What is the current maximum income limit for a family of four, assuming
    the family has three minors and no unusual deductions, such as extraor-
    dinary metdical expenses?
b. Unpublished data provided by HUD's Division of Economic Market Analysis.
Definition S.8 income is given in Appendix A.
c. PHA income limit is at least 80 percent of Section 8 limit.

and elderly households) or to impute an income from the assets
and add the imputed income to received income in determining
eligibility. According to the 1979 survey data for 22 of the 29
PHAs in the largest SMSAs, most (20) had some limitation on
assets, although it was sometimes, especially for the elderly,

quite generous; the majority simply had an absolute limit (generally higher for the elderly); 2 of the 22 added imputed income from the assets when applying the income eligibility tests.[3]

In concept, the PHA also has considerable discretion in defining income, but there are strong incentives for following the definitions developed by HUD.

There is little variance permitted, by contrast, in defining eligible household types. Simply put, single-person households (except for handicapped persons and those over the age of 62) are generally excluded from living in public housing. Exceptions to this HUD policy must be given by the field office and can only be justified, for example, when small units are not suitable for occupancy by eligible, single individuals, or when an Authority rents units in a project to "noneligible" individuals to make use of units that would not otherwise be occupied.

Although these rules establish the population of eligible households, PHAs may screen out undesirable tenants. "Noneconomic selection criteria" include evaluation of an applicant's history of paying rent, credit checks, home visits, and reports from former landlords to help assess the household's ability to maintain a unit. These criteria must not be applied so that they exclude classes of households. The PHA can also give preferential treatment on a variety of grounds; in the past, justification for preferences has included displacement, veterans' status, being elderly, living in substandard housing, having an emergency housing situation, or attaining a mix of tenants with differing incomes.

Evidence is limited as to how much PHAs use these options when establishing and executing admission policies. Two questions in The Urban Institute's 1976 survey of 119 Authorities bear on noneconomic screening. PHA personnel were asked if visits were made to applicants' homes before admission and whether references or previous landlords of applicants were contacted. Of the 11 PHAs included in this study and the UI survey, 5 responded that they did both types of checks, and 3 more said they checked references. Thus noneconomic screen-

---

3. Based on unpublished tabulations from the survey of "PHA (Re) Certification Policies and Procedures" conducted by The Urban Institute for HUD in 1979. The 22 cities are the same as those surveyed in 1976 and listed in table 22.

ing is far from universal; and even where it is policy, the consistency of its application is unknown.

Further information comes from the 1979 survey of admissions procedures, already mentioned, that included 22 of our 29 PHAs. The following question was asked:

> Suppose you had only one vacant apartment but had ten applicant families of the appropriate size who met the general income (and asset) limitations of the PHA. Please tell me each criterion you would use in deciding which household would be offered the vacant apartment. Please start with the most important criterion, then the next most important one, and so on.

The answers, tabulated in table 23, show a very strong emphasis on accepting first those in emergency housing situations, including families being displaced by private or public action. The second criterion stressed is position on the waiting list. Interestingly, getting "stable/nonproblem families" was men-

Table 23

CRITERION USED BY TWENTY-THREE LARGE PHAs IN SELECTING TENANTS [a]

| | Number of PHAs Mentioning Criterion | |
Criterion	Total	Mentioning First or Second
First come, first served	17	7
Income to increase PHA income level	9	4
Displaced families	22	20
Families living in substandard housing	9	0
Veterans	12	4
Stable/nonproblem families	3	1
Others [b]	16	8

Source: Unpublished tabulation of 1979 PHA (Re) certifications policies survey data.

a. Based on response to the question

Suppose you had only one vacant apartment but had ten applicant families of the appropriate size who met the general income (and asset) limitations of the PHA. Please tell me which criterion you would use in deciding which household would be offered the vacant apartment. Please start with the most important criterion, then the next most important one, and so on.

b. Dominant criteria were the household being in an "emergency" housing situation or PHA meeting equal opportunity goals.

tioned by only three Authorities; and only one mentioned it first or second. Raising the income mix of tenants—an objective mandated by the Congress in the Housing and Community Development Act of 1974—was mentioned by 9 PHAs, but given first or second priority by only 4. Thus it appears that these 22 very large PHAs are using their admissions policies to a quite limited extent to change their tenants to a group that would facilitate project management. This lack of initiative at first seems amazing. However, courts have intervened in a number of cases, the net result being that any rejected applicant is entitled to an informal hearing. In some states, certain types of preferences have been struck down. Faced with the requirement for a hearing, some Authorities may have decided that the cost of hearings are a greater burden than fully screening tenants.[4] Further, many PHAs believe that their mission is to serve those households with the greatest need. Some also complain that HUD guidance on how to pursue tenant mix objectives is inadequate, especially in light of court intervention.[5] (Preferences and screening are discussed further in chapter 10.)

The PHAs' power over tenant admission policies does not extend, however, to differential treatment of those on waiting lists. The waiting list is established on the basis of the type and size of dwelling required, the PHA's preferences as expressed in its written policies, and the time at which the application was screened. Once on these lists, "Eligible families must then be chosen in sequence from the waiting list as vacancies occur."

Evictions

Lease termination must be addressed in the lease signed by the PHA and the tenant. By regulation, all occupied units must be under a lease agreement, and terminations or refusal to renew a lease can only be for "serious or repeated violation of material terms of the lease." Termination requires a written notice that states the reasons for termination and advises the tenant

---

4. For a review of court actions, see J. S. Fuerst and Roy Petty, "Public Housing in the Courts: Pyrrhic Victories For the Poor," *Urban Lawyer*, vol. 9, no. 3, 1977, pp. 496-513.

5. These responses were given by six PHAs (five in the largest cities) in response to questions on lack of progress in meeting the income mix objective. See, "Serving a Broader Economic Range of Families in Public Housing Could Reduce Operating Subsidies" (Washington, D.C.: General Accounting Office, Pub. CED-80-2, 1979).

of his right to request a hearing. The tenant's request for a hearing begins the formal grievance process, whose structure is spelled out in elaborate detail in the federal regulations. An important point is that "in no event should the notice to vacate be issued prior to the decision of the housing office or the housing panel having been mailed or delivered to the complainant." The full grievance process could easily require 2-3 weeks; the eviction notice, then, provides varying maximum times for quitting the unit depending on the cause;[6] if the unit is still occupied, recourse to court action is necessary. This full procedure, resulting from a series of court suits brought by legal aid lawyers on behalf of tenants,[7] although providing due process, can leave a problem tenant in a project for a protracted period possibly causing additional difficulties.

HUD has sought to ensure basic tenant rights in detailing lease agreement requirements and grievance procedures. In so doing, it has left very little discretion to the PHA in setting policies, and the problem of evicting problem tenants is a major complaint of PHAs and other tenants as well.

TENANT RENTAL PAYMENTS

Regulations Set Boundaries

HUD's rules establish three rent-income ratio conditions that must be simultaneously satisfied for the PHA to be in compliance with the regulations. These are reviewed below. The reader should be aware of two different definitions of income that are used in calculating these ratios:

   a. Total family income or gross income—all of the household's income except for several classes of extraordinary income.

---

6. Minimum time periods for quitting the unit are (a) no minimum in cases involving the creation or maintenance of a threat to the health and safety of other tenants; (b) failure to pay unit, 14 days; (c) 30 days in all other cases.

7. A partial history of this litigation is in Roger Starr, "Which of the Poor Shall Live in Public Housing?" *The Public Interest*, no. 23, 1971, pp. 116-24; also see Fuerst and Petty, "Public Housing in the Courts"; and A. Hirsch and U. N. Brown argue the other side in "Too Poor for Public Housing: Roger Starr's Poverty Preferences," *Social Policy*, May/June 1972, pp. 28-32.

b. Family income or adjusted income—gross income less a set of standard deductions, such as $300 for each minor, certain occupation-related expenses, etc.[8]

Also note the difference between *contract rent*, that is, the rent actually charged by the PHA to the tenant, and *gross rent*, which is defined as contract rent plus an estimate of the cost, if any, of utility payments made directly by the tenant.

The three rent-income ratio conditions that must be satisfied can be stated as follows:

1. Maximum gross rent-to-income ratio: Gross rent charged to a household cannot exceed 25 percent of *adjusted* income.[9]
2. Minimum rent-to-income ratio: Gross rent shall not be less than 5 percent of gross income, or a higher amount specified by state or local laws.
3. Minimum *aggregate gross* rent-to-income ratio: aggregate gross rents for all units in the PHA must equal at least 20 percent of the *adjusted* income of all resident households.[10]

Of these three conditions, the first is designed to ensure that the tenant does not have to pay what has traditionally been considered an excessive portion of his income for rent,[11] while the latter two conditions ensure some minimum effort by tenants, individually and collectively, to meet expenses. Interestingly, the aggregate 20 percent ratio was initially created so that the 25 percent maximum contribution would not be interpreted as both a ceiling and a floor to tenants' contributions.

The effect of these regulations on the rent paid by tenants

---

8. See Appendix E for full definitions.

9. This was changed by the Housing and Community Development Act of 1979, which gave HUD the discretion of raising the maximum to 30 percent for households with incomes greater than 50 percent of the area median; but, at the time of this writing, implementing regulations had not been promulgated.

10. This condition is only applicable if the PHA is receiving operating subsidies; all of the large PHAs are.

11. On the appropriateness of this ratio see T. S. Lane, *Origins and Uses of the Conventional Rules of Thumb* (Cambridge: Abt Assoc., 1977); and J. D. Feins and C. S. White, Jr., *The Ratio of Shelter Expenditures to Income: Definitional Issues, Typical Patterns and Historical Trends* (Cambridge: Abt Assoc., 1977).

with monthly incomes of $200 and $500 is illustrated by the figures in table 24. The lower income household's gross rental
payments are between $22.50 and $10 per month. (The negative
minimum contract rent for the lower income household is due
to the utility allowance exceeding the contract rent amount,
when the minimum ratio is computed using gross rent.) The
range for the higher income household is $87.50 to $25.00 per
month. These simple computations suggest considerable latitude
on the part of the PHAs in setting individual rents.

In fact this latitude can be used in several ways. The PHA
does not have to employ the income definitions detailed in the
regulations. It may use whatever definition it sees fit; but, because it must report the specified ratios to HUD using the HUD
definitions, there is a strong incentive to use the HUD definition. Alternatively, the PHA can vary rent-to-income ratios in
numerous ways. Two ways suggested in the HUD handbook are
reducing the ratio as family size increases, or establishing a
lower rent schedule for less desirable projects.

Incomes and Rent Levels in Practice

To get some idea of the degree to which PHAs have used their
latitude, the 1976 tenant income and rent data gathered by The

Table 24

ILLUSTRATIVE RENT CALCULATIONS

Income on Rent Concept	Household A	Household B
1. Gross income/month (Total family)	$200	$500
2. Adjusted income/month (family)	90	350
3. Utility allowance	20	20
4. Ceiling maximum gross rent	225 [a]	225
5. Maximum gross rent (25% of adjusted income)	22.50	87.50
6. Minimum gross rent (5% of gross income)	10	25
7. Minimum contract rent (gross rent less utility allowance)	−10	5
8. PHA established rent (22% of adjusted income)	19.80	77

a. This is a rent ceiling which the PHA may establish, beyond which rent
does not increase as income rises.

Urban Institute have again been used.[12] Table 25 displays figures on tenant incomes and rents, defined under various concepts, for the 22 large PHAs that are among the 29 that are the focus of this monograph, and for the 5 PHAs that have large enough samples to justify reporting separate results. Four of the PHAs for which we have separate data include the same income sources and exclusions in their income definitions.[13]

The top panel deals with income definitions. Lines A.2 and A.3 report the mean annual family incomes, as defined by the PHA and by the HUD regulations, and line A.4 shows the difference between the two. Across the 22 Authorities there is close agreement, but there is substantial variation between and within the Authorities. The Chicago PHA's definition results in an 8 percent ($277) higher annual income than the HUD definition, and Philadelphia's is 10 percent ($350) less than HUD's. Furthermore the standard deviations for the differences within Authorities are impressive. For example, while the mean difference for the Atlanta PHA is only $14 per year, the standard deviation is $165; the standard deviation for all 22 cities is $547.

The differences between gross and net family income are reported in line A.7, and once more sharp variance among Authorities is evident. Among the five PHAs, the mean percentage reduction in gross income from the various deductions ranges from 16 percent (Chicago) to 28 percent (Philadelphia). Other entries in the panel indicate the effect of adoption of the more stringent income definitions used in the Section 8 program.[14] Annual incomes so defined would rise as much as $733 in Philadelphia and $343 for all the large PHAs.

To go a step further in analyzing adjusted incomes, a simple regression model was estimated separately for each of the five PHAs. In each, adjusted income was "explained" by gross income and a set of household characteristics to be used by the Authorities in determining adjusted income. These characteristics were whether the head of house was elderly, whether the head of house or spouse was handicapped, the number of minor children (under age 18), and the number of children over 18 who were full-time students. Several aspects of the estimated regressions, reported in Appendix F, table F-1, are worth noting. First, nearly all of the variance in adjusted income can be ex-

---

12. These data are described in chapter 3.
13. This information is not available for Baltimore.
14. These definitions are given in Appendix E.

Table 25

TENANT INCOMES AND RENTAL CONTRIBUTIONS UNDER ALTERNATIVE DEFINITIONS

	Twenty-two Cities	Five Cities	Los Angeles	Atlanta	Chicago	Baltimore	Philadelphia
A. Mean Annual Income Levels							
1. Gross family income ($)	4,906	4,332	5,330	2,581	4,693	4,136	4,584
2. Family income—PHA-defined ($)	4,142	3,421	4,329	1,869	3,956	3,250	3,279
3. Family income—HUD-defined ($)	4,054	3,394	4,231	1,883	3,679	3,281	3,628
Differences							
4. Family income HUD vs. PHA definition ($)	−88	−28	−98	14	−277	30	350
5. Family income S.8 vs. HUD definition ($)	431	436	475	262	555	360	383
6. Family income S.8 vs. PHA definition ($)	343	408	377	276	278	390	733
7. Gross vs. net family income (PHA) ($)	764	911	1,001	712	737	886	1,035
B. Mean Monthly Rents							
1. Contract rent ($)	72	59	72	33	60	63	64
Change in tenant contribution							
2. With HUD-allowed maximum ($)	12	10	13	3	13	5	11

3. With S.8 income and rent rules ($)	6	4	5	5	4	5	5
4. S.8 rules vs. HUD maximum ($)	11	7	11	1	13	3	2
5. With 15/25% rule and ($) PHA income	21	21	21	24	19	23	23
C. Rent-To-Income Ratio $\times$ 10 [a]							
1. Tenant gross rent contribution to PHA-defined family income	25	25	24	25	23	25	27
2. Maximum HUD gross rent contribution to PHA-defined family income	25	25	24	25	23	25	27
3. Tenant gross rents contribution to gross income	18	17	17	17	16	18	17

Source: Special tabulations of 1976 Public Housing Income Survey data.
a. All terms defined in Appendix E.

plained by these factors. Second, as one would anticipate, the level of gross income is by far the dominant variable. The coefficient of this variable indicates the rate at which adjusted income rises with gross income after taking account of the variables just listed; the values range from a low range of about .90 for three Authorities to 1.04 for Chicago. Finally, of the other variables, only the number of minor children is statistically significant for all five PHAs; the adjustment (deduction) in monthly income for each child ranges from about $19 in Los Angeles and Chicago to $29 in Philadelphia.

While these points clearly illuminate the variation in practices among Authorities, the same regression results can be used to estimate how the same family would be treated at those five PHAs. Our estimate of the average adjusted income for each of the five PHAs of a family of four, including three minor children, headed by a nonelderly woman with a monthly gross income of $300 is listed in table 26. This family would have $35 less adjusted income as defined by the PHA if they lived in Philadelphia rather than Chicago, a difference of 19 percent.

The effect of differences in income definitions on tenant rent levels can be offset or heightened by the PHAs' rental policies. Panel B shows current mean rents (B.1) and the increment in rents possible if the HUD-allowed maximum tenant contributions were charged (B.2). By this standard, Atlanta is charging high rents, and Los Angeles and Chicago are charging comparatively low rents. Again, the variation within all the PHAs is

Table 26

ESTIMATED ADJUSTED INCOMES AND RENTAL
CONTRIBUTIONS OF A FAMILY OF FOUR AT FIVE PHAs

Authority	Adjusted Income of "Standard" Household [a]	Rental Contribution of "Standard" Household [b]
Los Angeles	$209	$67
Atlanta	204	44
Chicago	218	55
Baltimore	194	53
Philadelphia	183	50

a. Based on regression models reported in Appendix F.
b. The standard household is defined as a family of four, including three minor children, headed by a nonelderly woman with a monthly income of $300.

high, suggesting either systematic differential treatment of tenants under the PHAs rental policies or simple errors in the computation of rents. Among all large PHAs, rental income could be increased by 16 percent by charging up to the HUD-allowed maximum.

The final panel of table 25 combines the information on income and rental policies by computing three gross rent contribution-to-income ratios. The first (line C.1) uses the PHA's definition of family income, and hence can be used to measure compliance with the aggregate rent-to-income agreement requirement defined earlier. The average of all the large PHAs is 21 percent, but varies among the five PHAs for which separate data are available from 19 percent for Chicago to 24 percent for Atlanta. The next ratio (C.2) uses HUD maximum tenant contribution rule, and none of the ratios for individual PHAs differs significantly from 25 percent. Finally, the ratio of gross rent to gross income shows most clearly the combined effects of rental and income policies. There is no significant difference in the mean values among the Authorities for which we have data. This consistency is remarkable in light of variance discussed in the previous paragraphs, and presumably results partly from the aggregate 20 percent ratio imposed by the regulations. At least as striking as the consistency is the low average level: households living in public housing are devoting only about half as much of their income to housing than all lower-income renter households and 5 to 7 percentage points less than those receiving assistance under the Section 8 Existing program.[15]

Another way to combine the information on income adjustments and rent policies is to estimate the rental contribution of the standard household defined above, using another estimated regression (table F-2 in Appendix F) and the adjusted income estimates for the household calculated above. Results of this exercise are listed in the second column of table 26, where a maximum difference in rental payments of $23 or—52 percent— is shown. The serious equity problems caused by local discretion in setting rents are vividly evident.

---

15. M. Drury, O. Lee, M. Springer, and L. Yap, *Low Income Housing Assistance Program (Section 8)* (Washington, D.C.: Office of Policy Development and Research, U.S. Department of Housing and Urban Development), adjustment of numbers on p. 67.

In conclusion, PHAs do exercise a good deal of discretion in establishing their rental policies and income definitions. While this leads to differences in rent payments as a fraction of PHA-defined family income, there is little variance evident among the few PHAs examined in the average fraction of the gross income that is spent by tenants on rent. However, consistency vanishes when the treatment of individual households is examined. If the pattern suggested here is endemic to the program, reduced local discretion will be required to ensure equitable treatment of tenants at varying locations.

Part IV

MANAGEMENT: PRACTICES AND INITIATIVES

Chapter 7

Management Within
The Authority

What is known about good housing management? At first impression, a good deal. After all, housing management courses are taught by the National Center for Housing Management and others; and, as described in the next chapter, HUD has developed a college-level housing management curriculum. Unfortunately, the basis for these courses consists of concepts and experience borrowed from other areas of business management (to some extent perfectly appropriate), common sense, and the knowledge of a few highly experienced managers. To date, there has been no rigorous testing of which management practices work well under alternative circumstances. Indeed, the definition of "works well" is largely unresolved. What is to be maximized: tenants' satisfaction; landlords' or PHAs' "profits," or the salutory effect of the project on the neighborhood? Which group comprises priority tenants? Alternative objectives often require rather diverse management practices. Furthermore, much of the applicability of conventional management wisdom is limited to a fairly narrow range of circumstances; by any standard many of the "super-block" projects are a managerial challenge quite beyond textbook examples.[1]

1. A series of sketches of distressed projects, which reflect the failings of proper management is in "Social Aspects of Low- and Moderate-Income Housing Programs," vol. 2 (Washington, D.C.: The National Commission on Urban Problems, 1968).

This chapter relies almost exclusively on the large body of work done by The Urban Institute, during almost a decade, on the management of public housing. This large and ambitious set of analyses, already partially described, is the dominant analysis of housing management; and it has the distinct advantage of being focused on public housing with its particular set of objectives and incentives. To be sure, there has been substantial debate about the specific procedures used by The Urban Institute in reaching various conclusions;[2] some even argue that the results are consequently invalid. Our view is that legitimate questions have been raised by outside reviews, but these reviews do not preclude using the results of the Institute's analysis. The Institute has always viewed its analysis as the first steps of a long hike on the road to conclusive results. At a minimum, the results to date point to priority areas for further analysis and standards' development.

As stated in chapter 5, the Institute's analysis included some 119 public housing Authorities, divided into three groups on the basis of the number of units under management, with those in the large group managing 1,250 or more units. The Authorities were divided into high performing and low performing groups, through an elaborate statistical process which attempted to control for the specific circumstances of the projects included in the analyses.[3] In the absence of agreed upon objective standards of performance, the criteria used to judge performance were residents' degree of expressed satisfaction with such things as project cleanliness, safety and security, maintenance, and management; the project manager's perception of the condition of the buildings and units, problems of deferred maintenance, and other factors; PHAs' employees' satisfaction with their jobs and the PHAs' performance; and, the perceptions of PHA management in certain areas of performance, such as occupancy rates, rent delinquencies, and vandalism. These diverse measures were used together to classify the PHAs into high and low performance groups.

One of the principal products of The Urban Institute's work

2. R. Shafer, "Operating Subsidies in Public Housing: A Critical Appraisal of the Formula Approach" (Boston: Citizens Housing and Planning Association, 1975). S. R. Merrill, J. Cromwell, D. Napior, D. Weinberg, "A Preliminary Working Paper on the Technical Components of the Performance Funding System" (Cambridge: Abt Associates, 1979).

3. See chapter 5 for a more complete description.

was a clear statement of the background circumstances of the projects in high and low performing Authorities (e.g., tenant composition and neighborhood conditions) and of differences in their management practices, at the project and PHA levels.[4] In the Institute's report, Sadacca and Loux contrast high and low performers for the population of 119 Authorities. Their findings are based on tests of the difference in the mean scores of management and control (i.e., background circumstances) between the high and low performing Authorities. For example, one finding in the Sadacca-Loux report is that high performing PHAs took significantly less time to prepare an apartment for a new tenant than low performing PHAs took—3 days versus 12 days.[5] This finding points out a poor management practice that really seems to make a difference. The causes of this problem would have to be ascertained for progress to be made at a specific Authority. Sadacca-Loux have defined a set of such practices which together can direct Authorities toward improvement, but not chart the course on how to achieve the objective.

This chapter differs from the Sadacca-Loux work in two ways. First, the 40 large PHAs are the focus of the analyses.[6] Second, we have tested for differences between the scores of the 11 PHAs in the largest cities that were included in the Institute sample,[7] and the means of the high and low performing PHAs for each of the management and control variables.[8] This

---

4. Robert Sadacca and S. Loux, "Improving Public Housing Through Management: A Technical Report" (Washington, D.C.: The Urban Institute, Working Paper 255-2, 1978).

5. It might be noted that regressions using the management and control variables explained about 80 percent of the variation in the individual performance criterion scores on average.

6. In fact, between the 1973 and 1976 survey years the Institute made several changes in their overall sample, based in part on the increase in the number of large PHAs. This resulted in the sample of large PHAs increasing to 45. None of the additional PHAs were in the largest cities. This augmented sample has been used for the analyses of the large Authorities separately reported in this chapter, although it is *not* used in other chapters. Also note that the set of performance variables shifted between the 1973 and 1976 analyses. The first set had been defined by experts (see chapter 5); those for 1976 were based on analysis of the data collected in 1973.

7. Washington, D.C., Baltimore, Atlanta, Memphis, Detroit, Columbus, Milwaukee, Houston, San Antonio, Los Angeles, San Francisco.

8. Differences in the control or background variables are reported in Appendix G.

makes it possible to determine if there are specific areas in which these 11 PHAs, as a group, are doing especially well or badly.[9]

This chapter basically restates the Sadacca-Loux findings for all 119 PHAs across the three size categories. It indicates when the findings hold for the large PHAs considered separately and among the large PHAs for the eleven largest Authorities compared to large high and low performance Authorities. This chapter should be considered essentially a quotation of the Sadacca-Loux findings, except where findings for the very large PHAs are separately noted.[10]

---

9. It is not known how representative, in management practices and in background conditions, these particular 11 PHAs are of the PHAs in the 29 largest cities with conventional public housing programs. Hence, the results of the comparisons of the 11 with the sample population of large Authorities apply only to the 11 PHAs included in the analyses.

Another difference between the findings reported here and those in Sadacca-Loux is that they also present results for changes over the three-year 1973-76 period in the performance of PHAs and relate these changes to management and control variables; this type of analysis is not presented here. This omission is due to the reduced clarity of the findings over a period of time and to the problem of too few observations in the four possible cells (e.g., high 76-high 73; high 76-low 73; etc.) for the 11 PHAs in the largest cities.

10. Two comments on the statistical findings are noteworthy. First, a substantial number of findings that are valid in distinguishing between high and low performance when all 119 Authorities are taken together are not valid (statistically significant) when tested only for the large PHAs. This is due to the greater homogeneity of background conditions and management practices among PHAs in the same size group. Hence, the difference in the mean of some characteristics, for example, number of days to respond to maintenance requests (as reported by the tenant, not from PHA work orders), between large high performance and low performance PHAs; the variance is smaller in the former case, which yields the difference insignificant among the large PHAs, although it *is* significant for all PHAs. Second, no significant differences between the 11 largest PHAs and the low performance large PHAs were found. The 11 largest PHAs on this item are essentially low performers. On the other hand, there are a substantial number of cases in which the 11 are not significantly different from either the high or low performers, although the two groups themselves differ. The 11 largest in these cases are "average." In summary, the 11 largest PHAs do exhibit some special characteristics compared to large high performers, but not compared to large low performers.

MANAGEMENT PRACTICES

Organizational Structure

The one aspect of organizational structure differentiating the high and low performance PHAs was decentralization—that is, more authority delegated to the project level rather than kept at the central office.

- Project managers at high performance PHAs believed they were given significant authority. But managers at low performance PHAs felt their authority was insufficient. These differences were most pronounced at the small and medium PHAs.

- Another measure of decentralization is the percentage of staff who work at the central office (rather than at the projects). High performance PHAs had a significantly smaller percentage of staff at the central office. The large PHAs had a significantly smaller percentage of central office staff than did the smaller PHAs (which would be expected since their projects are considerably larger and warrant having larger project staffs).

- Where maintenance is organized on a project basis rather than centralized and where larger inventories of supplies and parts are kept at the project, performance tends to be higher, both across all size groups and for the large PHAs separately. Maintenance organized at the project level probably permits the staff to be more responsive to the tenants' requests and enables the maintenance staff to become familiar with the specific problems of the project. High performance PHAs also had significantly larger inventories at the projects than did the low performance PHAs.

- More high performance PHAs overall and among large PHAs separately, had separate divisions for recreational activities and social services than did low performance PHAs. Perhaps this indicates greater organizational concern for residents' needs among high performance PHAs.

An overall measure of the effectiveness of PHA organizational structure is whether the central office staff and the project managers think the PHA's organizational structure should be modified to make it more efficient. Staff members at the high performance PHAs felt significantly less strongly than the staff at low performance PHAs that such reorganization was necessary. Not surprisingly, staff at the large PHAs (which have a more complex structure) felt significantly more strongly than those at smaller PHAs that reorganization was needed.

Internal Relationships
The ability of a PHA to deliver efficient service to its residents might well be influenced by the attitude of its staff toward their work and toward each other.

- Executive directors at high performance PHAs overall and among large PHAs separately felt that their staffs gave them significantly more support than did executive directors at low performance PHAs.

- Central office staff at high performance PHAs believed significantly more strongly than staff at low performance PHAs that supervisors supported them and worked with them as a team.

- Both central office staff and project staff at the high performance PHAs worried significantly less than their counterparts at low performance PHAs about being fired or laid off. In general, though, PHA staff did not report a high degree of concern about this possibility.

Management Strictness
Of the numerous measures of management practices analyzed in the Sadacca-Loux study, one practice with the strongest relationship to performance was management's practice in enforcing rules.

- Both residents and project staff at high performance PHAs reported more often than those in low performance PHAs that management was significantly stricter in enforcing rules (e.g., about the way residents handled garbage and trash, noise from parties).

- High performance PHA central office staff believed less strongly than low performance PHA staff that their PHA's eviction policy was too lenient. This result holds for the large Authorities separately, and among the large PHAs, the 11 largest Authorities voiced this opinion significantly less often.

- The time required to evict a tenant for rent delinquency was significantly different between performance groups. In 1976, time taken to evict a resident was significantly less at high performance PHAs than at low performance PHAs, although this did not hold across all three size groups.

Responsiveness of Management
In general, residents at high performance PHAs believed that management was responsive to their needs.

- Residents of high performance PHAs more often felt that they were treated well than did low performance PHA residents. This finding held for the large PHAs separately as well; further, among the large PHAs, the 11 largest had significantly lower ratings by their residents in this area than did the high performance large Authorities.

- At high performance PHAs overall and large Authorities separately, about three quarters of the residents felt there was enough staff, but only two thirds of the residents at low performance PHAs thought there was adequate staff. By contrast, only 60 percent of the residents at the 11 largest PHAs gave a positive response to this question, significantly less than at the high performance large PHAs. Interestingly, though, a significantly higher percentage of large PHA residents than medium/small PHA residents reported that there was not enough staff.

- A significantly larger percentage of residents at large high performance PHAs than at low performance PHAs thought the manager knew a great deal about how to do his job. Also, significantly more residents at high performance PHAs thought the manager or his staff (rather than staff at the central office or even someone outside the PHA) were the best persons to contact.

Other differences in management responsiveness between the performance groups were in maintenance responsiveness. For instance, project managers at high performance PHAs reported that it took significantly less time to prepare an apartment for a new tenant than managers at low performance PHAs reported —6 days versus 12 days. At the large PHAs, time taken was significantly greater than at the smaller PHAs, the difference here being attributable to the large low performance PHAs that had an average preparation time of 17 days. But among the large Authorities, those rated as high performers took only 6 days; the 11 largest PHAs took 18 days for these preparations. Additionally, although it took less time at the high performance PHAs to get apartments ready, a higher percentage of the residents at high performance PHAs than at low performance PHAs were satisfied with the way their apartments had been prepared. Again, there was a significant difference among the size groups: the large PHA residents reported less satisfaction than residents at smaller PHAs reported. Inasmuch as those measures are related to overall performance, the residents' first impressions of their apartments appear important.

Once the resident has moved in, maintenance responsiveness continues to be very strongly related to overall performance.

- At high performance PHAs, residents reported that it took significantly less time for management to respond to routine and emergency maintenance requests. As in the case of apartment preparation, in large PHAs, significantly more time was taken to respond to maintenance requests than was taken at smaller PHAs. Among large Authorities, high performers averaged an 11-day response time to routine requests, while low performers averaged 32 days—the latter being the same average as for the 11 largest PHAs.

- A higher percentage of residents at low performance PHAs overall and among large PHAs separately than residents at high performance PHAs thought that management should paint their apartments more often. And a higher percentage of residents at high performance PHAs than residents at low performance PHAs believed that they had enough paint colors to choose from.

Several measures of management's nonresponsiveness also differentiated between the high and low performance PHAs. Resident involvement in maintenance—such as doing their own repairs—is associated with lower management performance overall and among the large PHAs separately, although higher levels of resident participation in day-to-day project upkeep is related to higher performance, as discussed in the following section. These findings suggest that residents perform this maintenance when they feel management is not fulfilling its responsibilities.

Another maintenance practice which differentiated performance groups was whether the PHA charged residents for repairs, and the attitude of the residents toward the charges. A higher percentage of residents at high performance PHAs than at low performance PHAs thought that the amounts they had been charged for repairs were fair. The residents' views in the 11 largest PHAs were significantly less positive than the residents' views in the high performance large PHAs. This perception of "fairness" of repair charges may reflect the PHA's ability to explain to residents the need for such charges rather than be an indication of the appropriateness of the amount charged.

Although some aspects of increasing security, such as providing security guards, may be a responsibility of local government as well as the PHAs, other aspects are certainly within the PHA's responsibility.

- A significantly larger percentage of residents at high performance PHAs (about three quarters versus about a third at low performance PHAs) felt there was enough exterior lighting. Among the large PHAs the difference, while still significant, was much smaller (three quarters versus two thirds).

- A significantly larger percentage of residents in low performance PHAs overall and among large PHAs separately reported that they had either added locks or alarms to their apartments or had made their own security-related repairs. Again, when residents feel management is not fulfilling its responsibility, residents will act on their own.

- Managers at high performance PHAs (in 1973) reported that drugs and illegal activities by adults were not significant problems. Managers at low performance PHAs, however, did report such activities as significant problems.

Tenant Roles in Project Management

Tenants, of course, play an important role in project management. Sadacca and Loux grouped the measures of tenant roles in management into three categories: tenant cooperativeness, project cohesiveness, and tenant involvement in management. Although tenant participation in management through formal arrangements such as tenant organizations is frequently viewed as a positive factor, the Sadacca-Loux findings suggest that more informal tenant participation and supporting behavior are of equal if not more importance.

Tenant Cooperativeness. It is obvious that management, without the cooperation of residents, will be hard pressed to provide an acceptable living environment for the residents. There are strong relationships between management's responsiveness and tenant cooperation, and although such relationships do not indicate cause and effect, it is not unreasonable to assume that tenants will be more cooperative with management when they believe management is trying to respond to their needs.

- At high performance PHAs (in 1973), project managers and residents alike believed strongly that residents helped to keep up the buildings and grounds, and a lower percentage of residents at high performance PHAs than at low performance PHAs felt that unsupervised children were a problem. Similarly, managers and their staff at high performance PHAs (in 1976) thought that their residents maintained their apartments significantly better than did their counterparts at low performance PHAs.

- At high performance PHAs, the project managers, their staff, and the residents all thought that there was significantly less of a problem in the way tenants handle garbage and trash than did respondents at low performance PHAs. The large PHAs had a significantly greater problem (according to all respondent types) than the smaller PHAs.

Project Cohesiveness. Where management is responsive and the tenants are cooperative, a climate exists that is conducive to a harmonious living environment. Where managers and residents view each other as similar in outlook (rather than as opposing forces), the living environment is further enhanced.

- Managers at large high performance PHAs reported on the average that they knew about three quarters of their residents by name and sight versus low performance PHA managers who knew only an average of two thirds of their residents. But at the 11 largest PHAs, managers reported knowing only about 60 percent of the tenants. While this might be partly due to project size, it may also reflect the amount of time the manager spends in his office rather than out in the project itself.

• At high performance PHAs, a significantly higher percentage of residents said that they knew the name of the staff member they should contact to report maintenance requests.

• Managers at high performance PHAs reported having significantly less of a problem between residents and maintenance staff. Among the large PHAs, the 11 largest Authorities had significantly greater problems in this area than did the high performance PHAs.

• High performance PHA managers felt significantly more strongly that their residents had the same beliefs about right and wrong as they (the managers) had, that the tenants could be trusted, and that the tenants were not hostile toward management. At high performance PHAs, residents also thought that the other residents of the project were more similar to themselves.

• A significantly lower percentage of residents at high performance PHAs felt their project was too crowded.[11]

Tenant Involvement in Management. Although tenant involvement in day-to-day project upkeep is associated with higher performance, there is no pattern of formal tenant involvement being related to performance. However, several perceptions of the residents and PHA staff concerning tenant involvement are strongly associated with performance levels.

• A significantly higher percentage of residents in low performance PHAs than at high performance PHAs wanted more say and power. This holds among the large PHAs separately and is a clear characteristic of residents in the 11 largest PHAs.

---

11. This perception could, of course, be a measure of actual density, but given the strong relationships between this measure and other measures of tenant perceptions (such as whether there are tenants who should be evicted, or whether unsupervised children are a problem), it most likely reflects the residents' feelings of comfortableness with the other residents of the project.

It follows that residents want more say in management where management is not fulfilling its responsibilities (a finding similar to that of maintenance and security responsiveness).

• A higher percentage of residents at high performance PHAs than those at low performance PHAs believe that their tenant organization is doing a good job.

There is a high relationship between residents wanting more say and their evaluation of their tenant organization—where more residents believe their organization is doing a good job, a lower percentage want more say or feel that the tenants need more power. Wanting more say, then, may be a reaction to *both* management and the tenant organization not performing as well as the residents would like.

DOES GOOD MANAGEMENT COST MORE?

Reviewing the substantial variance in the per-unit-month operating expenses of the sample Authorities as well as the findings of differences in management practices of high and low performing PHAs leads to the question just posed. A related question is whether the variance among PHAs in operating expenses is due to conditions now largely beyond the PHAs' control, such as the age and design of projects.

Information on the relationship between operating costs and performance is also available from the work done by Robert Sadacca and his colleagues. It simply involves contrasting the operating expenses (on a per-unit-month basis) of high and low performing Authorities.

The link between performance and operating cost levels is shown in table 27. Perhaps surprisingly, high performance is associated with lower total operating costs and total routine expenses (as defined in the notes to the table). The gap is greatest for the large Authorities. Unfortunately, there is no way of telling where the largest Authorities fall within this scheme because data on individual Authorities have never been released, consistent with a confidentiality pledge made by the Institute to the PHAs to obtain cooperation. At any rate, the message of the work by Sadacca and his colleagues is that good performance as measured in this way should not be inherently more costly than a lower performance.

Table 27

PER-UNIT-MONTH OPERATING COST DIFFERENTIALS
OF HIGH AND LOW PERFORMING HOUSING
AUTHORITIES IN 1973 [a]

Performance Group	Authority Size		
	Large	Medium	Small
A. Total Operating Expenditures [b]			
High group	$56	$48	$39
Low group	68	52	43
B. Total Routine Expenses [c]			
High group	$51	$44	$37
Low group	62	45	39

Source: R. Sadacca et al., *Management Performance in Public Housing*, pp. 38-39.

a. Operating data are for the 1970 and 1971 fiscal years; 1973 refers to the year of The Urban Institute's field work.

b. Includes total routine expenses, extraordinary maintenance, casualty losses and capital expenditures.

c. Includes total administrative expenses, total utilities, total ordinary maintenance, and total general expense.

GOOD PEOPLE

Thus far the entire presentation has concerned "what to do?" and, to a much lesser extent, "how much does it cost?" All of the foregoing has tacitly assumed the presence of competent personnel or the ability of the PHA to attract such people to its key positions, most importantly to the position of project manager. This is not a safe assumption. The burden of many of the prior chapters has been to demonstrate that a good share of the projects under management by the PHAs in the largest cities are uncommonly difficult to manage by virtue of their size, architecture, density, and tenantry. Good managers are hard to attract to such posts even under the best circumstances. In addition, when PHAs are financially distressed, salary increases are often restricted across the board, and this makes recruitment still more difficult. Moreover, some Authorities are not completely insulated from having at least some staff positions subject to patronage appointments. These points are all recognized by the PHAs themselves. John Simons, executive director of the New York City Authority in 1978 said:

> I would also like to tell you that there is inadequate recognition of housing management as a skilled profession. . . . This is a great problem. . . . There are inadequate salaries and political influence in selection of managers in some cities. They have detrimentally affected the public and quasi-public housing program.[12]

In fact, despite the completion of project manager profile surveys, no one really knows how well this position is staffed.[13] Anecdotal evidence suggests scattered problems. For example, one story goes that work crews were sent to an ostensibly well-managed project in reasonably good condition to do moderate rehabilitation work on several supposedly vacant units. The work crew found them occupied by squatters—to the ignorance of the project manager. To quote one long-time veteran of public housing: There is no "substitute for someone getting off his ass and walking up to the top floor to see if the maintenance man really swept the landing."[14] Certainly, solid, aggressive managers are in the system: the elite, professional managers of the New York City Authority are legend.

Consistent excellence in key positions is essential.[15] The next chapter outlines and critiques a series of HUD initiatives designed to upgrade both the quality of management and managers; unfortunately, these initiatives have had little effect on the system to date.

---

12. "HUD's Troubled Housing Projects," U.S. House of Representatives, Hearings of the Committee on Government Operations, 95th Congress, 2nd Session, September 26, 1978 (Washington, D.C.: U.S. Government Printing Office, 1979), p. 17.

13. See C. W. Hartman and M. Levi, "Public Housing Managers: An Appraisal," Journal of the American Institute of Planners, vol. 39, no. 2, March 1973, pp. 125-37.

14. Richard Baron in M. Mayer, The Builders (New York: Norton, 1978), p. 197.

15. For a description of the role of good personnel in effecting improvement in public housing (based on case studies), see D. Carlson, "Public Housing Projects in Transition: 25 Case Studies" (Washington, D.C.: The Urban Institute, 1977).

Chapter 8

HUD Initiatives

Over the past decade, a series of initiatives to improve the operations of Public Housing Authorities has been undertaken under HUD auspices. Generally, they fall into two groups: those designed to improve management practices and those designed to improve the quality of the staff, in particular, project managers. This chapter provides an overview of those efforts and tries to place them in the perspective of other events occurring during the same period. The final section reviews an initiative to improve HUD area offices' management of the privately owned multifamily projects insured by the Federal Housing Administration, which has direct implications for public housing. These initiatives deserve our attention not because they have changed the delivery of public housing services to a major extent, but because cumulatively, lessons are being learned from them, lessons that with proper administration and incentives could produce fundamental change.

IMPROVING MANAGEMENT

Beginning at the end of the 1960s, the Department of Housing and Urban Development launched a series of efforts to improve the conditions in public housing, especially the large, distressed

135

Authorities. This section will review these initiatives; but, before turning to the specific projects, it is important to understand their genesis and their overall strengths and weaknesses.

All of these efforts were born out of the frustration that accompanied the decline of public housing as demonstrated in tenant rent-paying ability, building conditions, and problems in PHA finances that occurred in the 1960s. With one notable exception, the initiatives were not thought through, and they did not have the continuing push and high-level sponsorship, essential for a dispassionate evaluation and possible transfer of results, within the program office at HUD. Often the initiatives were conceived simply as a method of channeling additional resources to distressed or "deserving" Authorities, with evaluations being organized as an afterthought.

Ideally, a careful analysis of PHA problems on a holistic and and system-by-system basis would have occurred, then the design of alternative methods of improvement, and then a demonstration carefully structured to permit evaluation of the efficiency of the various approaches. Because of the perceived urgency, less methodical approaches were taken by successive HUD administrations, ranging from those taken by George Romney to those taken by Patricia Harris. Each time, the new initiative had little to build upon because of the lack of full attention to the prior programs after they had been started. Old public housing hands now expect initiatives on a regular cycle.

This is not to say that nothing useful has come out of these efforts. Indeed, as documented below, the projects receiving the infusion of extra resources were generally improved after the treatment, especially when measured by tenants' satisfaction with the management and physical environment. There was, however, a more fundamental change that has not been as well documented. The initiatives permitted and required the participating Authorities to augment their staffs with research and management specialists that they formerly had not the funds to hire (or sometimes been able to justify to their boards of directors). "Evaluation specialists" and "research analysts" made their debut in the PHA job title lists. This incremental staff examined not only the systems directly affected by the demonstration, but some others as well. This, in turn, created a small cadre of professionals who understood public housing on an Authoritywide basis. Equally important, a change in orientation of senior management occurred. For the first time, the techniques for measuring "efficiency" as well as the data were in hands of these decisionmakers. But limited post-demonstration finances often constrained exploiting these gains.

It is critical that these initiatives be kept in perspective. We have already noted that top program management at HUD gave them only fleeting attention. Furthermore, compared to the massive influence that changes in tenant profiles and finances experienced in the last two decades—one need only think of the Brooke amendments and the performance funding system—these programs could only have had modest effects.

Through events like the Brooke amendments and PFS, the Administration and Congress placed strong and continuous pressure on the Authorities to improve the efficiency of their operations. The initiatives were to give a one-time infusion of resources to salient projects to make service delivery efficient and, with luck, to provide lessons to the participating and non-participating Authorities on how to make progress in other projects. Today it seems clear that too few projects were caught up, too few concrete lessons were learned, and management skills were not transferred.

Housing Management Improvement Program (HMIP)

This earliest of the large-scale demonstrations was the most thoughtfully conceived of all the initiatives, although as actually executed it fell far short of the original design. The HMIP was announced in June 1971 and implemented during the 1972-75 period, with the design work beginning in 1970.

The initial conception was to systematically test the efficiency of management strategies by varying the location of decision-making power within the Authority and the emphasis between staff and tenant control at individual projects. This design recognized the problems of overcentralization induced by an earlier HUD decision to treat all the projects in a PHA as a group for financial analysis, thus causing the PHA to absorb budgetary and other powers away from project managers and tenants. The following chart shows the six alternatives that were to be tested, with at least two authorities adopting each of the six alternatives that were to be tested.

The plan was for whole Authorities to be "remodeled" along the lines of the alternatives. HUD was to provide substantial

	Locus of Power		Control and Responsibility
	Central Office	Projects	
1.	High	Low	Staff emphasis
2.	High	Low	Tenant emphasis
3.	Moderate	Moderate	Staff emphasis
4.	Moderate	Moderate	Tenant emphasis
5.	Low	High	Staff emphasis
6.	Low	High	Tenant emphasis

technical assistance to help effect the changeover. HUD's research office had given careful thought to the companion evaluation.[1]

The proposed project was developed by the research office within HUD and was proposed (and did) fund the demonstration with $25 million of research appropriations. Differences of opinion between the program office and the research office caused the original design to be abandoned and to be replaced with an almost unstructured demonstration.

In the program announcement, PHAs were invited to submit proposals "to design, implement, monitor, and document a comprehensive public housing management system that provides tenant services on a cost-effective basis." Guidance as to what specific tools to employ was extremely broad. The only requirement was that proposed activities should be consistent with one or more of the following objectives:

1. Recognize and satisfy tenant needs and interests while remaining cost effective.
2. Improve the general housing environment.
3. Increase management efficiency with respect to the conservation of Authorities' resources (money, materials, manpower).
4. Produce a management system that can be implemented rapidly and begin to produce benefits.
5. Create flexible management systems that can be adapted to other Authorities.

---

1. Urban Institute memorandum from M. Isler and R. Sadacca to H. B. Finger, Assistant Secretary for Research at HUD, "Design of an Experimental Demonstration of Public Housing Management," December 7, 1970.

6. Produce management systems with the capacity to collect performance data, analyze problems, and evaluate proposed solutions.
7. Create management systems that can adjust to changed operating conditions.
8. Create management systems that can be integrated with those of other Authorities.

Ultimately 13 PHAs were selected to participate, all together they undertook 150 separate programs.[2]

With no real design behind the demonstration, serious evaluation was impossible. The PHAs had the responsibility for general monitoring and documentation, and this led to highly uneven reporting. The value of specific improvements was never carefully analyzed, and given the design, probably could not have been. Under contract to HUD, The Urban Institute performed a general evaluation of extent of improvement at the participating PHAs compared to those in a control group. The analysis relied heavily on the perceptions of PHA central office and project staff and tenants about changes at their PHA or project over a three-year (1973-76) period. The overall conclusion was that PHAs participating in the HMIP did not have significant improvement over the period nor did they do significantly better than the control group.[3]

At the end of the demonstration period, many of the additional management activities ceased because of lack of funding. A 1978 survey of the participating Authorities found that of the 170 PHA-identified activities initiated through HMIP, 76 were still operating. Only six cases of actual transfer of activities to other PHAs are known.[4] The uneven documentation and lack of independent judgment made it very difficult for PHAs to decide whether some of the innovations that were imple-

2. Atlanta, Detroit, Greensboro, Hartford, Hawaii, Dade County (Miami), Milwaukee, New Haven, Puerto Rico, Richmond, Wilmington, National Capital (Washington), Worcester, and Sacramento; the last two later dropped out.

3. S. B. Loux and R. Sadacca, "Conditions Facilitating Implementation of Successful Management Improvement Programs" (Washington, D.C.: The Urban Institute, Working Paper 255-1, 1978).

4. Joan Gilbert, "An Assessment of the Public Housing Management Improvement Program" (Washington, D.C.: Office of Policy Development and Research, Department of Housing and Urban Development, draft, 1978).

mented were worthy of adoption elsewhere. HUD did virtually nothing in the way of dissemination. On balance, the $25 million seems to have purchased some short-term and few long-term improvements in management practices at participating PHAs, but nothing for the system as a whole.

Target Projects Program (TPP)[5]

TPP was the first program to single out distressed projects and make them the focus of attention. It was also far and away the most generously funded of the HUD management efforts. Rather than invite applications generally, HUD asked its regional offices to grade projects by the severity of their problems using the criteria listed in table 28. The highest scoring set was taken as the priority group from which to select participants, with others being selected based on recommendations from other sources. Eventually 142 PHAs and 332 projects participated in three "phases." The first and third emphasized large, urban PHAs; the second emphasized small and medium-sized agencies. An Urban Institute baseline survey confirmed that projects selected for TPP were indeed more troubled than the average project.

Although the program was intended to last only two years, because of delays and extensions, the demonstration actually continued from 1975 into 1978; and as of late 1979 some of the more troubled Authorities had not expended large amounts of their allocations. A total of $98.5 million in operating subsidies was committed to the TPP program, so that participating Authorities received amounts in excess of their normal operating subsidy allocations. In addition, contract authority, sufficient to fund some $341 million in modernization activity or an average of $3,300 for each of the $104,000 units involved, was alloted to the target projects. The PHAs in the 29 larger cities which are the focus of this study received 45 percent of all the TPP funds.

The instructions sent to the selected Authorities are remarkable in their emphasis on selected outputs. They gave no serious consideration to the relationship between the use of funds for capital improvements and the proposed goals for management improvement; nor is there sensitivity to the possibility

5. This section draws upon material in R. Kolodny, "Exploring New Strategies for Improving Public Housing Management" (Washington, D.C.: Report to Office of Research, U.S. Department of Housing and Urban Development, 1979).

Table 28

CRITERIA USED BY HUD FIELD OFFICES TO RATE
PUBLIC HOUSING PROJECTS FOR INCLUSION IN
THE TPP

1. Extensive physical deterioration and seriously inadequate maintenance.
2. Seriously deficient janitorial and other operating services.
3. Extensive "people" problems as indicated by high percentages of broken families, welfare families, families with serious social or behavior problems, and a high ratio of children per adult.
4. High crime and vandalism rates.
5. Inner-city or ghetto location.
6. Recent manifestation of tenant dissatisfaction, e.g., large volumes of tenant complaints, threat of rent strikes, etc.
7. Poor reputation in the community.
8. Vacancies and refusal of applicants to accept housing offers.
9. Closed and vandalized dwelling units.
10. Seriously adverse neighborhood influences.

that progress in one area might be achieved only by losing ground elsewhere. In short, the structure of the program created large incentives for a piecemeal approach to management improvement.

Table 29 lists the six goals and the 26 objectives from which the PHAs were to select the goals and objectives to be emphasized in their participant projects. The only objective universally required was effective management for the TPP plan. Actually, the implementation-evaluation process was laid out by the HUD central office in detail in a management-by-objective framework, with quantitative output measures for each objective specified, etc.

What did the TPP accomplish? Although fairly detailed descriptions of actual accomplishments were developed by the National Association of Housing and Redevelopment Officials,[6]

6. Amy Kell is the author of five reports: *The Target Projects Program: A Basic Resource Book, The TPP Experience—What Have We Learned?, Maintenance Management and Administrative Systems Under the Target Projects Program, Delivery of Human Resources Under the Target Projects Program,* and *General Management Innovations Developed Under the Target Projects Program* (Washington, D.C.: National Association of Housing and Redevelopment Officials, 1978.)

Table 29

TARGET PROJECTS PROGRAM

GOAL/OBJECTIVE CODES			
Goal No.	Title of Goal	Objective No.	Title of Objective
1	Improving Operating Effectiveness	1	Perform needed training of PHA personnel
		2	Reduce average time to satisfy maintenance service
		3	Reduce vacancy loss
		4	Reduce average rent collection time
		5	Reduce average eviction time
		6	Provide effective management for implementation of TPP plan
2	Improve Financial Condition	1	Increase operating receipts
		2	Increase ratio of operating receipts to total operating expenses
3	Improve Physical Condition	1	Improve janitorial services
		2	Improve exterminating services
		3	Improve condition of grounds
		4	Improve condition of structures
		5	Improve condition of elevators
		6	Improve condition of electrical systems
		7	Improve condition of heating systems
		8	Improve condition of plumbing
		9	Perform needed interior painting
		10	Perform needed exterior painting
		11	Provide needed replacement or repair of equipment
		12	Perform other needed physical improvements
4	Improve Security	1	Decrease incidence of crime
		2	Decrease incidence of vandalism
5	Improve Upward Mobility	1	Increase resident earned income
		2	Increase resident employment

Table 29

TARGET PROJECTS PROGRAM (Cont'd)

GOAL/OBJECTIVE CODES

Goal No.	Title of Goal	Objective No.	Title of Objective
6	Improve Resident/Community Services	1	Increase non-PHA support of services to residents
		2	Increase resident/community services

Source   U.S. Department of Housing and Urban Development, *Target Projects Program Handbook*, 7460.5 Rev., February 1976.

the question is almost impossible to answer in any rigorous way. The design followed in choosing participating projects and the treatments at the separate projects were completely divorced from evaluation considerations. One evaluation by an outside consultant examined the extent to which goals and objectives had been met; the conclusions were generally positive; a reduction in revenue losses from vacancies was the chief unmet objective.[7]

A broader evaluation of the success of the program was undertaken by The Urban Institute. This analysis employed very basic and mostly subjective measures of change at a sample of TPP projects and a group of control projects. Questions about perceived improvements in specific physical and management conditions at the projects were put to project staff and managers, tenants, PHA executive directors, and HUD area office personnel. The strengths and weaknesses of using these types of opinion questions are well known and not reviewed here. On the basis of these responses and analysis of the relationship between initial conditions at the project itself, overall management and conditions in the neighborhood around the project, The Urban Institute concluded

1. Both TPP projects and control projects showed significant improvement between 1974 and 1977, but in some aspects the TPP projects seemed to do better.

7. Coopers-Lybrand, Inc. *Target Projects Program: Preliminary Analysis* (Washington, D.C.: Report to the U.S. Department of Housing and Urban Development, 1978).

2. Neighborhood conditions had a strong effect on the likelihood of improvement.
3. Baseline tenant and project characteristics seemed to have little effect on likelihood of success, but projects with tenant behavior problems did have a lower likelihood of success.
4. Good management practices and close tenant involvement made success more likely.[8]

The Institute's conclusions are mostly general. However, the Institute did make specific recommendations for the structure of future management improvement programs—recommendations which seemed to have been forgotten or ignored in designing the Public Housing Urban Initiative Program (UIP) described in the following paragraphs.

Overall TPP seems to have accomplished its short-term goal of improving the projects which were the recipients of its massive funding. On the other hand, basic management improvements that would preserve those gains were often not effected and even where put in place were not guaranteed. Indeed, the piecemeal approach militated against broad-based changes. For this reason it is perhaps not surprising, but certainly discouraging, to find five of the TPP projects receiving massive funding only two years later under the Urban Initiatives Program. Finally, there was no way for the increased staff costs and other outlays to be sustained when TPP funding was exhausted. The underlying hypothesis was that a one-time, intense effort would set the project back on a "normal" course. This hypothesis is the continuing basis for HUD initiatives, and yet its validity has never been systematically tested.

Public Housing Urban Initiatives Program (UIP)
This is the latest of the HUD initiatives and in many ways the most complicated and the least well designed. HUD made no claim that this is a demonstration; rather it is an infusion of resources to public housing to accomplish special objectives. Evaluations of the effects of the resource expenditures were clearly an afterthought.

---

8. S. B. Loux, E. Castro, and R. Sadacca, "Evaluation of the Phase I Target Project Program" (Washington, D.C.: The Urban Institute, Working Paper 254-1, 1978).

The following are among the reasons given for needing this set of initiatives:

- The inability to target HUD funds through regular subsidy vehicles to projects in greatest need and at a level sufficient to bring about dramatic changes.
- The failure of some PHAs and city governments to work cooperatively to bring improvements to problem projects and adjacent neighborhoods.
- The failure to institute basic PHA-wide management improvements to guarantee that physical repairs will last.

These are similar to the problems acknowledged over a number of years and addressed by earlier initiatives. The results of the earlier efforts, however, were ignored in structuring the UIP.

The program was announced in the summer of 1978, and a year later participating PHAs for some of the elements had not even been selected. Hence, it is far too early to even qualitatively evaluate the outcomes. The following paragraphs, therefore, provide only a brief overview of the program as it had evolved by the fall of 1979.

The UIP involves total funding of about $260 million for several separate elements, especially the following four: (1) targeted rehabilitation and management assistance component; (2) a management accountability component; (3) interagency anticrime initiative; and (4) the urban partnership initiative. These four components are on separate tracks. There is minimum coordination in project selection, and the planning of project improvements is uncoordinated.

The targeted rehabilitation and management assistance initiative accounts for the majority of the resources. Participation is limited to PHAs managing at least 2,500 units. Additionally, the program is limited to projects of 200 or more units that have physical improvements needs requiring an average of $5,000 per unit or more, over and above that addressed in the past or currently through modernization program funding. Enormous latitude is allowed in the kind of rehabilitation plans that PHAs could propose. Three options are listed in the field notice: rehabilitation of the project for the same population at the same or lower density; conversion of family high-rise housing to elderly housing (contingent on availability of replacement housing); or modification of project design, including partial demolition to permit "thinning out" and elimination of various hazards. For thinning out to be included, the PHA must demonstrate that rehabilitation is "infeasible or excessively costly." The guidance on the management assistance portion, says only that those funds are to be used "toward upgrading PHA management capability on an agencywide basis."

To ensure that there was some relation between the management component and rehabilitation plans, the PHAs selected for participation would be required to have a management assistance plan (MAP) approved by HUD before commencing rehabilitation. The plan itself would be developed by a team comprised of PHA personnel, tenants, HUD central and field office staff, and local government officials. The MAP team would be responsible for directing the diagnostic and remedial phases of management assistance and for the selection of consultants used by the PHA. While this approach has definite merit, there were serious problems in its execution. Pressure for beginning rehabilitation took precedence over a fully considered plan for management improvements.

This initiative was administered as a competition for resources to overcome the problems of the most blighted projects in the largest PHAs. Thirty-three PHAs were selected (including 20 of the 29 PHAs included in this analysis), and the funded projects are a virtual roll call of those with infamous national reputations: Hunter's Point in San Francisco; Robert Taylor Homes in Chicago; Columbia Point in Boston; Herman Gardens in Detroit; and Somerset Homes in Baltimore.[9]

The management accountability component, by contrast, is designed to fund the implementation of a project-based budgeting system at those Authorities selected for funding. Years ago, HUD shifted to an Authoritywide consolidated accounting system—so that it could consider operating subsidy requests for an entire PHA rather than for specific projects. HUD thereby attained within PHA cross-subsidization among projects. This accounting system destroyed most incentives for project-level budgeting. It is now widely appreciated that this sacrificed a very important tool of good management, and the UIP initiative is to begin repairing the damage. Amazingly, however, HUD did not use the opportunity of the UIP to develop a preferred computerized accounting system that would ensure consistency

9. For a full listing of participating PHAs, specific projects, and funding levels, see HUD press release 78-239, October 3, 1978.

among Authorities, create an extremely efficient report generation capability, and save the cost of developing many separate
systems. Instead, each participating Authority is contracting for
its own budgeting system development, generally ignorant of
the systems developed under the HMIP.

The goal of the third UIP element, the anticrime initiative, is
"to encourage PHAs to think in long-term, comprehensive ways
about crime prevention and security problems." This initiative
was originally intended to be a genuine demonstration with an
accompanying rigorous evaluation. A substantial body of HUD-
funded research analyzing the extent and type of crime and
victimization in public housing and demonstrating ways to redesign project spaces to increase tenant control and thwart criminal activity was reviewed, background conferences with experts
held, and various research designs drawn.[10] Unfortunately, in
order to give the program office greater latitude in selecting participating PHAs, the competition for participation was designed
in such a way as to make any sort of rigorous evaluation extremely difficult, that is, the ability to link specific remedies to
reduce crime in a particular type of project. Although at congressional insistence some ex post facto adjustments have been
made in the demonstration and evaluation designs, it remains
to be seen if these can compensate for initial faulty planning.

Some $32 million from four agencies will fund 30 locally-
designed anticrime activities (including 12 of this study's 29),
which will address the following program elements: physical

---

10. The reviews and conferences are summarized in W. V. Rouse and
H. Rubenstein, *Crime in Public Housing: A Review of Major Issues and
Selected Crime Reduction Strategies,* vol. 1: A Report, and vol. 2: A Re-
view of Two Conferences and an Annotated Bibliography (Washington,
D.C.: U.S. Government Printing Office, 1979). Examples of the products
produced under HUD research funding include a set of manuals for use
by PHAs, e.g., William Brill Associates, *Planning for Housing Security:
Site Security Manual* and *Planning for Housing Security: Site Elements
Manual* (Washington, D.C.: U.S. Government Printing Office, 1979 pub.
nos. HUD-PDR-460 and 461); the series by William Brill Associates, titled
Victimization, Fear of Crime and Altered Behavior, reporting analysis of
Capper Dwellings in Washington, D.C., Murphy Homes in Baltimore, and
William Nickerson, Jr. Gardens in Los Angeles (Washington, D.C.: U.S.
Government Printing Office, pub. nos. HUD-PDR-174-1(-3), 1977); and
some actual implementations to housing projects, e.g., Brill Associates,
Comprehensive Security Planning: A Program for Arthur Capper Dwellings
(Washington, D.C.: U.S. Government Printing Office, pub. no. HUD-PDR-
280, 1978).

design and hardware changes; social services improvements; tenant employment; improved PHA or project management and maintenance; and stronger links between the PHA and local crimal justice department and other departments of local government. The breadth of the required elements is striking.

It was possible for the Authority to address some of these areas outside of the demonstration, either by having something adequate in place or by pursuing other funding sources. All twelve of the very large PHAs, in fact, received funding in all areas; except in six cases, funding from the the Law Enforcement Assistance Administration for improving community anticrime activities was not received. Coordination with other elements of Urban Initiatives, as indicated in the anticrime component application, is limited to a statement saying that projects that have been awarded modernization funds under the rehabilitation component cannot receive more modernization funds under the anticrime component.[11] In many other ways, however, the program guidance rates high marks for the amount of information conveyed and its comprehensive approach.

The final element, urban partnerships, is to use $2.5 million to encourage local governments to provide greater long-term support for public housing. Applications must be from local governments in cooperation with their PHAs. Eligible activities must be fundable under the Community Development Block Grant regulataions (since CDBG discretionary funds are being used) and must address at least one of the following:

- Development of plans and programs for reusing vacant or underused housing facilities;
- Development of neighborhood and community revitalization programs in areas where there are federally assisted public housing projects; or
- Development of plans and programs to improve the level and quality of municipal services provided to PHAs.

The applications were of such low quality that only three agencies were selected to participate and about one third of the

---

11. Office of Housing, U.S. Department of Housing and Urban Development, Notice H79-11(PHA), "Urban Initiatives Anti-Crime Program for Public Housing Agencies with 1250 or More Public Housing Units in Total Management," May 1979.

funds were awarded. Detroit received funds to rehabilitate and convert 136 one-bedroom units to 68 three-bedroom units in one project, Seattle is to establish an "urban agricultural park" for public housing tenants, and Washington, D.C., is to revitalize shopping areas near projects. The linkage between these projects and the program's intent is not immediately obvious.

While the good intentions of the UIP are immediately evident, so are a number of structural flaws. Most damaging is the lack of coordination among elements; indeed, the program structure seems at odds with one of the justifications given for its existence—the effective targeting of resources. In the end, the results will probably be similar to those of the earlier initiatives—the selected projects will have been improved, but there will be no idea whether these gains could have been achieved at lower cost or whether more could have been accomplished with the same amount of funding.

IMPROVING THE QUALITY OF PROJECT MANAGEMENT

With the growing recognition of the evolving problems in public housing, improving the quality of key staff, particularly project managers, is seen as important. Three initiatives sponsored by HUD are briefly reviewed here: development of a housing management curriculum; development of the concept of a certified housing manager; and tenant management. In addition, HUD had sponsored the establishment in 1974 of the National Center for Housing Management, which since then has developed and taught a wide range of management courses, generally on a fee basis. One initiative after another has been taken before any real progress has been noted on previous plans. Furthermore, each initiative has been conducted in isolation from the others. The developmental stage of these efforts is rapidly ending, and HUD now has the opportunity to combine the best elements of these activities into a program for upgrading key PHA staff. There is, unfortunately, no evidence that the necessary synthesizing work is being undertaken.[12]

---

12. HUD has also sponsored the development of a Hispanic housing management program, beginning in 1977. For an overview description, see R. Kolodny, "Exploring New Statistics for Improving Public Housing Management."

Housing Management Curriculum Development

Beginning in 1974, the concept here was for HUD to underwrite the cost of developing two types of housing training programs. With a set of tested courses available, it is the department's hope that these courses will be adopted as offerings by institutions of higher education. Graduates of the programs will learn systematically about housing management rather than simply "picking it up" on the job as is now the case.

The first type of training program is a set of several college-level courses which constitute a core curriculum:

> *Introduction to Housing Management*
> *Fiscal Management for Housing Managers*
> *Management of Physical Facilities*
> *Administrative Aspects of Housing Management*
> *Social Aspects of Housing Management*
> *Legal Aspects of Housing Management*
> *Field Internships in Housing Management*

The second element consists of fifteen workshops that have been based on the core curriculum plus special workshops in the areas of security, the elderly, and the handicapped. An estimated 50 persons have graduated from programs at the five institutions that participated in the development of the courses, and about 1,000 persons have attended the workshops. As of the fall of 1979 these courses were being prepared for general dissemination.

Certified Housing Managers

The concept of the certified housing manager (CHM) is very straightforward: only persons with a demonstrated minimal level of competence in relevant areas should be permitted to manage large public housing projects; the job is simply too difficult and the value of the assets involved too great for less qualified persons to be given this task. Certification will have the important effect of insulating these key manager positions from political patronage as well as from general hiring mistakes. As such it should, over the long term and assuming a rigorous testing program, result in genuine improvement in the quality of managers.

The certification program is now established for full implementation for all projects with 75 units or more as of January

1, 1981. It has taken almost a decade of persistent efforts to realize this goal.

HUD will use certifying organizations to perform the actual testing and certification tasks. There is no limit on the possible number of certifying organizations, but to qualify each must be a "national housing management organization" with experience in dealing with low-income housing and have developed an acceptable certification program.[13] Three organizations have passed those standards: National Association of Housing and Redevelopment Officials (NAHRO), National Center for Housing Management, and Institute for Real Estate Management. The remainder of this discussion is based on the NAHRO program.

There are two distinct paths for a person to become a certified manager:

1. *Four years of experience as a manager of public housing.* Any person who has acquired four or more years of experience as a manager of public housing, on or before January 1, 1981, may be certified by NAHRO upon review of his or her experience. The requisite experience is that acquired by one who, regardless of title, performs or supervises the tasks associated with the operation of low-rent housing developments or projects owned or administered by public housing agencies.

2. *Test and candidate review.* Any person employed by a Housing Authority or agency with fewer than four years of experience as a manager of public housing may be certified after successful completion of a job-related test and a candidate review administered by NAHRO. At the time of the candidate review, the person must be performing housing manager tasks. The requisite experience is that acquired by one who, regardless of title, performs or supervises the tasks associated with the operation of low-rent housing developments or projects owned or administered by public housing agencies.[14]

---

13. *Code of Federal Regulations,* Title 24, 867.303.

14. Paraphrased from "Certification Examination and Candidate Review Exercise, Public Housing Manager: Bulletin of Information for Candidates" (Washington, D.C.: National Association of Housing and Redevelopment Officials, 1978).

In the candidate review, a candidate must state how he or she would handle various situations that might occur at a project; for each situation, a scenario is given and the testee writes a response. The second part of the test is multiple choice and covers the areas of maintenance, residence services and relations, occupancy cycle, management, and administration.

While the testing looks solid, there is one anomaly in the structure of the program. It requires that a candidate already be performing housing management tasks to be eligible to take the test. It is unclear why others may not qualify for the test. The present arrangement would require the PHA to terminate or downgrade the candidate who repeatedly failed the test, although he or she has acted as a manager for some years. This contrasts with other professional testing where passing examinations are necessary for promotion but not for job retention. There is also no linkage between graduation from a course using the housing management curriculum described earlier and manager certification. Finally, no provision is made for decertification or reprimand; in effect the manager is being certified for life. Some long-term supervision of certified managers will be essential if the program's integrity is to be maintained.

Tenant Management

The Department of Housing and Urban Development began a three-year national demonstration of tenant management in June 1976 after about a year of planning. The demonstration—initially at seven projects in six urban Public Housing Authorities—is to test whether tenant management of "low-rent, family-occupied housing in urban areas can lead to improved operating performance, increased resident satisfaction, greater tenant employment, and general improved community conditions."[15] The central concept is that tenants with their special view of public housing and stake in its success as a living environment will do a superior job of management if they have adequate authority and training to carry out the job. Tenant management, then, is directed at improving the quality of the project managers, although the technical assistance provided often means management practices are improved as well.

---

15. Housing Management and Special Users Group, "The National Tenant Management Demonstration: Status Report through 1978" (Washington, D.C.: U.S. Department of Housing and Urban Development, Office of Policy Development and Research, 1979), p. 5.

The HUD demonstration grew out of the experience of the St. Louis Public Housing Authority with tenant management in two of its projects—Carr Square and Cochran Gardens. However, at least five other attempts at tenant management had occurred before HUD's national demonstration, and some of these were launched under HUD auspices.[16] In brief, the national demonstration has had the benefit of substantial prior experience.

Table 30 gives basic information on the demonstration projects. A comparison of these characteristics with a representative sample of 168 projects in large (over 1,250 units) PHAs showed the two groups were similar in size, age, and number of floors in the buildings; but the projects exhibited more management problems than other projects.[17]

The basic working relationship between the PHA and the tenant management corporation (TMC) is similar to that between an owner of rental properties and his management agent. Figure 3 gives a prototypical breakdown of responsibilities between the PHA and the TMC. Notes on a few key functions follow:

Tenant selection. The TMC does the actual selection in accordance with written PHA tenant selection policy.

Budget. The TMC and PHA negotiate the project's overall budget and its distribution among expense lines; the TMC administers the budget, although the PHA handles the accounting functions, furnishing the TMC with a monthly computer printout.

Project staff. Management positions created by the advent of TMC are filled by the TMC from the project tenants; further a TMC project manager replaces the former manager. Maintenance staff on site remains as PHA employees, but are super-

---

16. For a complete description, see William A. Diaz, *Tenant Management: A Historical and Analytical Overview* (New York: Manpower Development Research Corporation, 1979). See also, Anne Power, *Tenant Co-ops or Tenant Management Corporations in the USA* (London: North Islington Housing Rights Project, 1979).

17. T. Seessel, *The First Annual Report on the National Tenant Management Demonstration* (New York: Manpower Demonstration Research Corporation, 1977), p. 18; S. Loux and R. Sadacca, "Tenant Management Demonstration Projects: An Analysis of Base Line Data" (Washington, D.C.: The Urban Institute, Working Paper 5052-2, 1977).

Table 30

SELECTED ORGANIZATIONAL, PHYSICAL, AND SOCIAL CHARACTERISTICS OF THE DEVELOPMENTS: 1976

	TMC Development						
	Jersey City		*Louisville*	*New Haven*	*New Orleans*	*Oklahoma City*	*Rochester*
Characteristics	*A. Harry Moore*	*Curries Woods*	*Iroquois Homes*	*Que-View* [a]	*Calliope Homes*	*Sunrise Acres* [b]	*Ashanti* [c]
Total PHA dwelling units [d]	3,720	3,720	6,061	3,659 [e]	12,260	3,037	2,254 [f]
Development Characteristics							
Total dwelling units	684	712	854	260	1,550	537	211
Percentage of PHA units	17.8	19.1	14.1	7.1	12.6	17.7	9.4
Percentage of demonstration units	13.9	14.9	17.8	5.4	32.4	11.2	4.4
Number of buildings	7	7	72	24	95	[b]	46
Age of oldest building (years)	22	17	24	35	36	36	9
Building design	High-rise Elevator	High-rise Elevator	Low-rise Walk-up	Low-rise Walk-up	Low-rise Walk-up	Low-rise Walk-up	Low-rise Walk-up
Percentage minority households	95	65	35	72	100	99	99

Percentage AFDC households	68	35	37	53	35	48	61
Average annual gross family income	$4,651	$4,835	$2,947	$3,955	$2,000	$3,355	$4,700

Source: First Annual Report

a. Includes Quinnipiac Terrace and Riverview projects.
b. Includes Sooner Haven project and 387 scattered sites.
c. Includes the following projects: Olean Townhouses, Capsule Dwellings, Fairfield Village, Edith-Doran Townhouses, and Bronson Court.
d. Excludes leased housing.
e. Includes 742 state-assisted units.
f. Includes 364 state-assisted units.

vised on a day-to-day basis by the TMC. The TMC is governed by a board of directors, which in the start-up phase is critical to the TMC's success because it is responsible for policy formulation, selection of the project manager, and participation in other hiring decisions. Its members are elected by the tenants.

The demonstration projects have had substantial infusions of modernization and funds from the Target Projects Program described. Indeed, funds have averaged over $3,000 per unit while TPP funds per project per year have approached $250,000. (See table 31.) A good share of the TPP funds have been used to purchase extensive amounts of training and technical assistance, as well as to hire additional staff at the projects for improved maintenance, security, etc. Simply to institute tenant management required several of the Authorities to revise (and improve) their existing management systems. For example, project-based budgeting—a key management tool—was reinstated. The changes often affected some of the PHAs' other operations and would not have occurred without the special resources earmarked for such purposes.

Although the demonstration and evaluation are not yet complete, some lessons and conclusions have been tentatively drawn up by the HUD research office. These are listed in table 32. Overall, the lessons suggest that successful implementation of tenant management is a delicate operation requiring good will, good people, extensive external assistance, and substantial continuity. Tenant management clearly cannot work for everyone: even after enormous efforts by HUD and those providing technical assistance, the demonstration at one PHA collapsed. The conclusions suggest that if successfully begun, tenant management is competitive with conventional management.

THE PROJECT AUDIT-WORKOUT PLAN APPROACH

This initiative differs from all of the others reviewed in this chapter because it involved privately owned and operated multifamily housing insured under various HUD programs, but not public housing. In brief, by 1976 some 17 percent of all projects insured under selected programs had gone into an advance state of default; some 1,195 projects containing 122,000 dwell-

Figure 3

DIVISION OF RESPONSIBILITY UNDER PROTOTYPE TENANT MANAGEMENT

Function	TMC	TMC and PHA	PHA
Tenant selection and screening.		X	
Development of annual operating budget.		X	
Allocation of operating funds among selected budget line items.	X		
Preparation and disbursement of TMC payroll.			X
Provision to TMC of incentives to encourage cost saving and discourage overexpenditure.			X
Leasing vacant apartments.	X		
Adherence to rules and regulations. Institution of eviction proceedings and documentation of relevant information. Hearing tenant grievances.	X		
Processing of evictions including legal proceedings and physical removal, when appropriate.			X
Physical collection of rents.			X
Following up on rent delinquencies.	X		
Conduct of annual rent reviews.	X		
Processing work orders for maintenance service requests.	X		
Inspection and preparation of vacant apartments.	X		
Supervision of on-site maintenance personnel.	X		
Hiring, firing, and supervision of management personnel.	X		

Source: T. Seessel, *National Tenant Management Demonstration.*

Table 31

MOD AND TPP ALLOCATIONS TO PARTICIPATING SITES:
NATIONAL TENANT MANAGEMENT
DEMONSTRATION PROGRAM

Site	TPP Amount	MOD Amount	Total per Unit
Jersey City, New Jersey			
A. Harry Moore	$ 580,700	$ 997,000	$2,307
Curries Woods	581,000	1,015,000	2,241
Louisville, Kentucky	671,400	3,500,000	4,884
New Haven, Connecticut	442,100	1,650,000	8,038
New Orleans, Louisiana	2,010,500	6,524,000	5,505
Oklahoma City, Oklahoma	514,300	1,007,000	2,832
Rochester, New York	400,000	307,000	3,350
TOTAL	$5,200,000	$15,000,000	

Source: T. Seessel, *National Tenant Management Demonstration.*

ing units were effectively owned by HUD for an insurance loss of almost $2 billion.[18] In response to the rising rates of default, HUD's Office of Research launched two small-scale demonstrations to test new approaches to carrying out the "loan management" function assigned to the area offices. Under this function, the physical and financial condition of the project is monitored; and, for troubled projects, the loan servicer is to work with the managing agent and the owner to restore the project to sound condition.

Many of the general principles learned from these demonstrations—conducted by Advisory Services for Better Housing working with the New York Area Office, and National Housing Law Project working with HUD's San Francisco Office, and now being applied to the insured inventory—have direct applicability to improving distressed public projects and improving the overall management in their PHAs.

The genesis of the approach was an analysis of the highly distressed Woodlawn Gardens project in Chicago by Baron and McCormack in 1973. The main elements of their work were

18. R. D. Baron, B. B. Huckman, and R. Kolodny, "Preserving HUD-Assisted Multifamily Housing: An Affirmative Role for the Area Office" (Washington, D.C.: Report to Department of Housing and Urban Development, unpublished, 1977), exhibit 1.

- *Skilled Analysis and Intervention.* Proposed remedies were based on a disinterested, professional evaluation. While details of the analysis might be disputed, it was unlikely that the parties involved could effectively refute the overall diagnosis. The rights of each of the interested parties, including the tenants, were taken as roughly equal. Contributions toward the solution were apportioned according to an implicit standard of fairness which took account of the varying levels of resources.

- *A Comprehensive Workout Plan.* The approach expanded the definition of "workout" (previously denoting only those short-term financial arrangements required to restore a delin-

Table 32

PRELIMINARY LESSONS AND CONCLUSIONS
FROM THE NATIONAL TENANT
MANAGEMENT DEMONSTRATION

Lessons

Creating a viable management corporation takes much longer than the nine months initially projected.

Commitment to tenant management by the leadership of both the tenant management corporation (TMC) and the Housing Authority is of major importance.

Active participation of the Housing Authority top staff, including the executive director, is important in establishing the program.

Continuity in leadership is important.

Technical assistance to the TMC, whether supplied by the Housing Authority staff or outside consultants, is essential to the development of the program.

Conclusions

Although no clear pattern of consistent improvement in management performance has emerged from the research to date, it can be said that in some instances the TMCs have outperformed conventional management and, in all cases, not done any worse.

In the area of tenant employment, there has been to date a definite increase in the number of residents working on site.

While no final conclusions can be drawn at this time, there are some preliminary indications that tenant management is having a positive effect on community spirit and tenant satisfaction.

Source: T. Seessel, *The National Tenant Management Demonstration*, pp. 1-3.

quent project to a self-sustaining basis) to include a comprehensive review and set of proposals covering all major facets
of the project's life, on the assumption that a financial solution independent of attention to other elements was no solution at all.

- *Financial Relief and Forbearance.* The Plan faced forthrightly
  the substantial amount of financial relief and/or forbearance
  the project would require to become self-sufficient. It outlined
  alternative ways of closing the gap that went well beyond
  what was allowed under then existing HUD practice and
  HUD's interpretation of its authority.

- *Hands-On Technical Assistance.* The proposal envisioned
  close and continuing on-site assistance to the project in implementing the plan.[19]

These elements are based on several lessons, immediately applicable to public housing. First, a comprehensive audit of the
project's and the PHA's problems, management systems, financial records, and other areas is critical. The audit, that is, problem definition, requires experts in various areas and is likely to
take as long as three to six months. Second, a comprehensive
workout plan must be developed and agreed to by all of the
participating parties—tenants, the PHA, the city, and HUD. The
workout must address the physical condition of the projects,
the management systems, and tenant relations. Anything less
comprehensive is unlikely to have a sustained effect, a fact
attested to by the high decay rates in some of the TPP projects.
Further, adequate one-time funding for modernization and upgrading of control, accounting systems, and staff training will
have to be provided. Third, heavy technical assistance is needed
during the implementation of these improvements. This lesson
is one illustrated directly by many of the initiatives in the public housing area, especially the Housing Management Improvement and Tenant Management Programs. Finally, the area office
staff will have to undergo substantial training to adopt a more
pro-active management role and to understand the process of
change which the PHAs will experience.

If this approach has so much to commend it, why has it not
been applied to public housing? In fact, as part of the Urban

19. Baron, Huckman, Kolodny, "*Exploring New Statistics for Improving
Public Housing Management,*" p. 14.

Initiatives Program the Detroit and National Capital (Washington) Housing Authorities agreed to participate in an audit-workout, design-implementation program, which would be spearheaded by outside consultants who would be funded by HUD's research office. In both cases, political problems with the length of the implementation period aborted the process in the audit phase. Because of the small number of Authorities really needing such an approach, it would appear feasible for it to be applied to the target Authorities within a few years. Hence, the collapse of the initial application. The lack of any new attempt is unfortunate.[20]

---

20. An alternative form of technical assistance has been proposed by the National Association of Housing and Redevelopment Officials (NAHRO) but not tested by HUD. The proposal relies heavily on identification of superior practices (on the basis of informal judgment) and the communication of these practices to other PHAs ranging from the transmission of documentation to the provision of site visits by experts from an Authority having the superior practice. A strong and tacit assumption is that the receiving Authority will be able to fit the practice into its present system and that a piecemeal approach will prove effective. The proposal is described further in "NAHRO Concept for Technical Assistance to Large Housing Authorities" (Washington, D.C.: NAHRO, 1978).

Chapter 9

Fortress Public Housing

The public housing program has been discussed as though it were administered in complete isolation from other housing programs and community development activities at the local and national levels. This chapter presents fragmentary evidence available about how isolated public housing appears at the local level. Evidence from two areas is examined: (1) whether the Public Housing Authority uses the other assisted housing programs it administers in a strategic way to help reduce its problems;[1] and, (2) whether resources from the two major federal

---

1. A second type of isolation is the isolation of minority households in public housing located in predominantly minority areas, where areas are defined both as neighborhoods and as jurisdictions. HUD regulations now generally prohibit the location of new projects in such neighborhoods unless special circumstances are satisfied. Provision of housing opportunities for low-income minority households outside of their jurisdiction of residence requires substantial cooperation among jurisdictions of a type that has rarely been forthcoming. The Housing and Community Development Act of 1974 gave some impetus in this direction by requiring communities in preparing their Housing Assistance Plans (part of its CDBG application) to make provision for those households expected to reside in the community on the basis of employment opportunities. Both the neighborhood and interjurisdictional issues have long and difficult histories and are too complex to cover adequately here. See S. B. Kanner, "The Future of Public Housing," *Real Estate Law Journal*, vol. 6, no. 1, 1977-78, pp. 34-45; and D. Listokin, *Fair Share Housing Allocation* (New Brunswick: Rutgers University Center for Urban Policy Research, 1976).

community revitalization programs—the Community Development Block Grants (CDBG) and Urban Development Action Grants (UDAG)—are being used to complement efforts to improve or maintain public housing.

The evidence available is limited in important ways. In the absence of a comprehensive survey of local governments and PHAs on these points, we have had to use data drawn from several surveys each of which provides partial information. Further, we have not been able to find systematic information on the extent to which different organization of local administration has resulted in greater coordination among housing and CD activities, including public housing. So, for example, we do not know whether public housing is more strategically used by an integrated housing and community development agency, like the one in Baltimore, or whether some other form is better. Finally, we do not know anything about the aid received by PHAs from local governments out of general revenues. Hence, it is possible for CDBG funds to be used for street improvements and the construction of public facilities, and general revenues used for allocation to modernization of public housing or for improved city services to public housing projects. The data at hand do not permit disentangling the pattern just described.

Despite these limitations, available data form a picture with surprisingly good resolution. By and large, public housing at the local level appears isolated. Public housing is kept largely apart from the rest of the community in the administration of other programs, although many cities are funding public housing rehabilitation from CDBG funds. The isolation exists presumably partly because local government does not want to be stuck with greater continuing responsibility for public housing, something that might occur if local government initiated a more integrated approach. It is also partly due to lack of hustle and creativity by the executive directors at some PHAs and members of their governing boards. They do not take advantage of the possibilities that current regulations already offer them.

ASSISTED HOUSING PROGRAMS

The federal government sponsors a host of programs under which housing is provided to needy families at rents less than rents charged in the market. Two programs generally have a direct administrative link with conventional public housing: the Low-Income Rental Assistance Program (Section 8) and the Leased Housing Program (Section 23).

The Section 8 program, enacted as part of the landmark Housing Community Development Act of 1974, consists of three distinct program elements. One element assists households by leasing units which meet certain physical standards from the existing privately owned housing stock. The government pays the landlord the difference between the actual market rent (up to a HUD-determined maximum, the "fair market rent") and the rental contribution of the tenant, normally 25 percent of the household's adjusted income. Locally the existing Section 8 program has generally been administered by the Public Housing Authority.

The other two elements of the Section 8 program provide a guaranteed rental stream to developers who will build or rehabilitate units under the program. In this case, the HUD area office, or sometimes a state housing finance agency, advertises the availability of funds for building or rehabilitating units in a jurisdiction, and developers respond. If the developer's proposal is acceptable, HUD signs a 30- or 40-year annual contributions contract with him, which obligates HUD to pay him the difference between a tenant's rental contribution (25 percent of income) and the full rent for the units in his project. The developer obtains his mortgage financing from a private bank, from HUD through the Government National Mortgage Association, or from the state agency which raises funds by selling tax exempt bonds; and HUD (i.e., the Federal Housing Administration) generally insures the mortgage.

While most of the activity under these elements has occurred as just described, it has also recently become possible for Housing Authorities to be the prime mover. Under this arrangement, the PHA becomes the project sponsor, finds a developer willing to participate, and provides permanent financing by selling its own tax exempt bonds. Use of this vehicle is still exceptional, however.[2]

2. There is actually a fourth element of the Section 8 program, created by the 1978 housing act, which is a moderate rehabilitation program. This program allows rents up to 20 percent higher than those for "existing program" units when the landlord invests a few thousand dollars in the unit to meet program standards. It contrasts sharply with the original substantial rehabilitation program which requires very extensive or "gut" rehabilitation.

The number of households assisted is determined by a combination of the level of congressional appropriations, the housing needs of the jurisdiction compared to the nation, and the mix of assistance requested by the city between leasing existing units, rehabilitating existing units, or building new housing for income eligible households.[3]

The Section 8 program, with its several elements, is highly flexible; and it was designed to allow local governments to provide housing assistance consistent with the market conditions. Hence, in a very tight market with little prospect of private activity achieving relief for low-income households, the city could choose a strategy favoring new construction. Since its enactment in 1974, the Section 8 program has had high levels of activity. By July 1979, there were 840,000 units occupied under the program, including 162,500 newly constructed or rehabilitated, and 434,000 additional units committed for or actually under construction. By 1979 Section 8 was, in the aggregate, as large as the public housing program. The figures in table 33 show that in the largest 29 cities having public housing programs, the Section 8 program element that leases existing units (Section 8 Existing) is quite sizable in most cities compared to the number of public housing units. Since Section 8 Existing is usually administered by the local PHA, this substantial volume of Section 8 units means that the Authority can strategically use the public housing and Section 8 units.

The Section 23 program, initiated in 1965, was really a predecessor to the Section 8 Existing program; and it is probably best thought of in those terms.[4] As the leases under Section 23

---

3. For a basic description of the Section 8 program, see National Association of Housing and Development Officials, *Low-Income Rental Assistance Program (Section 8): Questions and Answers* (Washington, D.C.: NAHRO, 1975). The spatial allocation for housing funds is discussed in John L. Goodman, Jr., *Regional Housing Assistance Allocations and Regional Housing Needs* (Washington, D.C.: The Urban Institute, 1979). Finally, on the process leading to mix of assistance requested by local government, see R. Struyk, "Saving the Housing Assistance Plans: Improving Incentives to Local Governments" (Washington, D.C.: The Urban Institute, 1979).

4. For a description and evaluation see F. de Leeuw and S. H. Leaman, "The Section 23 Leasing Program" (Washington, D.C.: The Urban Institute, Reprint of Testimony given to the Joint Economic Committee of the United States, 92nd Congress, 2nd Session, 1972).

Table 33

NUMBERS OF SECTION 8 EXISTING AND PUBLIC HOUSING UNITS IN THE LARGEST CITIES

City	Section 8 Existing [a]	Public Housing [d]	City	Section 8 Existing [a]	Public Housing [d]
Phoenix	319	1,900	Boston	1,965	12,800
Los Angeles	8,300	8,200	Detroit [b]	1,896	10,300
San Francisco	598	7,100	Minneapolis	1,360	6,900
Denver	588	4,900	Kansas City	1,084	2,600
Washington, D.C.	756	11,200	St. Louis	2,000	6,700
Jacksonville	1,759	3,100	Buffalo	900	4,800
Atlanta	2,573	14,700	New York	21,590	116,600
Chicago	2,668	38,600	Cincinnati	635	6,800
Indianapolis	800	2,600	Cleveland [c]	4,434	11,500
New Orleans	2,707	13,600	Columbus	305	4,800
Baltimore	1,535	16,200	Memphis	794	6,800
Philadelphia	4,889	22,900	Dallas	3,024	7,000
Pittsburgh	1,398	9,800	Houston	4,518	2,600
Milwaukee	2,623	4,400	San Antonio	5,017	7,500
			Seattle	960	5,900

Source: U.S. Department of Housing and Urban Development, unpublished data.
a. Excludes Section 23 conversion; data as of October 1979.
b. Includes Michigan State Housing Development Authority administered units in the SMSA.
c. Cuyohoga County.
d. Data for fiscal year 1978.

expire, many of the units are being transferred to the Section 8 program if their owners want to participate.

How do the large Authorities use these programs? The information available comes from the 1979 survey of PHA income certification practices cited in chapter 6. Twenty-two of the 29 PHAs in the largest cities were included in that sample. All 22 of these PHAs administer either the Section 8 Existing or the Section 23 program; 21 of 22 administer the Section 8 Existing program.

The Authorities might easily use the lease programs to improve public housing. For example, if acquiring tenants with higher incomes is a priority, lower income applicants could be channeled into the Section 8 program, and those with higher incomes would be offered public housing units. Alternatively, if the Authority wanted to reduce the densities in their high-rise family towers to make proper management more feasible, some large families currently in the projects could be shifted out of the projects using Section 8 Existing, or large families generally could be served with Section 8.[5] The public housing units that are vacated, either by relocating in situ tenants or from the usual turnover, could then be leased to smaller households, assuming that the HUD area office grants an exception to the standard unit size-family size schedule.

Both of these examples assume a deliberate policy on the part of the Authority, which would be manifested in its intake procedures. Two questions posed to the PHA's occupancy specialist in a survey on tenant incomes and assignment to programs shed some light on these practices (see table 34). The first asks whether other programs administered by the PHA are men-

---

5. Some would argue against this strategy on the grounds that large units that rent for less than the HUD-defined maximum (the Fair Market Rent–FMR) are very hard to find. Two arguments can be posed in rebuttal. First, the FMR is to be set the level at which half of all units meeting the program's physical standard would be available to the program, if they were vacant. A comparison of the small number of units needed to meet program needs versus the number of units vacated during a year shows that this should not be a problem. The PHA may, however, have to provide significant assistance in searching for these units. Second, the PHA can at its own discretion grant "exception rents," i.e., higher rents for 20 percent of the Section 8 units it manages. These could be reserved for use with large families and overcome the problem of the FMRs being set too low, if the area office will not revise FMR schedule.

Table 34

RESPONSES OF TWENTY-TWO LARGE PHAs TO
QUESTIONS ON TENANT ASSIGNMENT TO PROGRAMS

	Response	
Question	*Yes*	*No*
If an applicant comes in to apply for housing in a specific program, do you usually mention the other housing programs to that applicant?	18	4
Which of these two statements best describes the procedures used when applicants come in (without a specific housing program in mind)?		
a. All available programs are explained to the applicant and the applicant then decides which one to apply for?	12	8 [a]
or:		
b. The applicant is asked to describe the situation and the agency tells the applicant what program would be best for him/her.	8	12 [a]

Source: Tabulations of data from the 1979 survey of "PHA CRE Certification
    Policies and Procedures."
  a. Only 20 usable responses.

tioned when the applicant inquires about a specific program. Eighteen of 22 do mention other programs, either to expand the applicant's choice or as part of a strategy to match applicants and programs. The responses to the second question are more revealing. This question concerned the applicant who did not have a specific program in mind. In 12 of the 20 cases for which usable responses were given, the PHA explained the programs and left the choice of program up to the applicant. In the other eight cases, the agency channeled applicants into programs. These responses, combined with the data presented in chapter 6 on the criteria used by PHAs in giving preferences to eligible applicants, strongly suggest that the PHAs are not using opportunities to control the tenant profile and hence eliminate some management problems.

Another way for the PHA to deal with the problem of concentrating certain types of tenants is for a PHA to use its funds for building new public housing to build or rehabilitate units on a scattered-site basis. Unfortunately, the information system at HUD central does not include this data, and it is not possible to provide any comprehensive description of unit activity.[6] Some cities, such as Baltimore, have effectively used scattered-site rehabilitation.

COMMUNITY DEVELOPMENT PROGRAMS

There is an enormous range for the use of community development programs in concert with public housing. At one end of the spectrum, the city might allocate funds to the PHA for modernization, with the PHA using the funds as it saw fit. At the other end of the spectrum is the presence of a housing project in an area targeted for a major set of upgrading activities, with the improvement of the project—and the integration of its tenants into the life of the surrounding community—as a critical element. Improvement to the project itself is one element. Adding or upgrading a park and other recreational facilities in the neighborhood may be another. In some cases, it would be very important to reduce the spatial isolation of the project, perhaps by street rearrangement, perhaps by the strategic location of other facilities on or adjacent to the public housing site.

In this section, PHA-involved activities under the Urban Development Action Grant (UDAG) and the Community Development Block Grant (CDBG) programs are reviewed using the data available from existing surveys, studies, and program files.

Urban Development Action Grants

The UDAG program was enacted in 1977 and by fiscal year 1979 had an annual budget of $400 million. It is a categorical program in that its funds are restricted in use and communities must compete for them. The program's purpose is to improve the economic base of the distressed cities in the United States. The actual definition of "distress" used in the program is fairly complicated; and it has received a great deal of attention from

---

6. Although the data are not computerized, the information should be on the form 1885 which is supposed to exist for each project, including scattered-site projects. Serious problems of missing forms and incomplete data were found when using these forms for the analysis in chapter 2. Further, since the OMB approval of the form expired a few years ago, its use has not been consistent; hence, it is likely that the data on monthly completed projects would be especially unreliable.

cities which have been classified as ineligible.[7] Eligible activities include all those under the CDBG program and others necessary to revitalize a city's economic base. A key UDAG objective is to maximize the involvement of the private sector in the funded projects; and one indication of the program's success is the number of private dollars "leveraged" with each public dollar. The intent is for UDAG to fund only those projects which are close to economic feasibility without the federal funds, and then to fund only that portion necessary to achieve feasibility.

The intent and structure of the program do not make the involvement of public housing projects, directly or indirectly, obvious. There is, however, a greater scope possible than might first appear. By the end of the second program year in September 1979, the UDAG office at HUD central was able to cite three UDAG-funded projects that involved public housing. Those projects, described in Appendix H, are only a trivial part of all UDAG activity. One of these, involving the Cochran Gardens project in St. Louis, is an unusually creative upgrading of public housing.

Community Development Block Grants

Enacted as part of the 1974 Housing and Community Development Act, the CDBG program replaced a set of categorical programs with funding provided to large cities on a formula basis with great certainty and comparatively few restrictions. Because the program is widely known, its general structure is not further discussed here.[8] The program is flexible enough to allow the assistance to public housing to take various forms—grants for modernization, construction of public facilities, funds to be used as the matching portion for Title XX day care services, site improvements, and some direct provision of services such as increased security patrols.

Two sets of data have been available to examine the use of

---

7. Office of Community Planning and Development, Department of Housing and Urban Development, *Urban Development Action Grant Program: First Annual Report* (Washington, D.C.: U.S. Government Printing Office, 1979).

8. A general description is in P. R. Dommel, R. P. Nathan, S. F. Liebschutz, and M. T. Wrightson, *Decentralizing Community Development* (Washington, D.C.: U.S. Government Printing Office, 1978).

CDBG funds in public housing. The first is the analysis done by the Brookings Institution's monitoring project of the CDBG applications filled out by 61 local governments as well as other local information on CDBG-supported activities. The Brookings project has been in place since the first program year and still continues. The second is a set of profiles of CDBG-supported activities generated for 14 large cities by the University of Pennsylvania. The profiles are part of an evaluation of the impacts of CDBG expenditures on households, the housing stock, and neighborhoods generally. The basic data in this case are the performance reports, that is, expenditures actually made. Obviously, neither data set is comprehensive across cities. Furthermore, neither project was designed to address the specific questions being asked here. As a consequence, any statements made here must be considered tentative; however, a consistent picture emerges.

The Brookings Monitoring Study. The Brookings project monitors the use of CDBG funds, especially the process backing the particular allocation of funds adopted, in 61 jurisdictions. Among those 61 are 14 of the largest 29 central cities in the country whose public housing is the focus of this monograph.[9] The Brookings project relies on a "monitor" in each of the 61 jurisdictions to observe the planning and expenditure process and then to accurately complete a highly detailed questionnaire devised by the core staff at Brookings in consultation with the monitors. The core staff then uses those reports as the basis for preparing general reports on the program for HUD, who sponsors the project.

The Brookings staff believed that the best way to isolate the use of CDBG funds for public housing was through expenditures of funds for housing rehabilitation, which would include grants to the Authority for modernization. Having identified these expenditures, it was possible to determine whether those expenditures were part of a concentrated neighborhood upgrading effort. This approach is limited since expenditures for public facilities on or adjacent to public housing sites, for example, would be missed. Still, it was thought the best approach.

Of the applications for the 14 largest cities, 5 planned to use

9. The cities are Phoenix, Los Angeles, Denver, Chicago, Atlanta, Boston, Minneapolis, St. Louis, New York, Cleveland, Philadelphia, Pittsburgh, Houston, and Seattle.

block grant funds in program years III and IV (1977-79) to support public housing modernization: Boston, Denver, Houston, Chicago, and St. Louis. From the materials available it appears highly doubtful that, except for St. Louis, these funds are not part of a concerted neighborhood upgrading strategy. Further, the variance in which plans are presented makes accurate comparisons of level of effort across cities infeasible.[10]

University of Pennsylvania Survey Data. During the summer of 1979, the CDBG program elements in 14 cities with populations of greater than 100,000 were identified and catalogued by staff from the University of Pennsylvania. Among these cities are 8 of the 29 cities included in our sample. The main source of information for this work was the Grantee Performance Reports for year IV (GPR), although these were supplemented with other materials, including data from interviews with local community development officials. The GPR provides information on a cumulative basis; hence, activities actually undertaken during the first four years of the Block Grant Program are reported.[11]

Table 35 summarizes the information found in the GPRs. Nine of the 14 cities have funded public housing rehabilitation; some have made very substantial outlays for this purpose. About half of these CDBG projects were geographically targeted in the sense that the GPRs indicated the specific census tracts in which the expenditures were made, that is, the location of public housing. The absence of such designation implies that the funds were turned over to the Authority to use systemwide,

---

10. It should be noted that in going through the applications there were a number of mentions of other CDBG funding that would benefit specific public housing projects. Still, there was no indication of a neighborhood strategy.

11. In coding the data on the GPRs for machine use, University of Pennsylvania staff used the 14 budget categories established by HUD guidelines, and an additional set of some 65 project "characteristics." An individual project could have up to 3 characteristics indicated for it. One of the characteristics defined is "public housing rehabilitation." We have examined every CDBG project with this characterization to get some idea of the complementary activities associated with rehabilitation. It has not been possible, however, to determine if any of the public housing rehabilitation expenditures have been part of neighborhoodwide upgrading projects. Further, because of the variance among cities in the way they report activities, the procedure followed is likely to provide a somewhat inaccurate picture for a given city.

but the Authority could have targeted their use. The final column in table 35 lists the other project characterizations which appeared with the public housing rehabilitation designation. Interestingly, there are several indications of the complementary provision of services: senior citizens' services, police services, and community services. There are also indications of other physical improvements occurring as part of the project. Together these bits of information suggest that CDBG-funded rehabilitation of public housing is often packaged with other improvements or services. This indicates genuine cooperation, at least on a spot basis between the Authority and city agencies.

Overall, a substantial number of cities are using CDBG funds to help public housing, although the level of funding appears to be a modest share of total CDBG funds. Even at these modest levels, however, the funds can be very important to the PHA. Because they are not governed by modernization program regulations, they can be used for badly needed work items that are not HUD priority items.

PUTTING IT ALL TOGETHER

This concluding section gives a brief overview of what can be done with the resources at hand. The example comes not from one of the largest cities but from Decatur, Illinois where the City and the Housing Authority have combined to fully integrate their resources to stabilize and rejuvenate the Longview-Torrence Park neighborhood. Longview Place is a 418-unit, low-rise multifamily public housing project set in a neighborhood of single-family housing. The project, built in 1942, was in need of modernization, but it suffered as well from excessive project density (1,275 occupants, including 700 children) and an almost total absence of play space and equipment.

The Torrence Park area was described in the opening paragraph of the joint Authority-City planning document as a "dying neighborhood . . . physically isolated and deteriorating."[12] By the time of the joint plan, a good share of the neighborhood's initial housing stock, which was deemed too expensive to reha-

12. S. C. Stone and J. W. Taylor, *Inner City Turnaround: An Evolving Plan for a Total Service Neighborhood, Longview-Torrence Park, Decatur, Illinois* (Champaign: University of Illinois, Housing Research and Development Program, 1976) p. 1.

Table 35

PUBLIC HOUSING REHABILITATION SUPPORTED WITH CDBG FUNDS IN FOURTEEN CITIES

City and Project Number [a]		Estimated Cost ($000)	Geographically Targeted	Other Characterizations of Activity [b]
Philadelphia [c]	59	200	no	Social and community services; Planning and development
Detroit [c]	45	500	yes	
	268	250	no	Acquisition of real property
	269	1300	no	Acquisition of real property
Los Angeles [c]	49	260	no	
	51	460	yes	Parks, playgrounds, and recreation
Chicago [c]	21	210	yes	
New York [c]	45	8512	no	
	44	5302	no	
	43	3800	no	
	42	4946	no	
	22	4110	no	Administration; relocation
	21	1870	no	Administration
	20	815	no	Administration
	30	1670	no	Administration; senior citizens' services
	27	1500	no	Senior citizens' services
	26	1000	no	
Lansing	52	38	no	Clearance and demolition

		Rehab for fire prevention	Senior citizens' services	Police support
Tacoma	44	26		yes
	45	109		yes
Boston [c]	174	1674		yes
	4	3835		yes
	92	3038		yes
	175	561		yes
	226	2250		yes
	227	109		yes
St. Petersburg	14	335		yes

Source: Grantee Performance Reports, year IV; data as compiled by the University of Pennsylvania.
a. Cities not reporting use of block grants for public housing rehabilitation are Gary, Oakland, Erie, Houston,[c] and New Orleans.[c]
b. Characterizations made by University of Pennsylvania in coding data.
c. One of largest 29 cities.

bilitate, had been demolished using urban renewal funds. More housing was expected to be lost in response to city code enforcement; indeed, even in 1975, only 151 houses out of 397 in the neighborhood were rated as meeting code or being able to meet it with only minor repairs. Since 1960 the incomes of households had fallen sharply, and more and more houses were operated by absentee landlords with a corresponding reduction in the incidence of owner occupancy. In these aspects, Torrence Park resembles many of the areas in which HUD's Urban Homesteading program has been initiated in response to high rates of foreclosure on homes whose mortgages were insured by the Federal Housing Administration.[13]

Under the plan developed, the city concentrated its early investments (financed by the CDBG program) on essential infrastructure: storm sewers, new sidewalks, curbs, and street surfacing. Funds are increasingly being devoted to residential rehabilitation. A major park adjacent to Longview Place will be constructed and more rehabilitation funded with an additional HUD Community Development grant from discretionary funds.

The Authority has been especially creative. It decided on a comprehensive approach to modernizing Longview Place, upgrading the units, and reducing project densities. In the first phase, items affecting the basic structural integrity of the buildings (e.g., new roofs, new electrical wiring) were funded. In later phases, some already completed, the buildings are individually overhauled. (Because the comprehensive approach is at variance with the "priority work task" system in HUD's modernization program, the Authority has not actually received regular modernization funds in some years!) The Authority is reducing the number of large families in Longview through two techniques. First, it has used some of its Section 8 existing resources for this purpose, when possible shifting households into the single-family houses of Torrence Park. Second, it has used its funds made available for the construction of public housing through the normal funds allocation system to build single-family homes in Torrence Park on sites made available by urban renewal and code enforcement. Finally, the Authority

---

13. Office of Policy Development and Research, U.S. Department of Housing and Urban Development, *Baseline Analysis of the Urban Homesteading Demonstration* (Washington, D.C.: U.S. Government Printing Office, 1979).

has formed a not-for-profit corporation to introduce various forms of homeownership into the neighborhood including an acquisition-rehabilitation program and a Section 235 federally subsidized homeownership program.

The Longview-Torrence Park initiative is in mid-term. Much has been accomplished, but plenty remains to be done. The marshaling and intelligent use of the available resources has been most impressive.

Part V

POLICY

IMPLICATIONS

Chapter 10

Suggestions For Improvement

To this point the chapters have catalogued public housing as it exists in the largest cities at the close of 1979. Many public housing projects are almost unbelievably difficult to manage due to a combination of project design problems including project scale and density, tenantry with a high ratio of minors to adults, and a share of problem families. Actual management is often below par because of the incentives HUD has created through its administration of the program and because of serious administrative deficiencies at the local level.

This chapter offers suggestions for positive change. It starts with a recapitulation of the relationships among the major institutions involved in order to help establish a realistic basis for considering the possibilities advanced later. The discussion includes a statement of principles that the system administering public housing should follow. Alternative approaches to an administrative system that differs in the locus of power (e.g., HUD, local government) and type of incentives produced for efficient management are then sketched. Among these, the existing approach still seems best; in concept this system is characterized by a direct relationship between HUD and the Authority, with the Authority having maximum freedom for day-to-day operations. However, the next section outlines a radical change in administration within the broad concept, including a simplified combined funding system for operations and modernization and explicit attention to correcting fundamental management problems at distressed Authorities.

The remainder of the chapter addresses these topics: who should be served by public housing; what could be done to improve the current funding systems (assuming that they remain in place); and, finally, a brief look at the problems and prospects at HUD central. Many of the changes suggested in these areas could be accomplished quickly under HUD's existing legislative authority.

Perhaps the most striking aspect of the existing system is the extent of the room for improvement. While there is much of merit in the current program, possibilities within the current structure have not been completely exploited.

THE POWERS THAT BE

To realistically discuss changes requires that existing institutional circumstances be understood and that modifications be considered in light of their compatibility with these institutions. The present situation need not be immutable. Rather, the prospects for altering institutions must be honestly assessed. Below a "prototypical" Authority-city-HUD relationship is described; in reality, of course, there are many variants, some of which affect the conclusions drawn. However, the prototype presented does convey a generally valid picture of the main elements in this relationship.

The typical local Public Housing Authority is a separate, legal entity, but it is an entity whose powers are sharply circumscribed. The municipality in which the PHA operates has several important powers. A municipality has a veto on additional development because of the requirement to provide municipal services to public housing projects. It also uses this power to determine the location of projects. Moreover, the members of the PHA's board of directors are appointed by the chief executive or the city council; thus, the Authority's policies are set, if not directly by the city, then by persons only once removed.

The municipality is in an enviable position. It has a great

deal of control over the Authority and little liability—save modest direct costs, the prospect of having dilapidated projects that may cause neighborhood deterioration, and some political liability. But even the latter may be viewed as a small cost if the projects are sited in neighborhoods of the politically disenfranchised and if the poor are not well organized. The municipalities' financial liability is the difference in the cost of providing certain services to the projects specified as part of the cooperation agreement between local government and the Authority and a payment made by the Authority in lieu of property taxes.[1]

What could the municipality do if it perceived poor performance on the part of the Authority and wanted to effect improvement? Clearly, it has a number of weapons at its disposal. Through the board of directors it could effect changes in top management. (This assumes that the mayor has "his" board, a situation which may not exist for new mayors.) The quality and quantity of public services provided to projects could vary, either across-the-board or at selected projects.[2] Development of future projects—sometimes highly valued by PHA management —could be dependent on the accomplishment of certain changes. Finally, municipal contributions of discretionary funds, such as the use of CDBG funds for project modernization, could be eliminated.

What must the municipality do if it perceives poor performance by the Authority? Nothing. Its incentive for positive action comes from the political power that public housing tenants and the households living around the projects are able to mobilize. In most cities this is not viewed as a particularly large or strong constituency.[3] Individuals less directly affected have been unlikely to support such causes.

---

1. The Authority realizes substantial savings from not paying taxes assessed at regular rates. For a discussion of the value of the tax reduction see S. K. Mayo et al., "Draft Report on Housing Allowances and Other Rental Housing Assistance Programs," vol. 2, pp. A-7 to A-50.

2. A good deal of latitude is possible here while still being in compliance with the letter of the agreement, although punitive variation is probably illegal.

3. In some ways the lack of political clout is surprising in light of the results of a 1978 national poll in which the respondents were asked whether the federal government should assist low-income families in meeting their housing needs. Seventy-three percent of all respondents and 80 percent of those in large cities answered affirmatively. The next

Note that there is a strong disincentive against the municipality becoming too involved. Financial responsibility is viewed as a federal responsibility, except for the provision of agreed-upon services. If municipalities become too heavily involved, the financial burden for operating subsidies might become joint, a prospect terrifying to any city controller. Indeed, the financial straits of some PHAs are causing cities to waive the payments in lieu of taxes—an ominous portent. In sum, most cities feel that they are providing their "fair share" of the resources needed to operate public housing.

Although the previous chapters have described HUD's financial and regulatory relations with the Authorities and explained the types of incentives embodied in the current set of institutional relationships, they have not addressed the question of what HUD can do with a badly performing PHA. HUD's principal sticks and carrots are financial: funds for developing new projects and modernizing existing ones can be denied until management makes improvements; likewise, HUD can refuse to approve an Authority's operating budget—a necessary step for the Authority to receive operating subsidies—until HUD is satisfied that the PHA made necessary changes. Of course, restricting modernization and operating funds may push a bad situation into becoming worse. Problems could worsen to a point where a decade or more of hard work by good management may be required for correction. The ultimate weapon in the small HUD arsenal is to take over the projects. This has only been done very reluctantly in the past, and for good reason. HUD is not equipped for the task. HUD's problems in operating privately owned, HUD-insured projects that have been foreclosed cast grave doubts on its ability to operate a major housing Authority over a sustained period. Furthermore, local gov-

---

question asked for the respondents' definition of low income (i.e., "For a family of four to be considered low income what would you think should be the upper limit of their annual income?") Of those responding the overall mean was $8,500, and the mean for respondents living in large cities was $8,800. The difference between these responses and local action may be attributable to the respondents supporting federal rather than local action. The data just cited are from unpublished tabulations of survey data. The survey is described in Office of Policy Development and Research, U.S. Department of Housing and Urban Development, *The 1978 HUD Survey on the Quality of Community Life—A Data Book* (Washington, D.C.: U.S. Government Printing Office, 1979).

ernments would try to block a takeover, by acting through their congressional delegations even if the department thought it could effectively operate PHAs. On the other hand, a few cities have pushed HUD to take full responsibility for an Authority.

The bluntness and limited nature of the instruments available to HUD to "enforce" good management practices are appallingly clear. Consequently, HUD works by caviling, cajoling, and threatening.

The foregoing suggests painfully little control over the truly recalcitrant Authority; or, stated differently, painfully little relief for the tenants of mismanaged Authorities. The lack of relief has, over the past decade, given rise to rent strikes and lawsuits by or on behalf of aggrieved tenants. The residents, heretofore effectively disenfranchised, have become an independent force often assisted by public interest lawyers and sometimes by technical and legal assistance provided by foundations. In many instances, assertive actions by tenants resulted in sufficient embarrassment to city officials to cause a positive response. In Newark, a protracted rent strike at the Stella Wright project led to tenant management and genuine improvements (some made possible by special HUD modernization funding) in this high-rise family project, although reforms were not PHA-wide. Rent strikes in St. Louis led to decentralized project-based management throughout the Authority—some projects under tenant management, others managed directly by private firms.

Not all strikes and lawsuits produce such sanguine, if hard-achieved results. In 1970, public interest lawyers began bringing suits on behalf of tenants in projects of the Boston Housing Authority (BHA) to have units brought up to minimum health and sanitary standards. After nine years in various courts, the issuance of a detailed consent decree by a state court and numerous management reviews and attempted corrective actions by HUD to force improvement by the BHA, the Superior Court of the State of Massachusetts in utter frustration ordered the BHA into receivership. To date, little progress has resulted from the direct and extensive intervention of the court. And there is little reason to assume that its giving further orders, albeit wtih the threat of contempt citations, will achieve much. At this point, it has ordered two things that may cause fundamental change (pending further appeals): the BHA's board of

directors has been abolished, with the receiver to report directly
to the court; and a receiver—in effect the Authority's executive
director—*can* be chosen strictly on his merits. On the other side
of the ledger, however, the court has to date found no way to
cause any infusion of additional monies for the Authority from
state or federal sources. Currently, the net effect of the court's
intervention is far from clear; but the court will obviously be
highly dependent upon the sagacity of the advice received from
the experts selected to assist it.

The need to strengthen the incentives for good management
in the routine aspects of the public housing program, and thereby lessen the reliance on ex post restorative measures is critical. However, the question of what to do ex post must also be
addressed. Several widely differing approaches are suggested.

PRINCIPLES AND APPROACHES TO IMPROVEMENT

The broad objective is to improve the quality of housing and
related services provided to the tenants of public housing and
to deliver these services in the most efficient way possible. To
achieve this goal, an effective public housing system must include several characteristics.

1. *Administrative simplicity.* Less complex systems are usually cheaper to operate; and, because their details are
   more easily understood, they can result in greater equity.
   The principle is to select an administrative system com-
   mensurate with the objectives at hand that is within the
   capabilities of system designers *and* those who must administer it.
2. *Incentives for good management.* These incentives must
   be built into funding systems and into the regulations,
   however broad or specific, that implement the approach
   selected.
3. *Getting back on track.* Some PHAs will perform misera-
   bly, regardless of the approach taken and the strength of
   the incentives provided. The responses available to the
   system when this situation arises must be defined in advance, and their likely effectiveness dispassionately evaluated. Will the necessary coercive power be there? Will

it be in the hands of those likely to want or able to use
such power?

4. *Realism.* The inherently difficult conditions under which
   some Authorities operate—poorly designed projects (some
   of massive scale), the large number of very large, single-
   parent families, and so forth—must be recognized in establishing funding levels, standards, and regulations.

5. *Orderly transition.* The difficulties of changeover—both in
   substance and the time required—must be assessed and
   reflected in implementation plans. While there is probably
   no change that could not be made, some changes will be
   more wrenching than others: can the system absorb the
   shock in a reasonable period of time?

These principles should be used to assess the comparative
merits of various approaches to altering the basic administrative structure of the public housing system. Four distinct alternatives are now sketched. They differ sharply in the location of
ultimate responsibility for efficient management and the types
of incentives offered to promote it. Each is briefly described and
some general comments are offered. An approach we have
chosen is detailed in the following section.

The first approach is to give the Authorities as much latitude
as possible in their internal management, to exert pressure for
efficiency through the funding systems, and to promote equity
in the treatment of tenants across Authorities through regulations. This is essentially the approach that HUD has pursued
for the past decade, albeit with major flaws in its execution.
The substantial freedom available to the PHAs in the areas of
tenant admission policies and establishment of tenant rental
contributions was discussed in chapter 6. The discussion of
PHA finances underscored the available latitude in fund allocations (and accounting procedures). Budget discipline is exercised through the performance funding system. This system
does not, however, have a cogent approach to the most distressed Authorities.

A sharply different approach revolves around the establishment of true performance standards. These standards would
measure how well an Authority discharged specific functions—
routine maintenance, income certification, emergency repairs—
against a norm derived from the more efficient of its peers, with

"peers" being defined with reference to project and tenant characteristics. The complementary funding system would reward good and improving performance, and funding levels would be tightly tailored to each Authority's "output." Progress in one area would be directly reflected in additional operating subsidies. The executive director of a poor performing PHA would have an objective report card to present to a board of directors who would be relied upon to require improvements. Of all the approaches considered, this one has the strongest incentives for solid management. Of course, the key ingredient, the standards, do not now exist; and many years of research would be necessary for their development, as would numerous, specific policy decisions.

A third approach is to accept local government as the natural administrator of public housing within its jurisdiction. HUD's responsibility as overseer would be largely vested in local government. Only the most basic questions would be referred to HUD; one example might be project demolition. Funds would be provided to the PHA through the city, and the city presumably would have the ability to allocate only some portion of the funds to the Authority. If efficiency gains were observed, the residual funds could be used for other housing and community development activities. Inefficiency would be paid for out of other city funds, whether Community Development Block Grants or general revenue. Since a genuine financial stake would be involved, the city would discharge its role as overseer more responsibly. Furthermore, when elected officials can no longer hide behind HUD's putatively unproductive restrictions and irrational funding allocations, tenants and the citizenry at large could confront these officials head on. Finally, HUD could have real power over the city's performance by making other housing assistance or CDBG funds dependent on good performance.

On the other side of this ledger are three serious questions about reliance on city government. One has to do with the incentives required for any city to willfully enter into an agreement that transfers so much responsibility to them. First, it seems doubtful that even generous initial funding levels would be sufficient inducement. Second, most cities have no record as competent managers of housing, since they have not previously had this type of responsibility. (Indeed, some PHAs seem able to perform well because of their independence from City Hall.) Third, it is far from evident that tenants have the political strength to protect themselves. This is especially likely when the services at a single project—located in a neighborhood that has little regard for its units' residents—are allowed to deteriorate.

The final approach is to make the PHA just another landlord; let the PHA compete in the market place under the same rules as private landlords. All of the in situ tenants would be given Section 8 Existing certificates, usable at PHA projects or in the market.[4] The Authority could rent to unsubsidized households, subject only to having a minimum share of its units in each project (perhaps 30 percent) available to Section 8 income eligible households. The PHA in its new entrepreneurial role—a role many PHAs would have difficulty playing—could buy and sell projects; if it sold them, outstanding ACCs would be paid off. The incentive for efficiency is bluntly clear: survival.

But what if the PHA fails the test? Should government be willing to watch the withdrawal of a large amount of low-income housing from the stock? Recall that in the absence of an entitlement Section 8 Existing program only a minority of eligible households will have certificates. Hence, a case might occur in which certificate holders move out of the projects, unsubsidized households move in, and the project, not covering costs, closes and evicts its new occupants. Another fundamental question is whether society is willing to have projects sold to investors for conversion to middle-income housing. Even if some replacement housing is forthcoming, is this the role for public agencies?

The first approach seems on balance to offer the greatest likelihood of success, when judged against the principles enunciated earlier, as well as certain political realities as they appear to us. This approach should not be taken, however, as business as usual. Far from it. The next section describes an almost completely new set of tactics within this broad approach. PFS and the modernization funding are completely replaced; incentives for management strengthened; and a serious solution to the "poor performers" problem advanced.

A NEW SYSTEM

Any reform consistent with the principles outlined above will

---

4. The Section 8 Existing program is described briefly in chapter 9.

be multifarious. For presentation, this reform is organized into four parts, which correspond to its major elements. However, each of the elements is essential to the system.

Funding

The heart of the system is the replacement of the present methods of allocating operating and modernization subsidies with a single payment which is based on the household income, size of tenant families, and the cost of providing housing services in the area.[5] That is, the PHA would receive the subsidy payments computed for each family occupying a unit managed by the PHA. This is the type of formula used to provide subsidy payments in the Section 8 program that was described in chapter 9. In that program, the subsidy paid to the landlord by the local agency (ultimately using federal funds) is computed as subsidy=(fair market rent)$_{ij}$–a (adjusted household income)$_j$. The i and j subscripts on the fair market rent (FMR) indicate that this is the FMR for the ith geographic area and jth sized dwelling unit, that is, units with the proper number of bedrooms for the family under consideration. Income adjusted for work expenses and other items, defined in Appendix E, is the same as that used in the Section 8 program.[6]

Because the FMR is the cost of renting adequate housing in the market place, it offers an objective, if imperfect, measure of the cost of providing public housing. Separate FMR schedules are produced by HUD central for existing dwellings and for dwellings built or substantially rehabilitated under the program. Beginning in 1979, the FMRs for existing units were set using data from the Annual Housing Survey, a large survey conducted yearly for the nation as a whole and on a rotating four-year cycle for 60 metropolitan areas. These data are, in fact, quite reliable and offer a realistic measure of housing costs at a point in time and changes in costs over time.

The PHA would use the subsidy payments for three purposes: making payments on the outstanding annual contributions contracts that funded project development and past mod-

---

5. This idea, in a somewhat modified form, was set forth in an internal 1973 HUD document, "Housing Management Report on an Interim Funding Strategy for the Public Housing Program," Appendix B.

6. Note that this would permit common income definitions across the assisted housing programs for the first time.

ernization; operating and maintaining the projects; and accumulating reserves out of which future modernization and replacements would be funded.

How does this scheme work out in dollars? Logically, the Authority, compared to private investors, should do well under payments computed using the FMR process because of its lower cost of capital. Recall that project development was financed by sale of municipal, tax exempt bonds; additionally, most of these projects are now 20 or more years old and their "purchase price" has remained their initial total development cost. Another reason that the FMR process is generous is that the PHA makes payments in lieu of property taxes to the municipality that are considerably below those paid by private landlords. Finally, the FMRs themselves are set to equal the rent of the median unit among those in the metropolitan area that pass the quality standards of the Section 8 program. In other words, half of the units in an area could be rented for the FMR.[7] This reaches fairly high into the quality distribution and should be comparable with the market rent of most public housing units.[8]

Detailed computations for five very large Authorities are presented in table 36 using data for the 1977 fiscal year. These particular five were selected because of availability of accurate tenant income data.[9] All figures in the table are on a per-unit-month basis. Two questions are foremost: will the FMR-based subsidy cover operating and capital costs? And, if so, how much more will the FMR-based system cost? The answer to the first question is given in line 3 of the table, which shows that for all five Authorities, total resources will exceed current total costs by at least 10 percent. The answer to the second question is that federal subsidies would indeed rise for the PHAs shown between $8 and $69 per unit month (line 5). For all five com-

---

7. For more on FMRs see E. O. Olsen and D. Rasmussen, "Section 8 Existing: Program Evaluation and Policy Options," *Occasional Papers in Housing and Community Affairs* (U.S. Department of Housing and Urban Development, forthcoming); J. Follain, "How Well Do Section 8 FMRs Match the Cost of Rental Housing" (Washington, D.C.: The Urban Institute, Working Paper 249-17, 1979).

8. This is the case in Pittsburgh and Phoenix according to the figures in S. Mayo et al., "Draft Report on Housing Allowances and Other Rental Housing Assistance Programs . . .," vol. 1, chapter 3.

9. The selection of these PHAs, and the income data used, is discussed in chapter 3.

Table 36

FINANCES OF FIVE PHAs UNDER REVISED SUBSIDY SYSTEM
BASED ON FAIR MARKET RENTS: FISCAL YEAR 1977

(all figures are on a per-unit-month basis)

	AUTHORITY				
	Los Angeles	Chicago	Philadelphia	Atlanta	Baltimore
1. Total resources available to Authority, based on FMRs [a]	$239	$296	$278	$198	$251
a. Tenant contribution [b]	94	81	81	47	77
b. Subsidy [c]	145	215	197	151	174
2. Total expenses (actual 1977)	152	204	202	174	173
a. Total operating expenses	109	144	154	110	122
b. Debt service [d]					
Development ACCs	24	50	42	56	44
Modernizations ACCs	19	10	6	8	7
3. Difference between total resources and total costs	87	92	76	24	78
4. Total actual subsidy in 1977 [e]	99	146	180	143	136
5. Increase in federal subsidy [f]	46	69	17	8	38

a. Computed as the weighted average of the Fair Market Rents (FMRs) applicable to the actual unit size distribution for each PHA; thirty percent of units are assumed to be in elevator units.
b. Computed using the Section 8 income definitions and adjustments, with the 1976 tenant survey income data, updated to 1977.
c. Subsidy equals FMR less tenant contribution.
d. Low Rent Program Division, Office of Finance and Accounting, Office of Administration, U.S. Department of Housing and Urban Development.
e. Equals debt service (line 2b) plus operating subsidy payments made through the PFS.
f. Equals difference between entries in lines 1b and 4.

bined, this would be an increase of about $50 million in FY 1977 or about 50 percent of the payments made that year for operating expenses. (Because of the high variance in treatment among Authorities, no simple extrapolation of these figures should be attempted. Computation of systemwide costs have not been made but could be simulated by HUD without excessive difficulty using the 1976 tenant income files.)

Several questions can be raised about the utility of the proposed system. For instance, why should the Authority receive a double subsidy, that is, partial property tax relief and tax exempt bond financing *plus* full Section 8 Existing subsidies? One response is that today no one really knows what it costs to operate public housing (including an allowance for investment). Even if the PFS was accurate six years ago, problems of adjusting for inflation and technical difficulties undermine confidence in the current estimate. Further, no reliable figures on "normal" modernization needs exist. For this reason the decision has been to tie public housing "rents" to actual market rents which can be accurately measured.[10] It is very hard to believe, for example, that the Chicago Housing Authority—whose projects and tenants were described in chapters 2 and 3—can "rent" its units for about two thirds of market rents (subsidy plus tenant contributions).

Some adjustments to the straight FMR formula may be appropriate. The increase in subsidy to any PHA might be limited to 40-50 percent. For new projects—perhaps those built since 1970—which do not have these problems, a FMR adjusted for property tax savings and tax exempt bond financing makes sense. On the other hand, the initial FMR would have to be set high enough for every PHA to cover current allowed operating expenses, ACC payments, and a minimum contribution for a modernization fund. However, too much adjusting for vintage, project size, and other factors will soon destroy the simplicity initially contemplated.

Another reason to use the apparently generous FMRs is that the Authorities provide a variety of social services that private landlords do not; unfortunately, these are highly variable both

---

10. Comparisons of current subsidy levels and those under the FMR system are complicated by the shift in the way in which modernization is financed. In effect, loan authority instead of contract authority is being appropriated each year.

among and within Authorities, and there has been no accurate accounting of their cost. Moreover, private investor-owners do get tax breaks in the form of accelerated depreciation write-offs and other factors. One recent estimate indicates these advantages are at least as large as the property tax relief.[11] Of course, if the market for rental housing is highly competitive, these savings should be passed on to renters; but for the poor, the assumption of competition—with its implied perfect information and absence of discrimination—may not be realistic. Finally, the vast majority of private market units can be more efficiently managed because they are not in projects of the scale of public housing, nor do they have the design problems and tenant profiles of public housing.

Another question about the FMR system concerns the unequal debt service levels among Authorities. Higher debt service reflects a newer mix of projects and/or greater modernization expenditures. In either case, the projects with relatively larger debt loads should be in better condition than others. The older projects without the benefit of modernization, often in older neighborhoods, will exhibit moderately higher operating costs and will require funds to set aside at a high rate to support needed improvements. Hence, a rough parity should exist between higher debt service and lower rehabilitation needs.

Problem Authorities

No matter how strong the incentives for efficient management and how generously the initial FMR level is set, it is certain that some Authorities will have severe financial problems, probably mirroring equally serious management problems. In addition to these, there will be another set of Authorities who are able to stave off financial collapse but who will be providing grossly inadequate services to tenants. No plan for revising the current system is complete without explicit consideration of how to deal with these Authorities.

PHAs with fundamental management deficiencies need strong medicine. Modest changes in management, such as the implementation of project-based budgeting, would be insufficient. While these PHAs might actually get a project-based budgeting system in place, for example, it would be unlikely to mesh with

---

11. F. de Leeuw and L. Ozanne, "Investment in Housing and the Federal Income Tax" (Washington, D.C.: Bureau of Economic Analysis, U.S. Department of Commerce, 1979).

other systems: personnel control system, tenant assignment policies, or maintenance organization and billing system. Without such coordination, accountability (and project-based management) is still not achieved. In fact, the introduction of a new system may do more harm than good; the parallel of providing Mirage jets to Bedouin tribesmen is not too farfetched. Similarly, providing these PHAs with large blocks of modernization funds—before considering any of a large number of possible management changes, for example, tenant assignment policies to facilitate management or whether centrally organized maintenance and storage is best—could waste resources. If management is badly deficient, the accomplished modernization could be quickly depreciated.

For these Authorities, the type of comprehensive diagnosis-workout plan development-implementation process outlined at the end of chapter 8 is essential. In such cases, HUD should fund the process to whatever degree necessary. It will not be cheap if done correctly because of the amount of technical assistance provided—both in terms of the specialists involved and the several-year period over which it will be in place. Because an important part of the technical assistance provided is the training of PHA staff, there is strong reason to expect the changes to be sustained. Although this type of workout has been successfully tried on individually assisted housing projects, there is no experience yet on the large PHA scale. For this reason, it should be implemented initially in two or three PHAs, and the experience should be carefully documented. After a year, that is, after the diagnostic phase was completed and the workout plan developed, work could begin on another set of Authorities, each year others could be trained who would develop expertise and understanding of PHA operations on a systemwide basis. In light of the process just outlined, and the fact that there are probably only a handful of "critical" Authorities in the very large cities, HUD, with direct congressional approval, should withhold funding for major system changes or comprehensive modernization until they can be made part of a coherent overall program. Politically, husbanding resources may be very difficult indeed, but the efficiency gains could be especially great.

Critical issues concern the selection of Authorities for this treatment, and the relationship between HUD and the Authority during the upgrading period. Obviously, no long-tenured executive director would want his Authority selected as one in such a problematic state that the full workout is needed. New directors and local elected officials may have opposite views. Faced with potential recalcitrance, the necessary authority to require a full workout should be vested in HUD. This would certainly have to be embodied in the Cooperative Agreement and may need explicit congressional approval. At the same time, some safeguards must be provided against ill-considered decisions on HUD's part. One safeguard is the magnitude of the enterprise; since HUD must bear the cost of upgrading management systems and possibly some rehabilitation expenses out of limited congressionally appropriated funds, few Authorities could be selected. Furthermore, a series of indicators of the physical condition of the projects, performance of management, and financial status of the Authority should be developed to make a prima facie case for selecting a particular Authority. Indeed, it is hard to imagine the selection process proceeding in any other way. To assure proper selections, the Congress could reserve a review of the selection to itself in the same way it now examines regulations proposed by HUD for promulgation. This step appears unnecessary to us but could be worthwhile if necessary to induce Congress to include this element in the revised system.

The other question concerns who is in control once an Authority has been selected. In the best of all worlds, the Authority and HUD would agree on the validity of the problems defined in the diagnostic stage and then agree on a plan for improvement. When such cooperation is absent, the HUD view as expressed through the team at the site and the local area office should dominate. However, an explicit appeal process must be defined, with, perhaps, HUD's assistant secretary for housing as the final arbiter.

There is no easy way to deal with pervasive, badly deficient management. The strongest feature of the approach suggested here is the likelihood of fundamental and sustained change resulting from the intervention.

Efficiency Incentives

The FMR funding system contains several incentives for the PHA to conduct its operations efficiently. Some stem from the joint funding of operating and modernization activities and some from the way in which distressed Authorities will be treated.

The incentive for linking the funding of operations and modernization is clear: any savings from day-to-day operations are clearly available for modernization.[12] Furthermore, the value of keeping current with routine maintenance rises sharply—and hence the amount of rehabilitation and replacements required falls—because there is no additional funding source available for this purpose. If the principles just enunciated for the Authority were effectively transmitted directly to individual projects through a capital-and-operations, project-based budgeting system, very careful strategic economic decisions could be made at this key level.

An additional incentive for efficiency arises by replacing the current modernization system that capriciously generates annual funding levels to the individual PHAs for priority work items only. The revised system provides greater certainty of future modernization funding, and greater freedom to the Authority to use its funds would foster comprehensive modernization planning and plan implementation.

But what if incentives are insufficient to guard against the increased funds simply being squandered? First, the requirement of an independent annual audit of every PHA's books would continue. This audit itself could be substantially strengthened to ensure proper allocation of cost items to specific accounts, for example.[13] Based on this information, improvements in performance could be requested where necessary. Second, a broad review of modernization plans and costs by the HUD field office would be implemented to assure reasonable standards and expenditures. (This would be much more passive than the current review.)

Ultimately, however, the principal incentive to the PHA

---

12. In theory, modernization funds cannot now be used to handle deferred maintenance but in practice these are the only funds available and they are used for this purpose.

13. The audits of new construction projects built and operated by private developers with HUD subsidies have recently been expanded to provide information on the consistency of project operations with HUD procedural regulations. See *Audit Guide for Mortgagers Having HUD Insurance or Secretary Held Multifamily Mortgages* (Washington, D.C.: Office of the Inspector General, U.S. Department of Housing and Urban Development, IG4372.1, 1978).

against gross mismanagement is the potential of its selection for the comprehensive workout. Selection would be a highly public criticism of the management of the Authority, affecting the careers of the entire echelon of top management.

The key incentive element lacking in the FMR system is one which makes the annual funding level contingent upon performance. As noted earlier, such a system requires overcoming the very difficult task of development of true performance standards. Instead, the FMR system creates incentives for the efficient use of the subsidies received by the PHA and a credible threat against long-term mismanagement.

The Transition
The funding changeover itself could be accomplished efficiently and easily. One major task would be to get reliable tenant income and other data from the PHAs for the computations. The second major issue is less tractable: the deferred maintenance and modernization backlog. Simultaneous with the funding switch something would have to be done about this.

The logical approach would be to provide funding to bring all projects up to a common minimum physical standard. This standard could be the Level II standard defined in the Office of Research's study of the investment needs of the public housing system, discussed in chapter 2. Note that the funds needed to accomplish repairs to Level II standard are being provided; the Authority itself could decide on the actual expenditure pattern. It might, for example, choose to bring some of its projects up to a higher standard immediately and defer action on some others for a time. This catch-up work should be funded outside the new payment scheme, that is, these ACCs would be paid for directly by the department whereas existing ACC obligations would be paid by the Authorities. There would be a strong incentive to expend these funds as soon as possible, consistent with comprehensive planning including tenant input, because of the erosive effects of current inflation levels.

Only badly distressed Authorities needing a comprehensive diagnostic, detailed management improvement plan, and implementation sequence, involving heavy technical assistance would need to delay modernization expenditures. In these cases, delay of modernization expenditures to complement management changes is strongly preferred.

The discussion now shifts from a system that might be to the public housing system as it is. In the remainder of this chapter, problems of immediate concern are raised and suggestions for their amelioration or resolution are offered.

WHO SHOULD BE HOUSED?

Tenant mix is critical to management regardless of the type of funding mechanism. The issues addressed here are tenant mix and the strategic use of other housing programs. In fact, use of programs in concert is one way to favorably change the mix of public housing tenants. Before exploring a complementary use of programs, we first look at what the Authorities could do for themselves within the public housing program.

What constitutes a good mix of tenants? This is, indeed, a difficult question. Congress (as part of the Housing and Community Development Act of 1974) and HUD have set economic integration as an objective;[14] and HUD has attempted to foster racial integration as well. Although the exact reasoning behind setting the economic integration goal is far from clear, it is at least in part that heterogeneity is valuable because people will observe "better" attributes of their neighbors and want to emulate them. Thus, households with higher incomes will probably have an employed member—a virtue others may emulate. Actually, the heterogeneity approach is based on unduly indirect reasoning. A more immediate rationale governing admissions could be that residing in public housing is a privilege and not a right; it is a privilege, made possible by a large housing subsidy for generally good quality housing, earned by a prior and sustained record of being an at least minimally responsible tenant. Heterogeneity may or may not be achieved, but more importantly, the manageability of public housing will be enhanced by careful tenant screening. At the same time, however, PHAs cannot adopt policies which clearly work against tenant heterogeneity or systematically exclude any group on arbitrary grounds.

---

14. On the history and rationale of the congressional action see Ellen Gesmer, "Discrimination in Public Housing Under the Housing and Community Development Act of 1974: A Critique of the New Haven Experience," *Urban Law Annual*, no. 13, pp. 49-80.

The income limits of 22 Authorities in the largest cities reviewed in chapter 6 demonstrated that several Authorities have decided only to serve the very poor. Income heterogeneity is effectively prevented. It is certainly unclear how these PHAs attempt to comply with congressional intent in this area. Indeed, the General Accounting Office has found little movement toward satisfying congressional intent.[15]

Furthermore, other data reviewed showed little consistent use of the screening tools available under the regulations—for example, home visits, credit checks, checks on rent-paying history. Given the management problems caused by difficult tenants and the time consuming and tortuous eviction procedures, this is simply amazing. Likewise, few PHAs in the largest cities have set changing their tenant profiles as an admissions objective; but this has been done by some Authorities.[16] Of course, where the PHA already has a tenantry which facilitates management, such an objective is unnecessary. But it is surely the case that the PHAs could do more to help themselves.

Several things might be done to sharpen self-interest. First, through legislation, Congress could clarify the screening latitude that is embodied in the regulations. While the basic injunction against screening criteria discriminating against classes of tenants must be sustained, the courts have tended to broaden the list of reasons for which a tenant cannot be rejected. Currently, every tenant who is denied admission is entitled to an informal hearing. This costly procedure may be justified, but the (actual or feared) incidence of applicants requesting such hearings would certainly be reduced by clarifying legislation. Similar clarification would be helpful on the ability of Authorities to actively seek an economically integrated tenantry; attempts by some Authorities to move in this direction have been blocked by the courts.[17] Removing the specter of further judicial intervention and reducing the likelihood of hearings would remove a major disincentive to more comprehensive tenant screening.

15. "Serving a Broader Economic Range of Families in Public Housing Could Reduce Operating Subsidies" (Washington, D.C.: U.S. General Accounting Office, 1979).

16. See Ellen Gesmer, "Discrimination in Public Housing Under the Housing and Community Development Act of 1974."

17. For more on these points, see J. S. Fuerst and R. Petty, "Public Housing in the Courts: Pyrrhic Victories for the Poor."

A second step, aimed at attracting some higher-income tenants, would entail a small modification to the performance funding system or the FMR system were it adopted. Under the current PFS, this year's rent roll (i.e., tenant contributions) becomes the basis of next year's projected rent which is subtracted dollar for dollar from the maximum potential subsidy payment. Thus there is little incentive to increase a tenant's contributions. If, by contrast, only 85 percent of incremental increases in the rent roll were deducted, the cumulative incentive over several years could be substantial. Indeed, it would probably be necessary to set a maximum reduction, that is, rent rolls used in calculating PFS could not be less than 80 percent of the actual rent rolls.[18] A similar procedure of discounting income increases, possibly above inflation, could also be implemented under the FMR system. Serious questions still remain about the value of a goal attracting higher-income tenants as opposed to more responsible tenants, when hard evidence is generally absent on the relationship of household behavior to its income or other characteristics for households residing in large public housing projects. Furthermore, the type of incentive discussed is in conflict with the goal of administrative simplification.

The third avenue to changing the tenant profile is to require more comprehensive screening by regulation. Authorities could be mandated to do credit checks and home visits, for example. This is a possibility, and one that deserves full congressional and Administration consideration. Two arguments against it come quickly to mind. One is that such a requirement on a universal basis is expensive and inefficient. A partial response to this objection is to make more rigorous screening applicable only to families (as opposed to the elderly) and possibly having some cut-off by Authority or city size. Or, the determination of those PHAs that must do additional screening might be left to the area office's discretion, but the HUD field staff is already overworked and seldom has the opportunity to really understand an Authority's problems. The second argument is that it

---

18. For example, an Authority with 2,500 units and annual tenant contributions of $1,000 per year, would, under a 15 percent rise in tenant incomes and being allowed to keep 15 percent of the rent increment, realize about $55,000 additional income in the first year. In the third year, its incremental income from this source would be about $200,000.

would not work: if the PHA is not behind it, it will be poorly administered, despite occasional HUD protestations. The past problems with proper certification of incomes, despite clear regulations on what must be verified, are especially instructive and discouraging.[19] In the end, Authorities must be convinced that careful screening and the establishment and implementation of tenantry goals, be they greater income heterogeneity or reduced family size, are in their own best interest; they must also be convinced that they are legally feasible.

In addition to using tenant selection criteria to alter tenant profiles in the projects now under management, the PHAs can also use other programs and newly developed public housing to this end. Unfortunately, the strategic use of programs was seen in chapter 9 to be exceptional. Reducing project density has been accomplished by a few PHAs by a combination of serving large family applicants through the Section 8 Existing program and replacing very large families as they leave the projects with smaller ones. Large families have also been served by scattered-site, preferably single-family, units developed as new public housing projects.

How might these and similar program uses be encouraged? The creative use of Section 8 Existing could be fostered by the allocation of "bonus" units from the secretary's resource pool to those PHAs using the program best. It would probably be wise to set this up initially on a formula basis, for example, one bonus unit for every 10 Section 8 units used to achieve a particular strategic objective. Given the constraint on resources, participation should be limited to projects with demonstrable problems of excessive density.

Several possibilities exist for the development of new housing under the public housing program or the Section 8 new construction or substantial rehabilitation financed through PHA bonds. Developers contend (probably rightly) that single-family housing is more costly to develop or rehabilitate than multifamily projects. Cost limits could be raised to facilitate development when it is part of an overall PHA management improvement strategy involving reduced project densities. If such a

19. The only data currently available are from PHA administration of the Section 8 Existing program. See J. L. Stucker, "Importance of Income Verification in the Section 8 Housing Assistance Payments Program," *Occasional Papers in Housing and Community Affairs*, U.S. Department of Housing and Urban Development, forthcoming.

strategy were coupled with the units being built in a neighborhood targeted for comprehensive assistance under the Community Development Block Grant program, the additional cost of single-family development could be made an allowable expense under the CDBG program and be paid for locally.[20]

Finally, the possibility of using development funds to purchase existing homes—so-called acquisition without rehabilitation—for use by families should not be overlooked. In the past, the Congress and the Administration have both opposed this use of development funds on the ground that there was no addition to the stock of housing. This approach may, however, retain public housing in the system for a longer period, thus increasing the net housing available to the needy. Likewise, it may be critical to preventing widespread abandonment in fragile neighborhoods, which would again reduce the stock of available housing. Note too that acquisition without rehabilitation might be the only way in which some communities will permit the development of any public housing (for families as opposed to projects for the elderly). In sum, there is again much that the Authorities could do if they so chose. Some initial incentive may be required, however, to introduce or reinforce strategic program use.

CHANGES WITHIN THE EXISTING FUNDING SYSTEM

Modernization Funding

The review of the current modernization program in chapter 5 pointed out several serious deficiencies. One concerned the level and distribution of appropriated funds. Because HUD has lacked any basis on which to make a firm estimate of the modernization needs of the public housing inventory, the modernization funding requests made to the OMB and the Congress have been skeptically reviewed although generally funded at the requested level. HUD's research office has now developed reliable estimates through surveys and physical inspections of some 400 projects.[21] These should become the basis for two major actions: (a) a multiyear program presented to the OMB

---

20. Land cost write down is now an eligible activity under CDBG but construction subsidy is not; it would require a legislative amendment, therefore, to permit this use of CDBG funds.

21. See chapter 2 for a further description.

and the Congress that would bring the modernization program up to date by funding the backlog of deferred maintenance; and (b) establishment of a system to allocate the annual national modernization appropriations among Authorities.

The hallmark of the revised system is to encourage comprehensive investment planning. The lack of such planning was documented as a major problem inherent in the current "priority work item" system, causing many improvements to be made inefficiently. Moreover, Authorities are not now encouraged to confront fundamental decisions. If the total modernization needs of a project are never considered in the aggregate, it will certainly not be possible to decide if the full incremental expenditure is justifiable on economic grounds. The value of comprehensive project modernization versus the cost of new projects must be considered, and these calculations must include not only the capital costs but operating costs and the length of time the project will be serviceable.

Part of comprehensive modernization planning concerns project "thinning." In recent years, thinning has virtually ceased to be discussed because of HUD policy statements opposing the loss of any units. Yet thinning may be essential to allow proper management of the remaining units. If this question is not confronted, modernization funds may simply be wasted as deterioration will quickly befall the investments. Furthermore, it is often not realized that there are three ways to thin out projects: (a) the actual destruction of some buildings and reuse of space for other purposes; (b) extensive rehabilitation where units are converted to either smaller ones (in which children density is reduced) or larger ones (where overall density falls); or, (c) leasing units to smaller households than would normally be placed in these units. The first option need only be used under extraordinary conditions where either the original site plan made inadequate provision for recreation space or adjacent alternative recreation sites are not available.

In this regard, it is important to note that draft regulations published at the end of 1979 on demolitions appear weak. They make tenant opinions and project densities "secondary criteria" in assessing the need for demolition. One primary criterion is the "current and projected needs for low-income housing in the jurisdiction"—presence of "need" requires a one-for-one replacement of demolished units. The other primary criterion is economic: rehabilitation is considered feasible if it is no more expensive than new construction; no mention is made of expected life of the rehabilitated structure. Marketability is a secondary criterion.[22] Marketability, management considerations, tenant views, and proper economic analysis should be given equal weight in making the demolition decision.

But what is the vehicle for accomplishing this? Beyond dismantling the work-priority system, the amount of modernization funds made available annually must be made adequate and dependable. Before modernization funds can be allocated, however, two tasks are essential. First, standards for modernization must be established. Today there are three distinct areas in which investments are being made in the public housing inventory—regular modernization, retrofitting projects to conform with handicap accessibility standards, and retrofitting for energy efficiency—and standards must be established for each area. In the modernization area, there could be at least three standards: one conforming with minimum safety and health regulations, a higher one that brings the units up to HUD's minimum property standards as modified for rehabilitation, and yet a higher one to make projects competitive with their private market counterparts. The standards must be chosen with the mission of the public housing program more precisely defined than is presently the case and in light of the cost of accomplishing the corresponding investment. Fortunately, the study just completed by HUD's research office does give investment requirements associated with alternative standards.

Once the standard is chosen, detailed guidance must be provided to every PHA so that the definition is clear. In the absence of consistency among Authorities, there are gross inequities: some will be able to rehabilitate to a very high standard and others will be able to do very little because the funds requested from Congress will be exhausted. Because most of the necessary material has been developed as part of the investment needs study, preparing the requisite guidance should not be a time-consuming or onerous task.

The second element that must be in place before the start of the revised program is a new method of allocating funds to individual Authorities. If all PHAs base their requests for funds on the same standard—and the amount appropriated by the Congress is also for this standard—a direct allocation based on PHA

---

22. *Federal Register*, vol. 44, no. 219, pp. 65369-70.

estimates would be possible. In the absence of such compatibility, an allocation formula like that described in chapter 5 would have to be used.

Once the funds necessary to bring projects up to the standards selected had been allocated, a different allocation formula would be required—this only based on anticipated decay and depreciation rates in different types of PHAs. The development of this formula, like the one already described, would require a substantial investment of scarce research funds.

The first part of this program will be expensive; how expensive depends on the standards chosen. During the years required to accomplish the program, part of the funds appropriated for development of new projects and modernization should be allocated together under the formula just described. One technical problem entailed by funds fungibility is that development funds have 40-year ACCs while modernization funds have 20-year ACCs. Since the budget authority needed for the program is the product of the annual contract amount and the contract term, funds fungibility introduces uncertainty into the budget authority calculations.[23]

In brief, the modernization program is in desperate need of reform, particularly change to promote comprehensive planning and the best use of the available resources by the PHA. HUD must revise its method of funds allocation, and serious consideration should be given to making the funds available for development and for modernization fungible in the aggregate between the two uses. All of these changes would require congressional acquiescence; indeed, initiative by the Congress may be essential in establishing multiyear funding and aggregate funds fungibility.

---

23. This approach seems preferred to the plan proposed by HUD as part of its fiscal year 1981 budget submission. Under it, individual Authorities would be allowed to switch up to half of the development funds to be used for modernization. Funds for development are allocated on the basis of an area's housing need. There is no necessary correspondence between this need and the need of public housing modernization. Logic would seem to favor making the two allocations separately, based on separate types of need. Of course, the PHAs are delighted at the increase in modernization funds afforded by the HUD approach, but the approach is more expedient than efficient or equitable. Also there is no clear relationship between this "initiative" and long-term comprehensive modernization, as the HUD proposal continues to be tied to the priority work system.

The Performance Funding System

Some basis for determining subsidy levels besides the combined judgment of PHA and HUD officials is essential, be it the PFS or the fair market rent approach discussed earlier. Such approaches have the significant advantage of introducing certainty of funding levels and of providing a basis for funding decisions besides raw politics; if well designed, they can embody substantial positive incentives.

The research underlying the PFS and its operation were outlined in chapter 5. There, the early results of a comprehensive evaluation of the system were also noted, which indicate serious problems with the inflation factor used in updating operating subsidy levels. The evaluation, due to be completed in late 1980, will find other areas that merit improvement; this is certainly to be expected since the PFS was viewed during its development as an interim system. Building on the evaluation findings, it will probably take years of further work to develop and implement a revised system.

It is only a slight exaggeration to say that the decisions to design and implement the PFS were taken when the limitations of social science research methodologies were less appreciated than they are today.[24] With a greater understanding of the inherent difficulties, a time consuming effort in developing a new system will necessarily result. Very important data problems will have to be resolved: what are the services provided by the Authority? What is the extent of the city's contribution? Comparability in cost accounting across Authorities is essential. Further, very difficult research questions must be tackled, for example, how do project design problems affect tenant behavior and operating costs? Granting that this difficult research effort should be undertaken as speedily as possible, what should be done in the meantime?

Two broad options are available; both involve fundamental change. One is to scrap PFS and adopt the FMR system or some other system. The other is to retain the PFS with some modifications until a new system embodying standards can be developed. An unacceptable choice is to simply patch up the

---

24. For an excellent discussion of the history of research and evaluation in federal decision making, see H. Aaron, *Politics and the Professors* (Washington, D.C.: The Brookings Institution, 1978).

PFS; it is possible to do better if the necessary energy is devoted to the task.

If the PFS is retained as the primary allocation device on an interim basis, then adjustments must be made to provide the PHAs with adequate resources while the system is being revised. The initial step is the creation of a sizable block of funds to be allocated by HUD on a discretionary basis to Authorities in dire straits.[25] This may have the effect in some instances of rewarding poor management; but in the face of problems with the funding mechanism, it is not possible for HUD to admit mistakes in its funding formula and say "make do." A revised inflation factor, a critical element in the PFS, could be developed quickly and implemented, alleviating the need for the continuing use of discretionary funding. The annual change in the fair market rents established for the Section 8 Existing program could be used as the factor. These adjustments should provide adequate funding until the more basic research is completed.

GETTING ORGANIZED AT HUD CENTRAL

The cheapest criticisms of any government program are levied at the seemingly nameless and faceless bureaucracy. It should go without saying, but seldom does, that those at the Department of Housing and Urban Development responsible for the centralized administration of the public housing program work hard to discharge their duty as best they can. There has been excellent leadership in the public housing program in the past two years. There are, nonetheless, fundamental problems. Here some of these problems are listed, some reasons for their existence given, and suggestions for change offered.

Three problem areas have been highlighted in earlier chapters. The first is that the basic data on public housing are inadequate. In chapter 2, the analysis was limited because of the lack of basic physical descriptions of the projects (data essential for organizing the modernization program); in chapter 3, the descriptions of tenants were found inaccurate (presumably a problem for estimating the size of needed operating subsi-

---

25. Consistent with this thinking, the HUD fiscal year 1981 budget submission includes a one-time request for a supplemental fiscal year 1980 appropriation of $52 million to assist a dozen or so badly distressed, very large Authorities.

dies); in chapter 4, the figures on current operating expenses and reserve levels were deemed woefully inadequate; and in chapter 5, deficiencies in the accounting of modernization loan authority given to individual PHAs were seen. This is not to say that HUD could not produce many of these data under pressure. HUD could; probably the field offices would be required to get most of such data so that their other duties would suffer; and the data would be collected without adequate quality control. The point is that basic policy decisions affecting the entire program continually take place with substantial ignorance of the basic facts.

The second problem is how scarce resources and, more importantly, time have been squandered in a series of poorly conceived and executed "demonstrations." These essentially relief operations have done little to benefit the system as a whole. Evaluations have been tag-ons, and even these weak efforts have been gutted by the program office's need to make changes in mid-stream or simple lack of cooperation. Since each new Administration makes aid to distressed Authorities in this now time-honored way, we can expect the announcement from the next Administration in the late summer of 1981.

The third fundamental shortcoming is the quality of the regulations governing the program, in particular the historic insensitivity to the perverse incentives they have created. The clearest case in point is the structure of the modernization program; a program that defies Authorities to do comprehensive planning. The excuse is that there are insufficient funds available for all that needs to be done. This has been true, but before 1980, HUD had failed to develop a solid estimate of necessary resources. Hence, HUD could not request the resources from the Congress nor even submit an estimate to the Office of Management and Budget. Problems within the operating subsidy system have also been noted.

What has produced this sorry state? For any program as complex and with the legacy of difficulties of public housing to be properly administered would require a deep and continuing active interest by the secretary of HUD. No secretary in HUD's 15-year history has devoted this kind of time to the program. For secretaries and assistant secretaries, fame comes from being associated with new programs that add new services or putatively administer existing ones more efficiently and, of course, from increasing the budget and most of all, the agency's domain. The problems of public housing are so serious and the possibility of making improvements seems so remote that few of the best young civil servants will choose to be associated with public housing for fear of finding themselves permanently in its backwaters.[26] Furthermore, most of the staff has not had any real experience with public housing outside the central office, nor do they often have the opportunity to spend time in the "field." Instead, they spend a large share of their time dealing with crises, which become even more numerous as tackling the underlying problems is perpetually postponed.

The public housing program's administration must be streamlined as much as possible. The central office must be involved as little as possible in program mechanics; minimum reliance should be placed on sophisticated funding systems that require the orderly and timely massing of data for calculation deployments. To some extent complex systems will be necessary, but the principle of Ockham's razor should be applied wherever possible. The byword is now to carefully tailor the subsidies to each PHA to fit each PHA's unique needs. But if the systems are beyond staff capabilities to properly administer, there ought to be a willingness to accept less tailoring in exchange for funding systems that work.

Realistic staffing levels and field experience must be developed. Improvement in staffing must be accompanied by changes in the way business is done with the PHAs if these resources are not simply to be absorbed into more efficient fire fighting. Of course, the size of the staff and its skill mix depend heavily on the type of systems chosen. Adoption of the FMR-based funding system would enormously lessen the staff burdens at HUD central compared to present operations.

Finally, HUD's data problems are legend, and OMB's frustration with them is chronicled in a drawer of memoranda. Within the central office, responsibilities are split between the program office which is responsible for submitting the data and the computer operators who simply process what they are given. Because the PHAs and the field offices have little to no incentive to submit high quality data, and the central office has virtually no capacity for checking it, the classic "garbage in, garbage out"

---

26. By this criterion public housing today is not alone; its most prominent companion is management of multifamily housing built under the Section 236 program in the late 1960s and early 1970s.

routine exists with a vengeance. Most data are required on a population basis; sampling techniques have not yet been used, except in back-up studies commissioned by the research office. It is a task that only the undersecretary can take on, but to date none has meaningfully done so.

* * * * *

A central theme of this chapter, and indeed of the entire book, has been to look comprehensively at public housing, to see it as a multifarious totality. The specifics of the modernization program, unit demolition regulations, tenant admission standards, and the operating subsidy funding system are closely interrelated. Ad hoc tampering with one element or another may achieve one goal but send disincentives reverberating through the other chambers in the system. Congress and the Administration must take a broad view and act constructively. Substantial improvement can be realized quickly and at modest cost to preserve this valuable housing resource for the nation's low- and moderate-income families.

APPENDICES

Appendix A

SUMMARY OF SAMPLING PROCEDURE AND
NOTES ON HUD MODERNIZATION STANDARDS

The contractor estimates from HUD records that there are 2,700 Public Housing Authorities with 10,000 projects containing 1,222,079 low-rent public housing units. In order to estimate the costs of modernization, accessibility and energy conservation retrofit, a 4 percent statistically significant random sample was drawn of 400 projects across the country. Detailed field surveys were performed on these projects so that sample cost estimates in each of the three study areas could be made. These costs were then to be stratified within the sample based upon quantitative cost models developed during the estimating process. Strata were identified based upon a random survey of the first 200 randomly selected projects.

It was found that after having surveyed 200 random projects, estimated costs per dwelling unit for Level I and II were in the $0-$800 range and $801-$10,000 respectively. The lower cost projects had characteristics that represented 85 percent of the total public housing stock. However, these projects required the least amount of modernization funds. Using an internally generated HUD list of 20 problem projects, that is, those projects requiring large amounts of modernization funds, a "distressed" stratum was identified that provided the basis for selecting random projects in the latter category. The total 400 projects were initially categorized or stratified as follows:

Note: Information from Perkins and Will and the Ehrenkrantz Group, *Preliminary Cost Estimates,* and from their detailed analysis plan, vol. 1.

Category	Characteristics	Number of Projects
DISTRESSED	200 dwelling units 10% Vacancy	75 including HUD 20 "distressed"
DISTRESSED CONTROL	200 dwelling units 10% Vacancy	75
RANDOM	Replacement/ Completion	50
RANDOM	First 200	200
	TOTAL	400 Projects

NOTE ON MODERNIZATION STANDARDS

The standards developed for modernization (Levels I, II, and III) are standards exclusively for existing building. There are, therefore, a number of limiting factors that would not be present in standards for new construction. Among the more important limiting factors are the following:

1. Design, planning, and dimensional considerations are addressed in the *Modernization Standards* only when they directly affect health, safety, or relevant qualities of living that can be addressed without major construction expenditure.

   Example: *Minimum Property Standards* room size requirements are not included in these standards whereas National Fire Protection Association requirements for egress exit door widths are included in Modernization Levels I and II.

2. The *Modernization Standards* are limited to observable and/or measurable criteria which can be evaluated without the disruption of any portion of the building.

3. Modernization performance standards for mechanical systems are limited to observable criteria that can be ascertained by the field inspectors through inspection and information obtained from project managers and residents.

   Example: *Modernization Standards* for elevators address the operation and physical condition of cabs, control panels and leveling whereas *Minimum Property Standards'* requirements for speed and capacity are not included.

4. Standards established in the *Minimum Property Standards Guideline for New Construction* that cannot be retrofitted to existing buildings without unjustified expenses have been omitted. In these cases, the satisfaction of the standard's intent is considered sufficient. All new work performed for compliance with the modernization Levels I, II, and III shall comply with the Guidelines for New Construction.

   Example: For Level II, MPS 508-7.1 requires that building entrance door hardware serving more than two families conform to Federal Standards FF-H-00106b, Series 161 or 86. It will be considered that existing locking systems that provide required security and are in good working condition will comply with Level II standards.

5. When the local Public Housing Authority considers it necessary, more stringent local codes and standards shall be met.

   Example: In areas receiving a greater than average amount of rain or snow, drainage and ramp ratio requirements become more critical to public health and safety. Where they are more stringent, adherence to local codes shall be required.

6. Modernization standards only address repair items that in aggregate, are substantial in scope, involve expenditures that would otherwise materially distort the level trend of maintenance expense, are not the result of PHA failure to perform adequate maintenance during the period after April 1, 1975, and may include replacement of structural elements due to normal wear and tear by items of substantially the same kind. Recurrent short-term items are not included.

   Example: The *Modernization Standards* address conditions of kitchen and bathroom sinks due to normal wear whereas they do not address leaky faucets or missing washers.

Appendix B

DEFINITIONS OF ACCOUNTING TERMS USED IN PUBLIC HOUSING

1. Administrative expenses include administrative salaries, legal expenses, staff training, travel, accounting and auditing fees, and "sundry" expenses.
2. Tenant services accounts are charged with cost incurred for services directly "related to meeting residents'" needs and supporting a wholesome living environment. Includes such things as resident transportation and admission fare to recreation sites; materials and expendable equipment for games; resident publications, etc.
3. Utilities: fees for water, electricity, gas, and other fuel plus associated labor costs to provide services, for example, boiler stoker.
4. Ordinary maintenance: labor, materials, and contract costs for routine project maintenance and operational services such as janitorial services, elevator services, extermination, and rubbish and garbage collection.
5. Protective services: labor, materials, and contract costs for services to protect projects and tenants.
6. General expenses include insurance, payments to local government in lieu of taxes, terminal leave payments, employee benefit contributions, collection losses, interest on administrative and sundry notes, and other general expenses.
7. Total routine expenses include expenditures for administration, tenant service, utilities, ordinary maintenance and operations, protective services, and general operations.

8. Nonroutine maintenance and capital expenditures are payments for maintenance, repairs, replacements, and additions beyond routine and preventive maintenance that are approved by HUD to be paid with operating funds. Excludes such expenditures financed from modernization program funds.
9. Total operating expenditures equals total routine expenditures plus nonroutine maintenance and capital expenditures plus rental payments for board units.

Note: For more complete definitions, see *Low Rent Housing Accounting Handbook* (Washington, D.C.: U.S. Department of Housing and Urban Development, 1969), and subsequent revisions.

Appendix C

ANALYSIS OF PUBLIC HOUSING
OPERATING EXPENDITURES

The substantial variation among the large Authorities in our sample in per-unit-month operating expenditures cries for an explanation. Numerous hypotheses can and have been advanced in this regard, some having to do with the vintage, configuration, and construction of the structures, some concerned with the practices of project managers, and some concerned with the characteristics of occupants.

Careful analyses of PHA operating expenses using a cost function approach have been conducted by de Leeuw and by Rydell. Both analyses have used a multiple regression model to explain variations in operating expenses among a sample of PHAs or projects at a point in time or over time in terms of project and tenant characteristics. They were both completed almost ten years ago and were part of the early attempt to understand the seeming explosion in public housing costs that began in the mid-1960s. De Leeuw analyzes Authoritywide expenses, and his data are plagued as a consequence by all of the limitations noted in the text. Rydell uses only figures for projects of the New York City Housing Authority, which may be on a more consistent accounting base than data from various PHAs.

As noted, de Leeuw analyzed the variance in operating costs per unit in 23 large Authorities for the four years between 1965 and 1968.[1] (Note that operating costs as defined here include

---

1. F. de Leeuw, *Operating Costs in Public Housing: A Financial Crisis* (Washington, D.C.: The Urban Institute, 1974).

utility costs.) Because the analysis uses the PHA as the unit of observation, it is necessary to account for regional differences in cost; variables for the cost of living, utility prices, and local government wage rates are included in the regression model for this purpose. The structural variable included is the average age of the units in the PHA. The included tenant attributes are minors per unit, the proportion of households on relief, the proportion of households with no wage earner, and the proportion of households headed by a nonwhite. The number of units under management is included to capture economies or diseconomies of scale.

The results of de Leeuw's analysis of the change in operating costs 1965-68 are summarized in table C-1.[2] The first column shows the change in the variables over the period; thus, the average increase in per month operating costs was $10.57. The second column gives the coefficients from the estimated linear regression,[3] and the final column shows how much each of the variables contributed to the rise in total operating costs. General inflation and utility prices (or cross-sectional differences in the cost of living)[4] account for over half of the difference. Older units are found to cost more to operate due to depreciation, and diseconomies of scale are found to raise per-unit-month (pum) costs for the largest PHAs. Interestingly, the additional costs associated with more minors and no-wage-earner households are of the same order of magnitude as are the vintage and scale effects.

These results confirmed the expectations of many observers. Of particular note was that according to this analysis only a comparatively small share of the variance in costs was under the PHAs' control; and to make changes in this area—some associated with tenant characteristics—could easily be at odds with HUD's occupancy regulations.

The second analysis of operating costs was conducted by

2. Tests for differences in the coefficients of models estimated for the individual years showed no significant differences. Hence, the models offer a cross-sectional explanation of variance as well as the time series one suggested in the text.

3. The model reported in the table explained 23 percent of the variance in total operating costs. All of the reported coefficients are significant at the 5 percent level or higher.

4. The cost of living and government wage rate variables were found to be highly correlated; so this conclusion applies to both variables.

Table C-1

EXPLANATION OF 1965-68 RISE IN PUBLIC HOUSING
OPERATING COSTS, TWENTY-THREE CITIES

	1965-68 change (Average of 23 cities)	Co-efficient	Contribution to the rise in total cost
Costs per unit per month ($s)	10.57	—	—
General cost of living ($s per month)	40.32	.15	6.05
Utility price (per month)	.64	.72	.46
Age of stock (years)	1.95	.50 [a]	.98
Units in stock (000 units)	1.05	.46	.48
Minors per unit (number)	.05	5.28	.26
Units with no wage earner (percentage)	2.36	.30	.71
Interaction of price level and other characteristics [b]			2.29
Total	—	—	$11.23 [c]

Source: F. de Leeuw, *Operating Costs in Public Housing*, table 13.

a. In the regression, the reciprocal of age times 100 (rather than age itself) was a variable. The regression coefficient of –1.12 is here converted to a linear form, valid for average ages of approximatly 15 years.

b. In the regression the physical characteristic variables and tenant characteristic variables were multiplied by the general price level. The contribution of these variables to rising costs thus depends on (a) their own increase and (b) the increase in the price level. These two effects have been separated, the latter being reported under "interaction of price level and other characteristics."

c. The total "explanation," $11.23, differs slightly from the total cost rise, $10.57, because of regression errors and the approximations described in notes a and b.

Rydell for projects in the New York City Housing Authority.[5] The variance in the vintage and physical configurations of the projects provided the needed variance; and New York is almost unique in having a very long time series of reliable data, stretching all the way back to 1921. Furthermore, the Authority has consistently had a "good as new" maintenance policy which provides a constant maintenance standard from which to consider changes in operating costs.

5. C. P. Rydell, *Factors Affecting Maintenance and Operating Costs in Federal Public Housing Projects* (New York: New York City Rand Institute, 1970).

Rydell's analysis examined only the effects of several physical attributes on costs; however, since one variable, average unit size, is undoubtedly correlated with family size, this may explain some variance actually associated with tenant profiles. Table C-2 presents the estimates of the 1959-67 time period separately for maintenance and operating expenses.[6] The body of the table gives the annual percentage changes in expense per unit associated with the variable listed in the table stub. The total increase is divided into two parts: those having to do with time factors (inflation and project aging) and those having to do with scale factors (project size, etc.).

The results of greatest interest for present purposes are comparisons between the two sets of estimates. While project aging causes a substantial increase in maintenance expenses, it has no effect on operating expenses. Larger projects are associated with both lower maintenance and operating costs. (Note by contrast that large *Authorities* were found by de Leeuw to have higher operating costs.) On the other hand, large unit sizes and more occupants per unit cause a very substantial increase in maintenance expenses and a less but still significant increase in

Table C-2

PERCENTAGE CHANGES IN MAINTENANCE AND
OPERATING EXPENSES IN NEW YORK CITY PROJECTS
1959–67

	Maintenance Expenses	Operating Expenses
Time Factors (percentage per year)		
Price inflation and other	4.03	3.78
Project age	2.01	−.17*
Scale Factors (percentage per 10 percent scale increase)		
Project size	−.86	−.80
Average building size	−.20*	−.16
Average unit size	7.57	2.29

Source: C. P. Rydell, *Factors Affecting Maintenance and Operating Costs*, tables 14, 16.
 * Variable not statistically significant at 5 percent level or higher.

---

6. The underlying regression models explain 57 and 78 percent of the increase in maintenance and operating expenses, respectively.

operating outlays. Finally, larger buildings are slightly cheaper to operate.

Both the de Leeuw and Rydell analyses confirm and quantify relationships that many experienced housing people find reasonable. They provide a ready basis for helping understand the variance in costs among Authorities, but they also provide precious little guidance on how to control costs in PHAs and projects that have costs greater than these models would predict.

Appendix D

ESTIMATES OF TOTAL SUBSIDY REQUIREMENT

To prepare budgets for action by the Office of Management and Budget and the Congress, it is necessary to estimate before the beginning of each federal fiscal year what the total operating subsidy requirement will be for that year. These estimates are calculated by simulating the expected PFS subsidy entitlement of each of a sample of 133 PHAs for the year concerned and then statistically generalizing from the sample to all PHAs receiving subsidies annually.

The individual subsidy amounts for the sampled PHAs are calculated by means of the funding formula described in chapter 5. In calculating the 133 expected entitlements, assumptions must therefore be made as to (a) the Allowable Expense Level of each PHA; (b) the rate of inflation by which each PHA's operating expenses will increase; (c) the cost of utilities to the PHA; (d) the expenses PHAs will incur in carrying out IPA Audits; (e) income; and (f) the Unit Months Available to each PHA. In order to generalize from the sample to the nation as a whole, a number of sampling multipliers are employed.

Further complicating the estimation process is the federal budget cycle which requires that the first subsidy estimate for any fiscal year be made more than 16 months before the beginning of that fiscal year. That estimate is then updated at the start of the federal fiscal year. The first estimate employs data from the sample PHAs describing their condition two years before the beginning of the federal fiscal year and three years before the subsidy funds in question will be spent. Therefore, this early estimate requires a 3-years-forward projec-

225

tion of the allocations to PHAs; the updated estimate is a pro-
jection two years into the future. Figure D-1 illustrates the
chronology of subsidy estimates.

Figure D-1

CHRONOLOGY OF SUBSIDY ESTIMATES

Date of Estimate	Budget Year and Status of Estimate	Date of Input Data	Year Subsidy Funds to be Obligated
June 1975	First FY 77 estimate	1974	1977
June 1976	Updated FY 77 estimate	1975	1977
	First FY 78 estimate	1975	1978
June 1977	Updated FY 78 estimate	1976	1978
	First FY 79 estimate	1976	1979

The assumptions underlying each of the subsidy estimates
are based on the best available information at the time. However, as the subsidy estimates are updated, changes in the input
assumptions are inevitable, and changes in the estimates themselves are, therefore, inherent in the PFS. In addition, the final
estimate is still only an estimate and may differ from the
eventual obligation when all of the PHAs have finally calculated their subsidy entitlements by the end of the federal fiscal
year.

Appendix E

DEFINITIONS OF INCOME AND TENANT CONTRIBUTIONS TO RENT

Var. No.	Variable Name and Method of Calculation
1	*Annual family income determined by PHA for rent:* This is the income calculated by the PHA upon which the tenant's rent is based. It may or may not be calculated in accordance with HUD low-rent, public housing regulations. If a tenant contact was required to obtain household income figures, this amount was computed by the Institute in accordance with the method the PHA uses to determine income.
2	*Gross family income according to HUD regulations:* (LRPH and Section 8): This amount is calculated by subtracting from total family income actually received, and "temporary nonrecurring or sporadic" income specifically excluded as income by HUD regulations, namely "(1) casual, sporadic and irregular gifts, and amounts which are specifically received for, or are a reimbursement of, the cost of illness or medical care; (2) lump sum additions to family assets, such as, but not necessarily limited to, inheritances, insurance payments, including payments under health and accident insurance and workmen's compensation, capital gains, and settlements for personal or property losses; (3) amounts of educational scholarships paid

Source: L. Loux and S. Sadacca, "Estimates of Rent and Tenant Income Levels in Public Housing Under Various Definitions," (Washington, D.C.: The Urban Institute, Working Paper 247-1, 1976), table 1.

directly to the student or to the educational institution
and amounts paid by the United States Government to a
veteran for use in meeting the cost of tuition, fees, and
books, to the extent that such amounts are so used; (4)
relocation payments made pursuant to Title II of the Uniform Relocation Assistance and Real Property Acquisition
Policies Act of 1970; (5) the value of the coupon allot-
ments for the purchase of food in excess of the amount
actually charged an eligible household pursuant to the
Food Stamp Act of 1964; (6) payments received by participants or volunteers in programs pursuant to the Do-
mestic Volunteer Service Act of 1973; (7) payments received by participants in other publicly assisted programs
as reimbursement for out-of-pocket expenses incurred
(special equipment, clothing, transportation, reimbursement for child care, and so forth, which are made solely
to allow participation in a specific program and cannot be
used for other purposes)."

These listed exclusions are quoted from LRPH regulations,
but are comparable to Section 8 excluded income. Therefore, this variable is used in both LRPH and Section 8 income computations.

3   *Family income as determined by HUD regulations (LRPH):
     This is the income that would be used in determining fam-
     ily contribution if the PHA followed the current LRPH
     regulations.* This figure is calculated according to the fol-
     lowing formula:

     For nonelderly: Gross family income as determined in
     Variable 2 above minus the following amounts:

     a. $300 for each minor (household member 17 or under)
     b. $300 for each full-time student age 18 or older
     c. $300 for each disabled or handicapped household
         member 18 or older
     d. If both the head of the household and spouse are
         working, the first $300 of the spouse's income
     e. The amount of unusual occupational expenses, "but
         only to the extent to which such expenses exceed nor-
         mal and usual expenses incidental to the type of em-

Var. No.	Variable Name and Method of Calculation

ployment engaged in." (The following expenses which were deducted by some PHAs were not considered "unusual" expenses for purposes of this study: the employee's Social Security tax (FICA), union dues, normal transportation expenses, and the like.)

   f. Payments for child care or care of the sick so the head or spouse can work

   g. Medical expenses in excess of 3% of total family income where such expenses are not covered by insurance

   h. 5% of gross family income (Variable 2)

For elderly: Gross family income as determined in Variable 2 minus the deductions listed in (a) through (h) above, except 10% of gross family income is deducted in item (h) instead of 5%.

4 *Maximum family contribution according to current HUD LRPH regulations* (monthly): This is the amount of family contribution that would be charged if the PHA charged the maximum family contribution according to current LRPH regulations. This figure is 25% of the family income calculated in Variable 3 above (divided by 12 to determine the monthly amount). NOTE: Welfare recipients in states which mandate that the amount designated for shelter allowance is the amount the PHA must charge for rent are assumed to continue paying that amount, that is, their current rent.

5 *Section 8 income for family contribution:* This is the income that would be used in determining family contribution if the Section 8 definition applied:

   A. If the household had 6 or more minors, or has medical expenses in excess of 3% of gross family income (Variable 2), this figure is gross family (Variable 2) plus 10% of family assets over $5,000. (NOTE: For purposes of this preliminary analysis, the Section 8 terms "Large, very low-income family and Very large lower income family" are defined as any family with 6 or more minors. Additional analyses will determine

Var.
No.   Variable Name and Method of Calculation

---

whether substitution of this definition for the actual
Section 8 definition has much impact on the statistics.)
B. For all other families, this figure is gross family income
(Variable 2) minus the following amounts:
   a. $300 for each minor (household member 17 or
      under)
   b. $300 for each full-time student 18 or over
   c. payments for child care for children 12 and under
      or for care of the sick so a household member can
      work
   d. medical expenses in excess of 3% of total family
      income.

6 *Section 8 family contribution determination* (monthly):
This is the amount of family contribution determined in
accordance with Section 8 income and family contribution definitions. The amount is calculated as follows:

For households with 6 or more minors or with medical
expenses in excess of 3% of gross family income, 15% of
gross family income plus 10% of family assets over $5,000
(Variable 5(A) above).

For all other households: 25% of the Section 8 income
determined in Variable 5(B) above.

7 *Amount of increase in family contribution if revenue
standard (25%/15%) were applied to current PHA-defined
income to determine family contribution:*
A. For families with 6 or more minors or families with
   medical expenses in excess of 3% of income, the current PHA-defined income (Variable 1) is multiplied by
   .15 and divided by 12 to determine monthly amount of
   family contribution;
B. For all other families, the current PHA-defined income
   is multiplied by .25 and divided by 12 to determine
   monthly amount of family contribution.

Note: Welfare recipients in states which mandate that the amount designated for shelter allowance is the amount the PHA must charge for rent
are assumed to continue paying that amount, i.e., their current rent.

Var. No.	Variable Name and Method of Calculation

The amount of current family contribution is subtracted from the amounts so calculated to determine the amount of increase.

8   *Monthly family contribution* (LRPH): This amount is obtained from PHA records only and is the sum of monthly contract rent paid by the tenant (Variable 16), plus estimated monthly tenant contribution for utilities (Variable 17).

Note: Welfare recipients in states which mandate that the amount designated for shelter allowance is the amount the PHA must charge for rent are assumed to continue paying that amount, i.e., their current rent.

Appendix F

REGRESSIONS OF AN ADJUSTED INCOME AND TENANT CONTRIBUTIONS

Table F-1

REGRESSION ANALYSIS OF ADJUSTED INCOME OF TENANTS IN FIVE PHAs [a]

Independent Variables	PHA				
	Los Angeles	Atlanta	Chicago	Baltimore	Philadelphia
Constant	-30.8	5.65	-34.4	10.0	-.16
	(5.13)[b c]	(2.03)[c]	(6.30)[c]	(1.46)	(.03)
Household's gross income	.99	.91	1.04	.90	.89
	(99.0)[c]	(100.)[c]	(106.)[c]	(75.0)[c]	(80.9)[c]
Household head or spouse is handicapped = 1; zero otherwise	- 9.60	-10.20	13.09	-12.37	-11.07
	1.00	(3.43)[c]	(1.31)	(1.61)	(1.69)
Number of students over Age 18 in household	-19.65	-25.10	- 3.56	-18.30	-28.43
	(2.63)[c]	(5.67)[c]	(.86)	(2.89)	(5.34)[c]
Household head is over Age 62 = 1; zero otherwise	4.06	7.06	-10.39	-10.81	- 2.90
	(.48)	(2.27)[c]	(1.02)	(1.43)	(.48)
Number of children under 19 in household	-19.05	-23.99	-19.89	-25.53	-29.16
	(12.9)[c]	(28.9)[c]	(17.0)[c]	(12.8)[c]	(27.8)[c]
R^2	.98	.98	.96	.96	.96
SEE	33.3	17.7	48.7	39.4	33.8
df	175	220	561	209	307
Mean value of dependent variable	360	156	330	271	273

a. Incomes are on a monthly basis.
b. Student t statistics are in parentheses.
c. Coefficient significantly different from zero at .05 level or higher.

Table F-2

REGRESSION ANALYSIS OF TENANT RENTAL CONTRIBUTION IN FIVE PHAs [b]

Independent Variables	PHA				
	Los Angeles	Atlanta	Chicago	Philadelphia	Baltimore
Constant	40.0	3.08	32.5	13.9	17.4
	(16.0)[b] [c]	(2.43)[c]	(35.0)[c]	(11.3)[c]	(6.02)[c]
Adjusted income	.08	.20	.08	.16	.17
	(15.08)[c]	(45.4)[c]	(46.6)[c]	(42.7)[c]	(36.6)[c]
Household head over age 62 = 1; zero otherwise	6.56	4.98	2.24	-3.18	5.11
	(1.95)	(3.55)[c]	(1.14)	(1.70)	(2.02)[c]
Number of students over 18 in the household	-4.74	-4.05	1.73	2.10	3.90
	(1.51)	(2.02)[c]	(2.16)[c]	(1.26)	(1.85)
Household head or spouse is handicapped = 1; zero otherwise	3.15	.72	-4.64	-.18	.44
	(.78)	(.54)	(2.49)[c]	(.09)	(.11)
Number of children under age 19 in household	3.54	.59	1.77	1.42	1.56
	(5.92)[c]	(1.68)	(8.04)[c]	(3.73)[c]	(2.40)[c]
R^2	.67	.90	.86	.87	.88
SEE	14.1	8.03	9.32	10.62	13.20
df	175	220	561	307	209
Mean value of dependent variable	75.5	36.5	63.8	64.0	63.3

a. Income and rental contributions are on a monthly basis.
b. Student t statistics are in parentheses.
c. Coefficient significantly different from zero at .05 level or higher.

Appendix G

CONTROL OR BACKGROUND CIRCUMSTANCES [1]
IN THE URBAN INSTITUTE'S ANALYSIS OF
PUBLIC HOUSING PERFORMANCE

Since the criterion variables (used to divide the PHAs into high and low performance groups) were partially adjusted to take into account their scores on the background or control variables, it is not surprising that there are relatively few significant differences between high and low performance groups on their control variable scores. Because of the high relationship between control and management variables, however, not all differences between the two performance groups could be eliminated without also eliminating important management differences as well. For example, the 13 control variables having significant high/low mean differences in 1976 were all highly related to the criterion variables. They were also highly related to the management variables, which probably partly explains their continued significance despite the adjustment process. All of the 13 control variables were significantly correlated (.05 level) with the management variable, "resident perception of management strictness," which was in turn significantly related to 18 of the 20 criterion variables.

The control variables measure four types of operating conditions or characteristics over which the PHA has little or no control (at least in the short run): PHA characteristics, project characteristics, tenant characteristics, and neighborhood characteristics.

---

1. This material again is largely a quotation from Sadacca and Loux, "Improving Public Housing Through Management."

NEIGHBORHOOD CHARACTERISTICS

Despite the fact that the performance measures were adjusted to control for some of the factors beyond the control of the PHA, five measures of neighborhood characteristics remained significantly different between the high and low performance groups. At high performance PHAs (in contrast to low performance PHAs) the following occurred:

- In general, managers reported less frequently that the neighborhood caused problems in management.

- Managers also reported fewer abanadoned cars (a general indicator of neighborhood conditions that has been validated in the data from the Annual Housing Survey[2]) had to be removed from the streets around the project. This result holds for the large PHAs separately, and among the large Authorities the 11 largest were found to have more problems in this area than the high performance PHAs.

- Residents expressed higher satisfaction with their neighborhood and with the municipal services.

- Residents also felt that litter and abandoned cars in the neighborhood were less of a problem. This result holds for the large PHAs separately, and among the large Authorities the 11 largest were found to have more problems in this area than the high performance PHAs.

PROJECT CHARACTERISTICS

In general, larger, older projects with less yard space for individual units tend to have poorer performance. (Of these three measures, only the amount of yard space was significantly different between high and low performance groups.) Project managers at high performance PHAs reported that poor project design caused significantly fewer problems in areas such as maintenance, security, and recreational facilities. Managers at

---

2. The Annual Housing Survey question actually deals with more general categories of trash, litter, or junk. See J. E. Goedert and J. L. Goodman, Jr., *Indicators of the Quality of U.S. Housing* (Washington, D.C.: The Urban Institute, 1977).

the 11 very large PHAs reported design problems significantly more often than managers reported such problems at the high performance large PHAs.

A significantly higher percentage of high performance PHA residents and residents at the 11 largest PHAs compared to all large high performance PHAs thought they had enough showers and toilets than did those at low performance PHAs. Also, a higher percentage of high performance PHA residents than residents at low performance PHAs said that they liked the view from their apartments. This result does not hold separately for the large PHAs.

TENANT CHARACTERISTICS

Although there were few differences between the high and low performance groups in the characteristics of their tenants (high performance PHAs had a larger proportion of elderly, and fewer children per unit), there were several important differences between the large and medium/small groups. The large PHAs served a tenant population with less elderly, more one-parent families with more children per unit, a higher proportion of unemployed families who received welfare, and who were in need of services such as day care and family counseling. As would be expected, many of these variables were interrelated, and all have strong relationships to the performance measures—the characteristics of the large PHAs listed above being related to poorer performance. Among the large PHAs, the 11 largest PHAs had a significantly greater share of their tenant households in one-parent families than the high performance large PHAs had.

Appendix H

DESCRIPTION OF URBAN DEVELOPMENT ACTION GRANT PROJECTS INVOLVING PUBLIC HOUSING

Two of the funded projects are providing a large number of jobs close to existing public housing projects. Many of these jobs will require minimal education and skills and could go to the public housing tenants, thus raising PHA income and reducing vandalism and other problems by reducing the daytime project population.

One project is the Goose Island Industrial Development Area in the city of Chicago, which is close to the Cabrini-Greene housing project. The estimates in the city's application are that 1,300 of the roughly 1,900 permanent (i.e., nonnew construction) jobs generated by the investment will go to low-income persons. The second project is the Jersey City 1 & 9 Industrial Truck Plaza, a comprehensive truck service facility offering motel accommodations, restaurants, brokerage service, banking facilities, and auto and truck maintenance and repair services. The project is very close to the Marian Garden's housing project, a badly distressed project that is being completely upgraded with modernization funds provided under the Urban Initiatives program. The project is expected to provide 243 permanent low-income jobs from a total of about 600. It is interesting to note that the Jersey City application effectively ignored the presence of the housing project, even though its upgrading had already been funded, while the Chicago application made the proximity to Cabrini-Greene a major selling point. To judge by the application, the spatial configuration in Jersey City was in essence a happy accident.

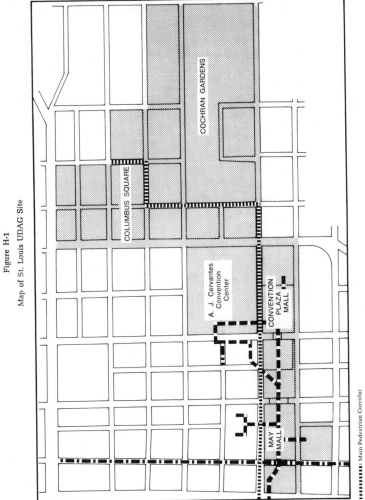

Figure H-1
Map of St. Louis UDAG Site

Main Pedestrian Corridor

Locust & 8th Street Malls

Existing & Proposed Skyway System

The third UDAG-funded project to be discussed here was awarded to the city of St. Louis and directly involves public housing. The driving force behind the application was the recognition by the city that expansion of its revitalizing central core to the north was effectively blocked by the presence of the large and badly distressed Cochran Gardens public housing project (704 original units in 12 buildings on an 18-acre site). The blockage had become acute since the 1977 opening of a new convention center and hotel complex only one block south of the project. The application proposed commercial revitalization (May Mall) to link the convention complex securely with the rest of the downtown area, upgrading Cochran Gardens, and the construction of additional housing around the project on a long-fallow urban renewal site to secure a genuine neighborhood. The overview summary in the application explains these elements as follows; figure H-1 gives a rough map for the area described.

The total amount requested in this application is $18.5 million. This money is to be received by two public agencies in the city of St. Louis, the Land Clearance for Redevelopment Authority (LCRA) and the St. Louis Housing Authority (SLHA). The LCRA will use the funds which it receives for writedown of land acquisition cost and the construction of various site improvements for the May Mall, Columbus Square, the Convention Plaza Mall, and the pedestrian linkages. The SLHA will use its funds for upgrading and renovation of buildings, construction of new turnkey housing, and various site improvements for the Cochran Gardens renovation program. Specifically, the distribution and use of funds for each of the components is as follows:

1. **May Mall**

The LCRA will receive $8 million in UDAG funds in order to write down the cost of land acquisition and to fund clearance and site improvements.

2. **Cochran Gardens**

The SLHA will receive $5.0 million of UDAG funds to be combined with $3.8 million of turnkey [public housing project development] funds; $5 million of "special mod" funds; and $6.2 million from Community Development block grants and other sources. This total of $20 million will be used by SLHA to assemble the land and promote construction of 100 turnkey units; contract for the conversion and renovation of a substantial number of units in the Cochran Gardens complex; construct a recreation center; and complete a substantial program of site improvements and amenities within the Cochran Gardens area.

3. Columbus Square

The LCRA will receive $2.5 million in UDAG funds for the assemblage of land and site improvements for the Columbus Square Apartments. The LCRA will reimburse HUD for its NDP advances totaling $350,000; acquire the remaining land; and contract for site improvements and extraordinary amenities planned for the Columbus Square Site.

4. Convention Plaza Mall

Again, the LCRA will receive the UDAG funds, $2.5 million in this case, for land writedown and site improvements. Approximately 70 percent of the land for the Convention Plaza Mall has already been acquired, but the remainder will be acquired by the LCRA and written down by approximately $1.5 million for purchase by the Convention Plaza Redevelopment Corporation. The remainder of the $2.5 million will be used by the LCRA to contract for site improvements and site amenities integral to the mall development.

5. Pedestrian Linkages

The LCRA will use $500,000 of UDAG funds to contract for street and sidewalk improvements—including lighting, landscaping, and street furniture—to improve the ground level pedestrian environment in the UDAG program area. This will be combined with $500,000 of other public funds.[1]

Of special interest for the entire analysis of this monograph is the treatment proposed for Cochran Gardens. At Cochran, the tenant management corporation set the following objectives for itself in carrying out the actual design improvements:

- Reducing the density in each building by reducing the number of families and giving more floor space to those who remain

---

1. *St. Louis UDAG: Report and Application*, 1978, pp. I-3, I-4.

- Moving larger families to lower floors and to properly sized units

- Designing one of the four 12-story buildings as an elderly congregate and care facility

- Creating recreation and community space on the site for day care, recreation, and other "software" activities

- Creating a site plan which addresses the shortage of parking, lack of play areas, the uncontrolled pedestrian walkways, and the meager landscape throughout the development

- Addressing the major deferred modernization items involving mechanical systems, electrical wiring, elevators, lighting, and apartment improvements

- Ensuring that no family which is in compliance with its lease will be dislocated from the Cochran Gardens neighborhood

Especially notable is the emphasis on reducing densities, moving large families to lower floors, and site improvements—all factors outside of normal HUD policies.

The rehabilitation plans call for townhouses to be created out of the second and third floors of 10 of the buildings with separate access to grade level from the units. This means that the 80 largest families (20 percent of all family units) will not have to use the elevators. Site improvements are being designed consistent with the "defensible space" principles to give tenants greater control; landscape elements are being selected to make areas easy to supervise and maintain; and, badly needed recreational facilities for children, adolescents, and adults that were omitted from the original design are being provided for the first time.

There are three final points about Cochran Gardens in the St. Louis UDAG that need to be noted. One is that the full spatial redesign will draw the project into the rest of the community and thus break down "fortress public housing." Second, the competence of the tenant management corporation at the project casts doubt on the durability of the improvements. Finally, while this UDAG project is on a particularly ambitious scale, its principles are applicable at much smaller levels. Such improvements could be financed with regular CDBG and public housing modernization funds.

Appendix I

ADDITIONAL TABLES

Table I-1

SELECTED MEAN 1970 CHARACTERISTICS OF NEIGHBORHOODS
WITH PUBLIC HOUSING FOR ELEVEN CITIES

	Wash-ington	Balti-more	Atlanta	Memphis	Detroit	Colum-bus	Mil-waukee	Houston	San Antonio	Los Angeles	San Fran-cisco
Mean Household Income ($)											
SMSA mean	11,812	9,959	8,769	8,244	11,645	9,302	10,497	10,128	7,822	10,290	10,445
City mean	8,917	8,084	6,603	8,475	8,984	8,088	8,760	9,840	7,855	9,802	8,759
Project neighborhoods	8,362	4,057	5,304	6,150	6,115	6,480	7,220	4,942	5,142	6,448	7,167
Mean Vacancy Rate											
SMSA mean	.04	.01	.05	.04	.04	.05	.03	.09	.07	.04	.04
City mean	.06	.06	.05	.04	.06	.05	.04	.09	.06	.05	.05
Project neighborhoods	.07	.13	.05	.11	.10	.06	06	.11	.10	.04	.05
Mean Homeowner-ship Rate											
SMSA mean	.46	.58	.57	.57	.72	.59	.60	.60	.64	.48	.52
City mean	.28	.44	.50	.56	.60	.51	.47	.53	.62	.41	.33
Project neighborhoods	.23	.15	.37	.34	.39	.23	.36	.26	.47	.17	.25

Source: 1970 Census of Population and Housing, Census Trade data, various volumes.

Table I-2

COMPARISON OF THE CHARACTERISTICS OF PUBLIC HOUSING TENANTS
AND THOSE ELIGIBLE TO BE TENANTS FOR FOUR PHAs

Household Characteristics	Atlanta In Public Housing	Atlanta Eligible [a] Renter	Chicago In Public Housing	Chicago Eligible [a] Renter	Philadelphia In Public Housing	Philadelphia Eligible [a] Renter	Los Angeles In Public Housing	Los Angeles Eligible [a] Renter
Social Distribution								
White	16	29	9	41	6	41	6	47
Black	84	70	89	46	90	54	54	22
Spanish	—	1	1	11	4	4	33	26
Household Types								
Husband-wife, no kids	3	15	2	13	2	13	3	15
Husband-wife, kids	4	17	11	19	8	13	25	20
Female-headed family	64	42	58	38	68	41	59	30
Single individuals	29	19	26	24	20	25	13	25
Age of Head								
65 or older	[b]	26	25	33	13	33	11	30
Under 65	74	74	75	67	87	67	89	70
Size of Household								
1 person	29	19	26	24	20	25	13	25
2 people	21	35	11	30	12	32	18	35
3-4 people	30	30	29	28	37	28	32	29
5 or more	20	16	34	18	30	15	37	12

Table I-2

COMPARISON OF THE CHARACTERISTICS OF PUBLIC HOUSING TENANTS
AND THOSE ELIGIBLE TO BE TENANTS FOR FOUR PHAs (cont'd)

Household Characteristics	Atlanta		Chicago		Philadelphia		Los Angeles	
	In Public Housing	Eligible [a] Renter	In Public Housing	Eligible [a] Renter	In Public Housing	Eligible [a] Renter	In Public Housing	Eligible [a] Renter
Primary Income Source [b]								
Wages, salaries, etc.	21	53	16	38	20	31	36	48
Welfare	44	15	58	24	65	28	57	17
Social Security	34	28	26	33	15	35	7	30

Sources: Same as table 9.
a. Income eligible by Section 8 program standards but not in public housing.
b. For eligibles those about 5 percent of population had primary income from other sources, e.g., dividends.

Bibliography

Aaron, Henry. *Politics and the Professors.* Washington, D.C.: The Brookings Institution, 1978.

_____. *Shelter and Subsidies.* Washington, D.C.: The Brookings Institution, 1972.

Baron, Richard D. *Tenant Management: A Rationale for a National Demonstration of Management Innovation.* St. Louis, Missouri: McCormack & Associates, 1975.

Barton, David M., and Olson, Edgar O. *The Benefits and Costs of Public Housing in New York City.* Madison: University of Wisconsin Institute for Research on Poverty.

Bauer, Catherine. "The Dreary Deadlock of Public Housing." *Architectural Forum* (May 1957).

Bowley, D., Jr. *The Poorhouse: Subsidized Housing in Chicago, 1895-1976.* Carbondale: Southern Illinois University Press, 1978.

William Brill Associates. *Comprehensive Security Planning: A Program for Arthur Capper Dwellings.* HUD-PDR-280. Washington, D.C.: U.S. Government Printing Office, 1977.

_____. *Planning for Home Security: Site Security Manual.* HUD-PDR-460. Washington, D.C.: U.S. Government Printing Office, 1979.

_____. *Planning for Housing Security: Site Elements Manual.* HUD-PDR-461. Washington, D.C.: U.S. Government Printing Office, 1979.

_____. *Victimization, Fear of Crime and Altered Behavior.* HUD Series PDR-174-I(-3). Washington, D.C.: U.S. Government Printing Office, 1977.

Brown, Douglas M. "An Evaluation and Synthesis of the Target Project Program Evaluation Reports." Georgetown University, 1978.

Brown, R.K. *The Development of Public Housing Programs in The United States.* Atlanta: Georgia State College of Business Administration, 1960.

Catz, Robert S. "Historical and Political Background of Federal Public Housing Programs." *North Dakota Law Review* 50 (Fall 1973): 25-43.

Coopers and Lybrand. *Cost Effectiveness and Status Report—Target Projects Program (TPP) Phases I and II, 1 April 1975-30 April 1976.* Washington, D.C.: U.S. Department of Housing and Urban Development, 1976.

de Leeuw, Frank. *Operating Costs in Public Housing: A Financial Crisis.* Washington, D.C.: The Urban Institute, 1974.

_____. *Operating Expenses in Public Housing, 1968-1971.* Washington, D.C.: The Urban Institute, 1973.

de Leeuw, Frank and Leaman, Sam. *The Section 23 Leasing Program.* Washington, D.C.: The Urban Institute, 1972.

Diaz, William A. *Tenant Management: A Historical and Analytical Overview.* New York: Manpower Development Research Corporation, 1979.

Dommel, P. R.; Nathan, R. P.; Liebschutz, S.F.; and Wrightson, M.T. *Decentralizing Community Development.* Washington, D.C.: U.S. Government Printing Office, 1978.

Downie, Leonard, Jr. *Mortgage in America.* New York: Praeger Publishers, Inc., 1974.

Drury, Margaret J.; Lee, Olson; Springer, Michael; and Yap, Lorene. *Low Income Housing Assistance Program (Section 8).* Washington, D.C.: U.S. Department of Housing and Urban Development Office of Policy Development and Research, 1978.

Eisenstadt, Karen. *Factors Affecting Maintenance and Operating Costs in Private Rental Housing.* New York: New York City Rand Institute, 1972.

Feagin, J.R. "America's Welfare Stereotypes." *Social Science Quarterly* (March 1972):921-933.

Feins, J.D., and White, Charles S., Jr. *The Ratio of Shelter Expenditures to Income: Definitional Issues, Typical Patterns and Historical Trends.* Cambridge, Massachusetts: Abt Associates, Inc., 1977.

Fisher, Robert Moore. *Twenty Years of Public Housing.* New York: Harper & Brothers, 1959.

Follain, James. *How Well Do Section 8 FMRs Match the Cost of Rental Housing.* Working Paper 249-17. Washington, D.C.: The Urban Institute, 1979.

Freedman, Leonard. *Public Housing: The Politics of Poverty.* New York: Holt, Reinhart and Winston, Inc., 1969.

Friedman, Lawrence. *Government and Slum Housing: A Century of Frustration.* Chicago: Rand McNally & Company, 1968.

Fuerst, J.S., and Petty, Roy. "Public Housing in the Courts: Pyrrhic Victories for the Poor." *Urban Lawyer* 9 (Summer 1977):496-513.

Gesmer, Ellen. "Discrimination in Public Housing Under the Housing and Community Development Act of 1974: A Critique of the New Haven Experience." *Urban Law Annual* 13(1977):49-80.

Gilbert, Joan. *An Assessment of the Public Housing Management Improvement Program.* Washington, D.C.: U.S. Department of Housing and Urban Development, 1978.

Glazer, Nathan. "Housing Problems and Housing Policies." *The Public Interest* 7(Spring 1967):38.

Goedert, Jeanne E., and Goodman, John L., Jr. *Indicators of the Quality of U.S. Housing.* Washington, D.C.: The Urban Institute, 1977.

Goodman, John L., Jr. *Regional Housing Assistance Allocations and Regional Housing Needs.* Washington, D.C.: The Urban Institute, 1979.

Gordon, Nancy M. "Institutional Responses: The Social Security System" in *The Subtle Revolution: Women at Work.* Edited by Ralph Smith. Washington, D.C.: The Urban Institute, 1979.

Hartman, Chester W., and Carr, Gregg. "Housing Authorities Reconsidered." *Journal of the American Institute of Planners* 35(January 1969):10-21.

Hartman, Chester W., and Levi, Margaret. "Public Housing Managers: An Appraisal." *Journal of the American Institute of Planners* 39(March 1973):125-137.

Hirsch, A., and Brown, U.N. "Too Poor for Public Housing: Roger Starr's Poverty Preferences." *Social Policy* (May/June 1972): 28-32.

Hirshen, Al, and Brown, Vivian. "Public Housing's Neglected Resource: The Tenants." *City* (Fall 1972).

Kanner, S.B. "The Future of Public Housing." *Real Estate Law Journal* 6 (1978):34-45.

Katz, R.D. *Intensity of Development and Livability of Multifamily Housing Projects.* FHA Technical Study No. 509. Washington, D.C.: U.S. Government Printing Office, 1963.

Kell, Amy. *Delivery of Human Resources Under the Target Projects Program.* Washington, D.C.: National Association of Housing and Redevelopment Officials, 1978.

_____. *General Management Innovations Developed Under the Target Projects Program.* Washington, D.C.: National Association of Housing and Redevelopment Officials, 1978.

_____. *Maintenance Management and Administrative Systems Under the Target Projects Program.* Washington, D.C.: National Association of Housing and Redevelopment Officials, 1978.

_____. *The Targets Projects Program: A Basic Resource Book.* Washington, D.C.: National Association of Housing and Redevelopment Officials, 1978.

_____. "The TPP Experience—What Have We Learned?" Washington, D.C.: National Association of Housing and Redevelopment Officials, 1978.

Kolodny, R. *Exploring New Strategies for Improving Public Housing Management.* Report to the Office of Research. Washington, D.C.: U.S. Department of Housing and Urban Development, 1979.

Kreisberg, Louis. "Neighborhood Setting and the Isolation of Public Housing Tenants." *Journal of the American Institute of Planners* 34(January 1968):43-49.

Lane, T.S. *Origins and Uses of the Conventional Rules of Thumb.* Cambridge, Massachusetts: Abt Associates, 1977.

Listokin, D. *Fair Share Housing Allocation.* New Brunswick: Rutgers University Center for Urban Policy Research, 1976.

Loux, Suzanne B.; Castro, Ena; and Sadacca, Robert. *Evaluation of the Phase I Target Project Program.* Working Paper 254-1. Washington, D.C.: The Urban Institute, 1978.

Loux, Suzanne B., and Sadacca, Robert. *Conditions Facilitating Implementation of Successful Management Improvement Programs.* Working Paper 255-1. Washington, D.C.: The Urban Institute, 1978.

_____. *Estimates of Rent and Tenant Income Levels in Public Housing Under Various Definitions.* Report 247-1. Washington, D.C.: The Urban Institute, 1977.

_____. *Tenant Management Demonstration Projects: An Analysis of Baseline Data.* Working Paper 5052-2. Washington, D.C.: The Urban Institute, 1977.

Lyn, Glenn Robert. "Effects of a Public Housing Project on a Neighborhood: Case Study of Oakland, California." *Land Economics* 43(November 1967):461-466.

Macey, John. *Publicly Provided and Assisted Housing in the U.S.A.* Working Paper 209-1-4. Washington, D.C.: The Urban Institute, 1972.

Mayer, A. "Public Housing Architecture Evaluated from PWA Days up to 1962." *Journal of Housing* 19(June 1962):447-458.

_____. "Public Housing Design." *Journal of Housing* 20(April 1963):133-143.

Mayer, M. *The Builders.* New York: W.W. Norton and Company, 1978.

Mayo, Stephen; Mansfield, Shirley; Warner, David; and Zwetchlenbaum, Richard. *Draft Report on Housing Allowances and Other Rental Housing Assistance Programs—A Comparison Based on the Housing Allowance Demand Experiment, Part I: Participation, Housing Consumption, Location and Satisfaction.* AAI #79-139. Cambridge, Massachusetts: Abt Associates, Inc., 1979.

_____. *Draft Report on Housing Allowances and Other Rental Housing Assistance Programs—A Comparison Based on the Hous-*

ing *Allowance Demand Experiment, Part II: Costs and Efficiency.* Cambridge, Massachusetts: Abt Associates, Inc., 1979.

Meehan, Eugene J. *Public Housing Policy: Convention Versus Reality.* New Brunswick, New Jersey: Rutgers University Center for Urban Policy Research, 1975.

_____. "The Rise and Fall of Public Housing: Condemnation Without Trial." *A Decent Home and Environment: Housing Urban America.* Edited by Donald Phares. Cambridge, Massachusetts: Ballinger Publishing Company, 1977.

Merrill, Sally R.; Cromwell, J.; Napior, D.; and Weinberg, D. *A Preliminary Working Paper on the Technical Components of the Performance Funding System.* Cambridge, Massachusetts: Abt Associates, Inc., 1979.

Meyerson, Martin, and Banfield, Edward C. *Politics, Planning and the Public Interest.* New York: The Free Press of Glencoe, 1955.

Moore, William, Jr. *The National Ghetto: Everyday Life in an Urban Project.* New York: Random House, 1969.

Murray, Michael. "The Distribution of Tenant Benefits in Public Housing." *Econometrica* (July 1975):771-88.

Muth, Richard F. *Public Housing: An Economic Evaluation.* Washington, D.C.: American Enterprise Institute, 1973.

Nathan, R.P., and Adams, C. "Understanding Central City Hardship." *Political Science Quarterly* 91(Spring 1976):47-62.

National Association of Housing and Redevelopment Officials. *Certification Examination and Candidate Review Exercise, Public Housing Manager: Bulletin of Information for Candidates.* Washington, D.C.: NAHRO, 1978.

_____. *Low-Income Rental Assistance Program (Section 8): Questions and Answers.* Washington, D.C.: NAHRO, 1975.

_____. "NAHRO's Testimony Before Senate Subcommittee on April 12: Myths/Realities of Public Housing." *Journal of Housing* 30(April 1973):179-191.

_____. *Public Housing Management in the Seventies: Readings.* Washington, D.C.: NAHRO, 1974.

_____. *Trends in Housing Management.* (Reprints from the *Journal of Housing,* 1972-1976.) Washington, D.C.: NAHRO, 1977.

Newman, Oscar. *Defensible Space.* New York: Collier Press, 1973.

Olsen, Edgar O., and Rasmussen, David. "Section 8 Existing: Program Evaluation and Policy Options." *Occasional Papers in Housing and Community Affairs,* forthcoming.

Perkins-Will and the Ehrenkrantz Group. *An Evaluation of the Physical Condition of Public Housing Stock.* Washington, D.C.: Report to the U.S. Department of Housing and Urban Development, 1979.

Polikoff, A. *Housing the Poor.* Cambridge: Ballinger Publishing Company, 1978.

Power, Anne. *Tenant Co-ops or Tenant Management Corporations in the U.S.A.* London: North Islington Housing Rights Project, 1979.

Prescott, James Russell. *Economic Aspects of Public Housing.* Beverly Hills: Sage Publications, Inc., 1974.

Rabushka, Alvin, and Weissert, William G. *Caseworkers or Police: How Tenants See Public Housing.* Stanford, California: Hoover Institution Press, 1977.

Rainwater, Lee. *Behind Ghetto Walls: Black Family Life in a Federal Slum.* Chicago: Aldine Publishing Company, 1970.

Rouse, W.V., and Rubenstein, H. *Crime in Public Housing: A Review of Major Issues and Selected Crime Reduction Strategies, volume 1, A Report.* Washington, D.C.: U.S. Government Printing Office, 1979.

_____. *Crime in Public Housing: A Review of Major Issues and Selected Crime Reduction Strategies, volume 2, Review of Two Conferences and an Annotated Bibliography.* Washington, D.C.: U.S. Government Printing Office, 1979.

Rydell, Peter C. *Factors Affecting Maintenance and Operating Costs in Federal Public Housing Projects.* New York: The Rand Institute, 1970.

Sadacca, Robert and Loux, Suzanne. *Improving Public Housing Through Management: A Technical Report.* Working Paper 255-2. Washington, D.C.: The Urban Institute, 1978.

Sadacca, Robert; Isler, Morton; and DeWitt, Joan. *The Development of a Prototype Equation for Public Housing Operating Expenses.* Paper 11900. Washington, D.C.: The Urban Institute, 1975.

Sadacca, Robert; Loux, Suzanne; Isler, Morton; and Drury, Margaret. *Management Performance in Public Housing.* Paper 61000. Washington, D.C.: The Urban Institute, 1974.

Schussheim, Morton, and Smith, Anne. *The Future of Conventional Public Housing: Some Views of Local Housing Officials.* Washington, D.C.: Congressional Research Service, 1979.

Scobie, Richard S. *Problem Tenants in Public Housing: Who, Where and Why Are They?* New York: Praeger, 1975.

Seessel, Thomas. *The First Annual Report on the National Tenant Management Demonstration.* New York: Manpower Demonstration Research Corporation, 1977.

Setlow, Carolyn E. "A Study of Public Attitudes Toward Federal Government Assistance for Housing for Low and Moderate Income Families." *Housing in the Seventies: Working Papers, volume 2.* Washington, D.C.: U.S. Government Printing Office, 1976.

_____. "A Survey of the Attitudes and Experience of State and

Local Government Officials and Federal Housing Programs."
Housing in the Seventies: Working Papers, volume 2. Washington, D.C.: U.S. Government Printing Office, 1976.

Shafer, Robert. *Operating Subsidies in Public Housing: A Critical Appraisal of the Formula Approach.* Boston: Citizens' Housing and Planning Association, 1975.

Smolensky, Eugene. "Public Housing or Income Supplements—the Economics of Housing for the Poor." *Journal of the American Institute of Planners* 34(March 1968):94-101.

Solomon, Arthur D. *Housing the Urban Poor.* Cambridge, Massachusetts: MIT Press, 1974.

Starr, Roger. "Which of the Poor Shall Live in Public Housing?" *Public Interest* 23(Spring 1971):116-124.

Stone, S.C., and Taylor, J.W. *Inner City Turnaround: An Evolving Plan for a Total Service Neighborhood, Longview—Torrence Park, Decatur, Illinois.* Champaign: University of Illinois Housing Research and Development Program, 1976.

Struyk, Raymond J. *Saving the Housing Assistance Plans: Improving Incentives to Local Governments.* Washington, D.C.: The Urban Institute, 1979.

Stucker, Jennifer L. "Importance of Income Verification in the Section 8 Housing Assistance Payments Program." *Occasional Papers in Housing and Community Affairs,* forthcoming.

Sumka, Howard J., and Stegman, Michael. "An Economic Analysis of Public Housing in Small Cities." *Journal of Regional Science* (December 1978):395-410.

Taggart, Robert III. *Low Income Housing: A Critique of Federal Aid.* Baltimore: Johns Hopkins Press, 1970.

U.S. Bureau of the Census, *Annual Housing Survey, Metropolitan Area Reports.* Washington, D.C.: U.S. Government Printing Office, 1974 to 1976.

_____. *Annual Housing Survey: 1976, Part A, General Housing Characteristics of the United States and Regions.* Washington, D.C.: U.S. Government Printing Office, 1978.

_____. *Population Reports and Estimates,* Series P-25, Nos. 649-698, Washington, D.C.: U.S. Government Printing Office, 1977.

U.S. Department of Housing and Urban Development. *Baseline Analysis of the Urban Homesteading Demonstration.* Washington, D.C.: U.S. Government Printing Office, 1979.

_____. *Housing in the Seventies: National Housing Policy Review.* Washington, D.C.: U.S. Government Printing Office, 1974.

_____. *Low Rent Housing Accounting Handbook.* Washington, D.C.: U.S. Government Printing Office, 1969 and subsequent revisions.

_____. *Low Rent Housing Guide: Orientation to the Program.* HMG 7401-3. Washington, D.C.: U.S. Government Printing Office, 1971.

_____. *The National Tenant Management Demonstration: Status Report Through 1978.* Washington, D.C.: U.S. Department of Housing and Urban Development Office of Policy Development and Research, 1979.

_____. "The Need For a National Urban Policy" in *Occasional Papers in Housing and Community Affairs.* 4 (July 1974):7-190.

_____. *The 1978 HUD Survey on the Quality of Community Life—A Data Book.* Washington, D.C.: U.S. Government Printing Office, 1979.

_____. *Problems Affecting Low Rent Public Housing Projects.* Washington, D.C.: U.S. Government Printing Office, 1979.

_____. *Public Housing Occupancy Handbook.* (7465.1 Revised.) Washington, D.C.: U.S. Government Printing Office, 1978.

_____. *Target Projects Program Handbook.* 7460.S Revised. Washington, D.C.: U.S. Government Printing Office, 1976.

_____. *Urban Development Action Grant Program: First Annual Report.* Washington, D.C.: U.S. Government Printing Office, 1979.

U.S. General Accounting Office, *Serving A Broader Economic Range of Families in Public Housing Could Reduce Operating Subsidies.* CED 80-2. Washington, D.C.: Government Printing Office, 1979.

White, E.; Merrill, Sally R.; and Lane, T. *The History and Overview of the Performance Funding System.* Cambridge, Massachusetts: Abt Associates, Inc., 1979.

Wolman, Harold. *Politics of Federal Housing.* New York: Dodd, Mead and Company, 1971.

Index